The Carpool Detectives

THE *CARPOOL DETECTIVES*

A TRUE STORY OF
FOUR MOMS, TWO BODIES,
AND ONE MYSTERIOUS COLD CASE

Chuck Hogan

RANDOM HOUSE

NEW YORK

Random House
An imprint and division of Penguin Random House LLC
1745 Broadway, New York, NY 10019
randomhousebooks.com
penguinrandomhouse.com

LIBRARY OF CONGRESS CATALOGING-IN-PUBLICATION DATA
Names: Hogan, Chuck author
Title: The carpool detectives / Chuck Hogan.
Description: First edition. | New York, NY : Random House, [2025]
Identifiers: LCCN 2025008425 (print) | LCCN 2025008426 (ebook) |
ISBN 9780593733226 hardcover | ISBN 9780593733240 ebook
Subjects: LCSH: Criminal investigation—United States—Case studies |
Criminal investigation—United States—Citizen participation |
Cold cases (Criminal investigation)—United States—Case studies
Classification: LCC HV8073 .H5975 2025 (print) | LCC HV8073 (ebook) |
DDC 363.250973—dc23/eng/20250428
LC record available at https://lccn.loc.gov/2025008425
LC ebook record available at https://lccn.loc.gov/2025008426

Printed in the United States of America on acid-free paper

2nd Printing

FIRST EDITION

BOOK TEAM: Production editor: Dennis Ambrose • Managing editor: Rebecca Berlant • Production manager: Angela McNally • Copy editor: Emily DeHuff • Proofreaders: Taylor Teague and Shannon Barr

Book design by Mary A. Wirth

The authorized representative in the EU for product safety and compliance is Penguin Random House Ireland, Morrison Chambers, 32 Nassau Street, Dublin D02 YH68, Ireland. https://eu-contact.penguin.ie.

*To "Carrie," for allowing us to reopen
an old wound in hopes of
finally healing it*

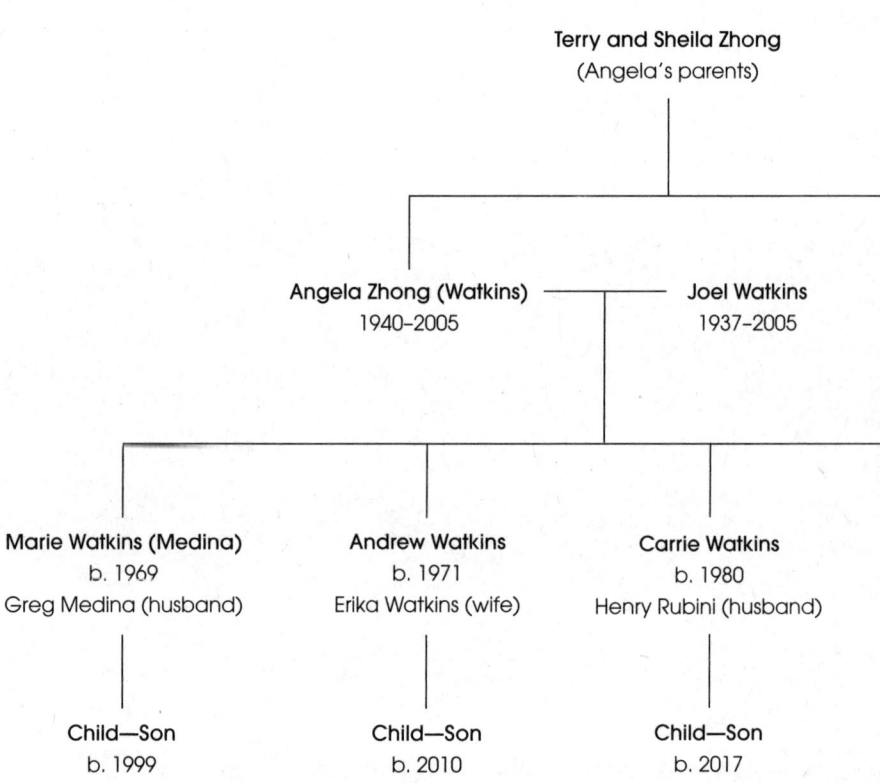

Terry and Sheila Zhong
(Angela's parents)

Angela Zhong (Watkins) —— Joel Watkins
1940–2005   1937–2005

Marie Watkins (Medina)
b. 1969
Greg Medina (husband)

Andrew Watkins
b. 1971
Erika Watkins (wife)

Carrie Watkins
b. 1980
Henry Rubini (husband)

Child—Son
b. 1999

Child—Son
b. 2010

Child—Son
b. 2017

WATKINS FAMILY TREE

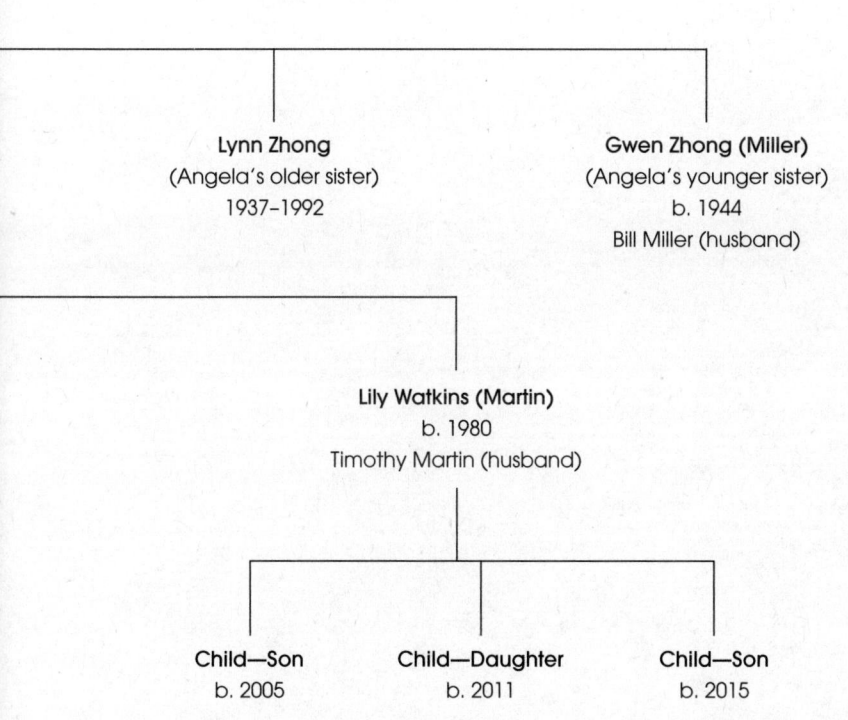

Lynn Zhong
(Angela's older sister)
1937–1992

Gwen Zhong (Miller)
(Angela's younger sister)
b. 1944
Bill Miller (husband)

Lily Watkins (Martin)
b. 1980
Timothy Martin (husband)

Child—Son
b. 2005

Child—Daughter
b. 2011

Child—Son
b. 2015

*A*ngela felt like a ghost walking through her own home. As evening fell, she paused to gaze out the window at the orange tree in the yard and the plants she'd carefully tended. *Is this the last time I'll see my garden?*

Her husband, Joel, had informed her a few days ago that they were losing the house. They'd been on the brink of financial collapse before, but this time felt different. The business was down and he had fallen deeply into debt again. "I'm sorry," he'd told her. He had been able to right things before, but now they were in their late sixties and their timeline was short. Angela tried to be hopeful, tried to remember the faith she'd always had in Joel. He'd always been able to find a way.

Last night, though, he'd come home from work reeking of alcohol, despite swearing he had put all that behind him. She looked at her husband of over forty years and, for the first time, saw not the man she wanted to see, but the man who was really there.

She saw that Joel was scared.

In the years since the kids had grown up and moved on, Angela's world had become progressively smaller and simpler, while Joel's became more complicated in ways she didn't fully understand. Now, looking out at her garden, the small patch of earth that meant so much to her, she wondered whether she should have wanted more for herself. She'd relied on Joel to take care of everything, including their finances, and in doing so, she had allowed her fate to become inextricably tied to his.

The orange tree caught a shaft of moonlight as she thought back to the other things she'd been trying to block out since he told her about the debt. Secretive telephone calls. Late night drives. Something was very wrong—she knew that now. Were she another person, and they another couple, she'd have confronted him the first time she'd woken up in the middle of the night to find his side of the bed empty, his car missing. She imagined yelling at him, demanding he tell her what was going on, but then she pictured his rage and felt a twist of dread.

Instead, she stayed at the window in the falling darkness, fear coursing through her as she saw headlights sweep into the driveway. What was going to happen to them?

What have you done, Joel?

THE BEGINNING

*M*arissa *was so bored.*

She was sitting in a college classroom, enrolled in a continuing education course promising an introduction to television journalism. The coursework she thought would be compelling involved viewing unedited B-roll footage to be inserted into news reports: filler, such as a police officer unspooling yellow caution tape around an accident scene or a bored public official giving a canned press briefing or bib-wearing walkers participating in a charity 5K. She had signed up for night school to study investigative journalism, determined to follow her passion a decade after leaving a career in forensic accounting to become a full-time parent. She thought she would be learning how to tell exciting and impactful stories, not compose boilerplate local interest pieces.

What she did not expect was that she would view a piece of film that would alter the trajectory of her life.

The soundless footage showed a red Skyhook helicopter hovering low inside a deep canyon. From massive straps hanging from the bottom of the helicopter, a wrecked SUV dangled slowly, corpse-like, beneath the rotorcraft, high above the hilly forest.

Marissa sat up in her seat. Something about the footage captivated her.

The helicopter set the vehicle gently down on the roadside, its long straps slackening and then, released, collapsing to the gravel around the SUV. Sheriff's deputies and California Highway Patrol officers surrounded the vehicle, which had been damaged almost beyond recognition. The location of the retrieval was not identified, but it was familiar to Marissa.

California State Route 2 ran from the Pacific coast in Santa Monica—near where she lived now—east and north through the San Gabriel Valley and up into the rugged mountains of the Angeles National Forest. Marissa used to hike in that area on summer day camp excursions when she was young—running barefoot with friends, catching frogs, a world away from the tension and dysfunction of her home.

What followed chilled her.

To demonstrate how dry footage was incorporated into the finished product, the instructor played the actual news segment as it had aired in August 2006. "Accident Investigated as Double Homicide." The costly helicopter retrieval had been performed after the vehicle had lain at the bottom of a ravine for more than a year.

The report raised so many questions in Marissa's mind. Why wait so long to bring it up? How could a one-car accident be a double homicide? And had this crime ever been solved?

For the first time in that class, she was paying attention. The segment included a still image of a Los Angeles County Sheriff's Department "Information Wanted" poster showing driver's license photographs of a man and a woman, Joel and Angela Watkins,* an older married couple who looked so ordinary, so everyday, so *anyone*—Marissa could not get the image of the two victims out of her mind. She had recently renewed her driver's license, and it had not occurred to her that the resulting image could, in the event of a crime, be the image that forever defined her. She thought of the two victims running errands that forget-

---

* The victims' names are pseudonyms, and all identifying details have been altered. For reasons of privacy and security that will become clear, every name in this account is a pseudonym, with the exception of those of the four detectives and their spouses.

table day, putting up with the inconvenience of going to the Registry of Motor Vehicles, another chore in another day of comings and goings—until it all stopped. Stopped forever.

The couple were close to Marissa's parents' ages, and something about their expressions seemed familiar to her, looking so normal, and yet at the same time she detected tension in their faces—similar to the tension she'd known in her own parents.

Who would want to murder this older couple, and why?

This was in early 2020. Marissa had found herself at one of life's crossroads.

For more than a decade, motherhood had defined her life. Marissa always wanted to be a mother, and she and Brian had married young, at twenty-five, planning to start a family almost right away. But just thirteen weeks into her first pregnancy, after hearing the fetal heartbeat and watching the little bean move on the ultrasound, she suffered a devastating loss. She woke up covered in blood and miscarried shortly after. Six months later, she suffered another miscarriage. She was distraught. Of all her plans, hopes, and dreams in life, becoming a parent was one thing she had simply taken for granted.

Ultimately, she picked herself up and they tried again, this time seeking the help of a reproductive endocrinologist. She did everything she was supposed to—ate wholesome organic foods, got regular exercise—while avoiding everything she was supposed to—coffee, alcohol, deli meats, unpasteurized cheese. So when her daughter was born and placed in her arms, healthy and wailing, her joy was beyond what she'd ever known. Halfway through her maternity leave, Marissa knew there was no chance she would go back to work. Two years later, her second daughter arrived, and the family she once feared might not materialize now felt complete.

She loved being a mom. Marissa's childhood had been tumultuous at times, such that much of her approach to parenting was an attempt to compensate for what she felt had been lacking in her own upbringing, devoting herself to giving her girls everything she could. Brian worked in advertising for a major movie studio, and for most of their thirties he worked long hours in order to establish himself professionally. Marissa's career in forensic accounting had never felt like her identity, while being a full-time mother did. It was the most fulfilling and rewarding job in the world—until it wasn't.

Now, her girls were eleven and nine, the ages when children first show signs of becoming their own selves. The oldest was a typical first child, a perfectionist, somewhat anxious, endearingly empathetic. The youngest was shy, but also brave, exactly as Marissa had been as a child. She and the girls were particularly close, and she was proud of that. Marissa still felt needed, and with adolescence on the horizon, she understood that as a mother she had a long, long way to go. But she was no longer their entire world. The days of swinging her kids around or playing tag were fading. Her daughters were blossoming and no longer required one hundred percent of Marissa's focus and energy. Being on the cusp of forty had something to do with it as well.

With both girls now in school for much of the day, Marissa began considering the second half of her life. She threw herself into school-focused volunteer work, ultimately becoming president of the parent association and overseeing the class fundraisers. While this work was important and challenging in its own way, it did nothing to fill the void she was feeling.

She shared her thinking with Brian, telling him that there was a course of study at a local university through which she could earn a certificate in investigative journalism. This was out of the blue, and it seemed to Brian like a lot for her to bite off all at once. "Okay," he said. "I guess let's look into it."

"Oh, no need," Marissa told him cheerily. "I already enrolled."

She was still thinking about the footage of the wrecked car dangling from the helicopter as she arrived home that night after class. She lived in a Spanish-style house in a quiet but densely settled neighborhood, a dozen or so blocks from the Pacific coast. Tall palm trees lined the wide sidewalks outside single-family homes separated by hedges or short fences, not far from one of the Westside's main thoroughfares for stopping and dining. She checked in with Brian, got the girls to bed, then brought her laptop to her favorite spot on the living room sofa and began googling. Fifteen-year-old news stories came up in the results, and she began reading them in roughly chronological order.

The initial stories focused on the lack of information related to their vanishing. "No trace," "family members have not heard," "no indication of foul play in the disappearance." A son, Andrew Watkins, was quoted as saying, "We have no idea what could have happened." The Watkins children, all adults, had last heard from their parents by telephone over the weekend, and the father, Joel, had last been seen at his office in Pasadena that Saturday. The son was also quoted as saying that they enjoyed taking weekend drives and there was concern they might have met with an accident.

Two weeks later, the story was still being updated. There were no further developments as to Joel and Angela Watkins's fates, but, as one article's subheadline stated, "Questions Surround Missing Elderly Couple." The family business, Wattkins LED, an importer of commercial lighting equipment, had been closed overnight, and the company's telephone line was disconnected. A Sheriff's Department spokesman said that the disappearance was "an active investigation and we are looking into anything and everything."

The details became even stranger over time. Not only had Wattkins LED closed down for good, but the company's bank had filed a lawsuit claiming fraudulent financial activity and was seeking to recover significant losses. After issuing conflicting statements regarding the business's closing, family members had ceased communicating with the press altogether.

Then, in July 2005, five weeks after the Watkinses' disappearance, two bodies were discovered near a wrecked SUV below Angeles Crest Highway, north of their La Cañada Flintridge home, as Marissa had seen in the news footage. Three days later, the "skeletal remains" were positively identified as those of Joel and Angela Watkins. Family members issued a short statement saying that they were devastated and thanking law enforcement. "They were great parents and grandparents who will be missed." An official cause of death would not be determined for several weeks, pending toxicology tests.

And then—nothing. For thirteen months, no further news stories, no updates. Until the bombshell.

The car had been retrieved from the canyon by helicopter "as part of an ongoing investigation." The articles referenced the couple's still unexplained disappearance. Apparently new evidence had come to light indicating that the accident was not an accident at all. The story confirmed that what was once thought to be a tragic motor vehicle crash was now being investigated as a double murder. A sheriff's detective was quoted saying, "All evidence points to another person or persons being responsible for their deaths."

Another person or persons being responsible for their deaths. This phrase set Marissa's mind buzzing.

The following April, an article reported that a $5,000 reward had been offered for information regarding Joel and Angela's disappearance and death. Specifically, the Sheriff's Department statement mentioned the hope that someone driving on Angeles Crest Highway that night might have seen something. To Marissa's mind, a plea for two-year-old information from the general public indicated that the investigation had hit a total standstill. At the same time, the extraordinary expenditure of money and manpower involved in physically recovering the car more than a year after its discovery pointed to continued law enforcement interest.

The reward offer was apparently unsuccessful. After 2007, there were no further news articles about the Watkins murders. The story never went national, with only one small article appearing in a major daily newspaper, at the bottom of a page in the *Los Angeles Daily News* in 2005, under the headline MISSING COUPLE FOUND DEAD. The story had received frequent coverage on local television stations after the initial mysterious vanishing, and then again upon the discovery of their wrecked Ford Explorer and skeletal remains. But without any further revelations—no arrests, no explanation, no resolution—the coverage had faded away.

Many of the archived articles from local papers included the original comments section. At that time, in 2005, internet trolling was not yet an art form, and the readers' real-time comments more closely resembled a message board, with people trading theories, correcting other commenters' inaccuracies, and expressing empathy.

In the earliest articles, most readers simply noted their concern for the missing couple and for their families. Some commenters claimed to be acquaintances of the Watkins family.

I know Joel and have shared many conversations with him and I am certain he did nothing shady. As a business owner myself, I know my first priority would be to make sure my employees are paid. Prayers for a happy ending to this mysterious story . . .

The Watkinses are some of the nicest people you'll meet. They are definitely in my prayers! . . .

The lack of public information about this incident is frustrating. Don't these people carry cell phones? Can't

*they trace them from their cell phones? Are there any in-
dications of foul play? . . .*

But as the days went on and the business was inexplicably
shuttered, the readers and commenters sensed a deeper mystery
unfolding.

*I hope the missing couple are all right and no harm
comes to them, but it is all so strange. Does their family
not want them back? The fact that the company is closed
and the website is down concerns me . . .*

Nobody vanishes nowadays unless they want to . . .

*I do think this is getting fishy. Why did the family close
the business? This man has been missing only seven days!
I read that some of the couple's children worked there.
They must know the business. I hope they are okay, but
did they take the money and run? . . .*

*These parents would not leave their children without
reason. There is a reason the police are not releasing any
information. I hope some news outlet is working on the
real story . . .*

In the absence of answers, new theories took root with dark
undertones.

*I always had the impression that Joel Watkins was a little
crooked . . .*

*Their bank is suing so I hate to bare [sic] bad news but
neither the money nor Joel Watkins is ever coming
back . . .*

After the discovery of the bodies, there followed a lot of predictable *I-told-you-so*'s and *This-is-so-tragic*'s. When, more than a year later, their murders were publicly confirmed, enough time had passed that the commenters had lost their passion for, even interest in, the case.

While Marissa thought her curiosity about the case would be satiated after reading a few archived articles, she instead felt herself getting sucked further into the narrative and wanting to know more. Lacking any other information on the criminal investigation, she set about compiling as much basic biographical and background information on the Watkinses and their immediate family as she could find using various common websites and search engines.

She learned that Joel Henry Watkins was born in 1937 in Irvine, California, south of Anaheim. He was sixty-eight when he died. Angela Mei (Zhong) Watkins was born in 1940 in San Lorenzo, California, outside Oakland. She was of Chinese American heritage, sixty-six years old when she died. They were married in Las Vegas, Nevada, in December 1963, forty-two years earlier. At the time of their deaths, they resided in a 3,049-square-foot four-bedroom, three-bathroom midcentury house on Shadow Peak Road in an area of La Cañada Flintridge known as Paradise Canyon. They had purchased the home two years earlier, in February 2003, with a substantial mortgage.

They had raised their four children in nearby Pasadena, where they lived from 1978 until 1996. Marie, the oldest, was born in 1969. She was thirty-six at the time of her parents' deaths, fifty years old in 2020. Her married name was Marie Medina, and her husband, Greg Medina, two years older than she, ran various businesses and appeared to be tangentially involved with Wattkins LED, though not as an employee. Marie and Greg had one young child, a boy.

Their son, Andrew Watkins, was born in 1971. He was thirty-four at the time of his parents' deaths, forty-nine years old in 2020. Andrew was single at the time of his parents' deaths, a former certified public accountant whose accounting license had been either suspended or allowed to lapse in 2002. He began working for his father's company in 1997, a position that did not require a CPA license. Almost immediately after his parents' estate probate closed, Andrew relocated to Charleston, South Carolina, where he married and had one son.

The youngest children were twin girls, Carrie and Lily Watkins, born in 1980. They were twenty-five at the time of their parents' deaths, forty years old in 2020. Carrie was married to Henry Rubini at the time of her parents' deaths and later had one son. She had kept her maiden name and worked as a software developer for a major insurance company, living in Pasadena, California.

Twin sister Lily's married name was Martin, and she had lived in Indiana with her husband, Tim, and was pregnant with her first child at the time of her parents' deaths.

Angela Watkins had two sisters, one of whom predeceased her, the other one still living. Joel had no other surviving family members.

Marissa turned her research to the company. Wattkins LED operated out of leased office space in Pasadena, California, not far from La Cañada Flintridge. The company did not produce anything, but imported LED lighting into the United States, almost exclusively from factories and companies in China. In an industry publication interview in 2001, Joel identified "horticultural usage"—which sounded like a euphemism for cannabis cultivation—as the largest potential growth area for LED lighting.

From the outside, there was nothing terribly remarkable about the Watkins family or their family company, a detail that only further piqued Marissa's interest. The couple had entered their midsixties with an enviable lifestyle. They appeared to be successful, with a large (if highly leveraged) house and a young grandchild who lived nearby, with a second on the way. They had a lot to live for. Who would want to murder Joel and Angela Watkins, and why?

It wasn't as clear to Marissa at the time as it would become in retrospect, but what drew her so deeply into the initial research was the familiar family dynamic: a seemingly normal couple with secrets that had major implications for their family. This she understood.

Marissa had grown up in Echo Park, currently a trendy, hip neighborhood close to downtown Los Angeles, but a much grittier area in the 1980s. It was a rough neighborhood then, with cars often broken into and new graffiti appearing nearly every night. The day her parents brought her home from the hospital, they discovered a homeless man hiding in their basement. Her family lived in a towering old Victorian house that so closely exemplified her family's identity, her mother's license plate read TOWRHSE. The building stood four stories high, with six bedrooms and three bathrooms, its ramshackle wooden exterior painted all different colors. But as the years went by, the house fell into disrepair. The fence became ridden with termites. One time her younger brother fell through a rotted plank in the back deck. The interior floors were so warped and creaky that you had to tiptoe, as through a minefield, to the bathroom at night or else wake up everybody in the house.

But when she was young, the house was a dreamland, full of mystery and adventure. She would lead her brother and much younger sister into the attic and under the house looking for treasures. She was always searching for something, daring to climb the highest walls and then jumping off them. They kept many animals, all of them strays, most scarred or one-eyed. Marissa's first action upon coming home from school was to check the backyard for escapees and clean up the mess on the floors.

Her love for pets and her particular affection for strays came from her mother, a special education teacher. Marissa's father was a lawyer. Both parents were emotionally distant, her mother present but extremely secretive, while her father was withdrawn and often depressed. One reason their house was in a constant state of disrepair was because her parents, together and individually, had a troubled relationship with money. They spent money they didn't have and often borrowed from Marissa's grandparents. The family got away from the Tower for only seven days each year, on their annual road trip to Yosemite. When she was older, Marissa would use some of the camp counseling money she earned to help patch up the place where she could. She learned how to put down tile and wire outlets. She became handy because she had to.

One night in her freshman year of high school, she vividly remembers watching *The Simpsons* and laughing along with her siblings when she heard a huge crash downstairs. She left her brother and sister in front of the television and ventured down alone, hearing raised voices. From a hiding spot on the stairs, she saw her parents fighting. The subject was money, of course. The grocery store had called after multiple bounced checks. As their yelling rose, Marissa couldn't take it anymore, and spontaneously burst from the stairs into the kitchen, crying out, "*What's going on?*" Her parents turned to look at her, blankly, silenced. Neither one spoke. Neither of them thought to console their daughter or explain. It was at that moment Marissa realized she was on her own. *I have to be successful,* she decided. *I can't rely on anyone else to take care of me.* She would do whatever it took not to live like her parents, a life of constant strife and uncertainty.

Despite not doing much in the way of homework and skipping most of the assigned reading, she managed to sail through high school with good grades. Life at home had become uncomfortable, and so on most school nights, she slept over at friends' houses, observing her friends' family dynamics, seeking positive examples of domestic life.

Secrets ran deep in Marissa's family, and when they were revealed, it was usually in a shocking and disturbing fashion. Accordingly, Marissa hated surprises, because she had experienced so many negative ones. When she was seventeen, her father one day decided he was taking a sabbatical from his law firm to spend an entire summer at Yale University studying the Icelandic language. Then, one week before returning home from Connecticut, he sent Marissa a message via AOL Instant Messenger.

Subject line: Hi.

Message: I'm divorcing your Mother. Can you pick me up at the airport on Friday?

When Marissa picked him up at the airport, he didn't understand why she was surly.

"I thought you'd be happy," he told her. "I was when my parents split up."

Happy? Maybe he meant *relieved?* But she wasn't relieved, and she wasn't happy. She didn't speak to her father for many years after that.

Marissa worked twenty hours a week in order to help put herself through USC. Her natural inclination was to be a psychology major, but the moment of clarity she had experienced that night of the *Simpsons* crash never left her mind, and after one semester she switched her major to business.

Upon graduating, she landed a consulting job, bought herself a car, and even earned enough money to give some to her mother. She lived at home for one year, but it was unendurable, so she moved in with Brian, whom she had met in high school and started dating in college. She switched jobs, moving into real estate development finance with Westfield malls, and worked for them until her first daughter was born.

Her mother's issues with money and secrets worsened over time. Marissa was seven months pregnant with her first child and out for what seemed like a casual brunch with her mother when her mother revealed that she had lost the family home—the symbol of their family's identity—to foreclosure. She had neglected to pay the mortgage for nearly a year, and the Los Angeles County Sheriff's Department was coming to padlock the Tower House in two days. Marissa had to oversee everything being packed up and loaded out in forty-eight hours while resettling her mother in an apartment, all at her advanced stage of pregnancy.

As Marissa looked at her adult life, she felt a sense of accomplishment and also gratitude. She had succeeded in building the life of which young Marissa had dreamed: having a devoted husband and partner; two beautiful, well-adjusted daughters; a historic but renovated and well-maintained home in a safe and walkable neighborhood; an obedient and well-trained dog; a newer-model car kept serviced and clean. All things she didn't have growing up but desperately wanted.

And while there were moments when she felt she had everything she needed, at other times it seemed to her that she had nothing at all. As night would fall at the end of another exceptionally busy day, she wasn't ever sure what, if anything, she had actually accomplished. Shuttling kids to and from school, activities, and playdates, making lunches and dinners, helping with geometry homework—all so necessary and yet so mundane. Where was that scrappy kid who could take on anything, who was voted "Most Brave" in her sixth grade class over all the boys, who always seemed to find adventure without ever looking for it? Somewhere along the long and winding path of motherhood, she had lost that part of her identity.

Perhaps if she could get to the bottom of the Watkins mystery, she might acquire a better understanding of her own family's dysfunction. Maybe she would find that families harboring secrets were more common than she assumed.

Marissa was convinced that if she could somehow shine some light on why the Watkinses died, or bring renewed attention to this cold case, it had the makings of a good article—maybe even a great one.

Coincidentally, around this same time, Marissa's lifelong friend Eileen had called to connect her with another friend named Jeannie who had mentioned a similar interest in embarking upon a second career in investigative journalism. Marissa was excited to meet someone else who shared her interests, and she and Jeannie exchanged phone numbers and set a midweek lunch date at Lulu, a restaurant in the courtyard inside the Hammer Museum in nearby Westwood Village.

"We've actually met once before," Jeannie told her. After a rare free hour spent surfing off Malibu Point the previous summer, Jeannie had run into Eileen and Marissa getting lunch at the Malibu Farm Cafe. The restaurant was at the end of the pier and had a casual walk-up counter and tables with a view of First Point, where Jeannie had been surfing for the previous thirty years.

Lulu had a more refined vibe, charming and intimate, and over dishes inspired by seasonal local produce, the two women learned they were facing similar crossroads in midlife. Blond, green-eyed Jeannie had also given up her corporate career when her child was born, and she was now asking the very same questions as Marissa, such as *What is the rest of my life going to look like?* and *Is it too late to make the second act of my life meaningful?* Jeannie seemed to Marissa like her kind of person. She had written freelance articles for surfing magazines in her twenties. "It was difficult to get a staff writing job," Jeannie said. "The magazines were written almost exclusively about, for, and by male surfers—with the noted exception of the swimsuit issue." For her part, Marissa shared with Jeannie an article she had published the month before on an online environmental advocacy website as part of a class project. As Los Angeles's oil boom slowed in the 1950s, many active wells in and around the Vista Hermosa neighborhood, just north of downtown Los Angeles, had been carelessly plugged with cement or abandoned outright. In the 1960s and 1970s, new neighborhoods had been constructed atop these long-festering toxic sites. Gases seeping from cracks in sidewalk concrete exposed residents to concentrations of hydrogen sulfide at levels "immediately dangerous to life and health." A penny left out on the street overnight would become corroded by the next day—all within sight of the skyscrapers of downtown L.A. Marissa's article related stories of residents dealing with noxious odors and high rates of respiratory illnesses and cancer.

Jeannie was impressed. "Did anything come of it?"

"Sort of," said Marissa. "A reporter at the *Los Angeles Times* ran a piece that expanded on what I'd found. But the story didn't mention my article at all." They connected on another topic, too, one that everyone was talking about: the 2019 novel coronavirus outbreak, which the World Health Organization had officially christened COVID-19. Eleven million people in the city of Wuhan, China, where the "atypical pneumonia-like illness" had originated, had been placed under lockdown. More recently the entire country of Italy had been shut down as well. Just the day before, the Centers for Disease Control had forecast that even in the United States, "the disruption to everyday life may be severe."

"What does that mean?" wondered Marissa. "School closings?"

"I don't know," said Jeannie. "Canceling large gatherings? How bad can it get?"

At that moment, there were fewer than twenty documented cases in the United States, yet both women had become obsessed, having followed news of the virus since January as it spread westward across the globe. Marissa had ordered hospital-grade disinfectant in February, and she was already in possession of some masks and supplies thanks to a FEMA-sponsored readiness course she had taken, Community Emergency Response Team (CERT) training.

"Crap," said Jeannie, suddenly worried that the Costco run for toilet paper she'd made the day before wasn't nearly enough. "I heard about a medical supply company near LAX that sells old medical masks and cleaning supplies in bulk, I might try them tomorrow." As they finished their lunch at the enchanting museum restaurant, neither woman had any real grasp of what was to come.

Marissa left feeling she had made a connection with Jeannie, but even more strongly that she had reaffirmed her ambition to pursue journalism. Though she had been tempted to mention her interest in the Watkins murders with Jeannie, she never did, for fear that her growing obsession with a fifteen-year-old cold case might come off as crazy.

In Marissa's first investigative foray beyond the resources of Google, she tracked down one of the reporters who had initially covered the story for the *La Cañada Valley Sun* in 2005. The writer had left journalism about ten years ago as the industry contracted and now owned and operated a power washing company in San Marino. The former reporter didn't remember much about the particulars of the Watkins story, except for one thing that had stuck in his mind: After early and eager participation from the distraught family of the missing couple, the adult children soon fell silent. He recalled reaching out to them for comment and their not returning his phone calls—the opposite of what one would expect from a family desperate for answers about their parents' overnight disappearance.

February became March, with Marissa continually tracking COVID-19 news in this most uncertain time. Marissa had become involved with a fundraiser for the girls' school, a midweek bowling night for parents, something she felt she couldn't get out of attending despite her worries. She'd added hand sanitizer to the budget for food and supplies. More than sixty parents originally RSVP'd for the event, but on that Tuesday night, only nine attended, all mothers. In hindsight, that was for the best. Close quarters chatting over chicken wings and communal bowling balls? It could have been a super-spreader event before the term had even been invented.

Instead of the usual small talk common to most parent gatherings, that night there was only nervous energy. The moms discussed Covid in terms of an impending storm, sharing tips about essential pantry items, the best places to get paper goods, the shock of encountering bare shelves in the liquor section at Costco. Everyone seemed to be measuring their anxiety against the group's, deciding where they needed to be on the spectrum from making doomsday jokes to being legitimately terrified. Marissa was near the terrified end of the range—Brian had a work trip coming up that she was frantic about—whereas others laughed off the thing that would soon overtake their lives. In an effort to change the subject, Marissa pounced on a lull in the conversation. "I came across this news story about an unsolved double murder case involving a married couple whose car went over a cliff, and I can't get it out of my mind."

Almost immediately, she regretted bringing it up. Marissa had a tendency to overshare—perhaps an overcompensation for her particularly secretive childhood.

While Marissa laid out some of the particulars of the Watkins murders, she was actively gauging the others' level of interest in the case as a way to check her own obsession. Was this mystery worth the time and energy she was pouring into it? Would others find the case as compelling as she did?

As she took them through the circumstances of the case, what she was really doing was seeking connection, wondering whether anyone else among the group thought and felt the same way she did.

A few of the women she spoke to were totally into it. Nicole, an outgoing and energetic working mom, audibly gasped at the family angle and wanted as much dirt as possible. "All of it, tell me everything, more, now," she said, making Marissa laugh out loud.

Samira, a confident and self-possessed mom whom Marissa knew vaguely from PTA volunteering, immediately leaned in, asking all the same questions about the case that Marissa had asked.

"Was there a will?" asked Samira. "Life insurance policies?"

"I don't know yet," said Marissa. "But the business debt was apparently settled somehow, so I'm guessing there was at least a will."

"I wonder how much the kids benefited from their parents' deaths?" asked Samira.

"It's the husband," said Nicole, laughing. "Always the husband. If I ever go missing, you know what to do."

"But he died too," said Marissa. "The news stories say it was definitely two homicides."

"Maybe he hired someone to take out him and his wife?" said Nicole. "Couldn't do it himself. Suicide negates life insurance, right? He did it for the kids."

"The kids who stopped cooperating with the police?" said Samira, her eyebrows raised.

"Ooh, right," said Nicole. "Much more interesting if their children did it, anyway."

"But why would they kill their own parents?" said Marissa.

"Do they need a motive?" said Nicole. "My own kids are already killing me."

Nicole's ability to process information so quickly and with such levity made Marissa want to hang out with her more. And she was relieved that what she originally mistook for amused engagement on Samira's part was actually a deep, judgment-free curiosity.

"I worked in deep background research in my previous life," Nicole told Marissa. "If you're ever stuck trying to look up something, I can probably help."

The women ended up bowling together in a group that night. They could have never guessed that this would be the beginning of a powerful, life-altering bond.

The following Monday, March 9, Marissa's Covid anxiety reached full panic mode. Brian had his bags packed and was insisting on going through with his business trip to San Francisco. Maybe he could duck out early and head back home before Friday, he offered. Sixty confirmed cases across the country didn't sound like much to him. The health risk of air travel was so obvious to her, so present and preventable, that she felt as though she were losing her mind. As the town car arrived to take him to the airport, Marissa stood in the doorway and made her last stand—literally begging him not to go. She was so freaked out that he relented. He had never seen her like this before. He sent the driver away with his apologies, and unpacked his bag.

On the morning of Wednesday, March 11, Marissa received an email announcing that officials at the girls' school would be meeting during the day to discuss next steps in light of the growing health threat. At 2:45 p.m., she received a follow-up email: The girls' school would be closing for two weeks. (Two weeks became fifteen months.) That evening, Marissa's classes were canceled as well. Citing 118,000 cases across 114 countries and 4,291 deaths globally, the World Health Organization officially declared COVID-19 a pandemic.

Pandemic. Okay. Serious and scary, but in a way, it was an exciting novelty, too. No school for the girls, which they loved. Tales of isolated panic-buying begat actual widespread panic-buying. Marissa heard the term "social distancing" for the first time.

On March 19 came the California statewide stay-at-home order, shutting down all but essential businesses.

Quarantine. The unthinkable. The entire world ground to a halt.

The ensuing days and weeks blurred together. Brian worked from home, setting up shop in the converted garage at the rear of the property. Remote school started up part-time at first, Marissa glimpsing the beleaguered teachers holding class from their kitchen or dining room table in the *Brady Bunch*–style Zoom box. Order-ahead groceries were placed in the trunks of vehicles in supermarket parking lots. Life became contactless and sterile.

Marissa, craving distraction beyond card games, jigsaw puzzles, and Netflix, was never more grateful for her obsession with the Watkinses. As she was just about to exhaust the resources available on the internet, a lawyer friend suggested she search Superior Court files to find the lawsuit the bank had filed against Joel Watkins's business in the weeks following his disappearance.

The lawsuit had been filed on June 13, 2005, sixteen days after the Watkinses disappeared. The plaintiff, Pacific Heritage Bank & Trust, wished to freeze the assets of the defendant and levy any outstanding funds owed to the bank. This turned out to be one of the most illuminating documents of the case.

The filing began by defining the factoring agreement between Wattkins LED and Pacific Heritage Bank & Trust. Invoice factoring provides advances of up to 85 percent of an invoice's value up front. Businesses with cash flow issues need to pay expenses immediately, while customers might take thirty, sixty, or ninety days to pay for goods delivered. For Wattkins LED to remain solvent, it needed access to working capital to bridge the period of time between delivery and payment. Wattkins LED would essentially sell its invoices (accounts receivable) to Pacific Heritage Bank & Trust (the factor) at a discount and receive cash immediately. Once the client paid the invoice to the bank, the bank would pay the remaining percentage of the invoice to Wattkins LED, minus a fee.

The liability limit of the amount of money to be fronted to Wattkins LED by Pacific Heritage under the terms of the agreement had been $900,000 in 2004. However, on February 18, 2005, three months before his disappearance, Joel Watkins signed a new guaranty increasing the bank's liability to $1,000,000.

The lawsuit made explicitly clear that Joel Watkins's guaranty was important because "Watkins was the business." The contacts and relationships were all his; he had started the business in the early 1990s, and only he could sign checks.

Much of the document was dry legalese—"Legal Basis for Default," "Representations and Warranties," "Code of Civil Procedures," and the like—but the comprehensive declaration of the vice president of Pacific Heritage Bank & Trust also revealed a great deal of practical information. Compellingly, it established a tick-tock of the circumstances of Joel Watkins's disappearance, beginning two days after he was last seen.

> On or about Monday, May 30, 2005, I appeared at the offices of WATTKINS LED pursuant to a pre-arranged meeting with Mr. WATKINS at approximately 2:45 PM. He had sent me an e-mail the previous Saturday indicating that he would be available at the office after 1:00 PM on Monday May 30. I had sent him an e-mail that morning giving an ETA at his office of about 2:30 PM, mentioning an unpaid receivable. We were also to discuss the renewal of the receivables facility, which was expiring June 7, 2005, one week away. When I arrived at his Pasa-

dena office, I was greeted by office manager Bonnie Salazar who informed me that Mr. WATKINS was not there,
and that she thought he had a doctor's appointment. I
asked her to have him call me, and I returned to the
bank.

On or about May 31, 2005, the next day, not having
received a call, I called and asked if Ms. Salazar had
heard from Mr. WATKINS. She indicated she had not,
that people were concerned, and that his son Andrew
had gone by the WATKINS's house the previous evening,
only to find that neither Mr. WATKINS nor his wife were
there. I asked her to keep me advised of any developments.

On Wednesday, June 1, 2005, I called again. Bonnie
said that Andrew had filed a missing persons report for
Mr. WATKINS and his wife. She said Mr. WATKINS's
cell phone had been found inside his office at WATT-
KINS LED. I asked to speak with Andrew, who stated he
had no idea where his parents were, and that a detective
would probably be calling.

I then advised various personnel at the bank inter-
nally that Mr. WATKINS was missing. Later that afternoon, I spoke with a detective from the Los Angeles
County Sheriff's Department for approximately 10 minutes. He wanted to verify the invoice factoring agreement and the existence of the meeting scheduled for
May 30, 2005. He asked several things about Mr. WAT-
KINS's business, some of which I could not disclose
due to privacy laws.

On Thursday, June 2, 2005, the bank sent out letters
to the various customers of WATTKINS LED asking
them to make checks payable to Pacific Heritage Bank &
Trust, to make sure that monies were properly paid.

On Friday, June 3, I received a voice message from

Andrew Watkins saying that the business was being shut down.

Since my first inability to contact Mr. WATKINS on May 30, 2005, I have received no e-mails or other communications from him or his wife. After May 30 and prior to June 10, 2005, when the WATTKINS LED accounts at the bank were closed, there were no checks written during that period by WATKINS on the business accounts.

I had no prior notice Watkins was leaving town or that anything was amiss with him or his wife. He had sent an e-mail to me on Saturday, May 28, 2005, to the effect that he was having meetings with potential investors in WATTKINS LED to seek additional capital and would be in contact with me that afternoon or Monday.

I spoke again with Andrew Watkins on June 7. He indicated that the business had no money, that all employees had been terminated, and that the bank in effect owned the business now.

It was a lot to process. The two touchstones for Marissa were family drama and financial stress. She did not know where this was going but it felt like a riddle she was emotionally and intellectually equipped to solve. It was immediately apparent to her that Andrew Watkins had some complicity in or knowledge of what had occurred. There was no other reason to shut down his father's company when his parents had been missing for less than a week.

The filing contained a list of the couple's assets, including the house on Shadow Peak Road in Paradise Canyon, then valued at approximately $1.5 million while "encumbered" by mortgages and loans in excess of $1 million. A copy of the Watkins Family Trust was included as an exhibit, bearing both Joel's and Angela's signatures. Also to be "attached" to the bank's claim was a small sum of money in a personal account at Pacific Heritage, and a life insurance policy in Joel's name in the amount of $1 million, of which Angela was the beneficiary. If she didn't survive him—as ended up happening—the estate would be the beneficiary.

In the bank's investigation into Joel Watkins's holdings, it discovered that at the end of May 2004, the time at which Joel was negotiating the invoice factoring arrangement with Pacific Heritage, he had also set up a separate limited liability company with exactly the same name, Wattkins LED, LLC, in the state of Nevada. "The Nevada entity, about which we have no information at present, is listed in good standing with the state," the filing added. This struck Marissa as highly irregular. Two LLCs in separate states? Was Joel Watkins using the Nevada shell corporation to launder the factoring payments from Pacific Heritage for his personal profit?

Then came the bombshell.

Pacific Heritage Bank & Trust began evaluating its position regarding WATTKINS LED and the Guaranty. It discovered as the result of its investigation that the invoices purchased were, by reason of apparent misrepresentation and concealment on the part of WATKINS, in some instances not bona fide.

Bank personnel immediately dispatched receivable collection letters to the payors of the WATTKINS LED invoice receivables Pacific Heritage had purchased. At least two of the responses claimed that the receivables they ostensibly owed were in fact fraudulent invoices. The receivables in question did not exist. One of those two responding parties frankly acknowledged that they had verified phony invoices at WATKINS's request because WATKINS said he needed more money.

Upon further review of the accounts receivable, it

appeared that there are no fewer than 7 and as many as 15 suspect customers of WATTKINS LED supplying receivables which may not have been bona fide. More may yet be uncovered.

Marissa read this again. This was theft, clearly and incontrovertibly—the whole reason the bank was suing Wattkins LED. Joel had asked vendors to falsify invoices on his account, which the bank had paid to Wattkins LED. If Joel Watkins thought or suspected that his crime had been found out by the bank, that would explain why he and his wife skipped town ahead of the Monday afternoon meeting with the bank officer. But what did Andrew Watkins know that led him to close down the business so suddenly?

That total amount owed to the bank by Wattkins LED and by Joel Watkins personally was just under $1 million. With various documents and exhibits attached—including a lengthy ledger of transactions, copies of news articles regarding the disappearance (which Marissa had already compiled), and the demand letters from the bank to Joel Watkins and Wattkins LED—the entire filing ran 110 pages long. Curiously, the last attachment was an online search of the California Board of Accountancy regarding Andrew Watkins, indicating that his CPA license was inactive. Marissa thought it intriguing that the bank official included a document concerning the professional status of the defendant's son.

This was progress, moving on from readily available internet news articles to an actual court document. She felt she had a framework for the case and the makings of a timeline, but there was much that still felt scattered. Marissa wished for a fresh set of eyes, a clear perspective. Someone with whom she could toss around different ideas. If she was going to do this, she wanted to do it right.

That's when she thought of Jeannie. Their lunch at the museum restaurant seemed so long ago now, a world away. It was a bit crazy, inviting a near-stranger to partner with her in investigating a double murder. In all likelihood, Jeannie would think Marissa was a weirdo going through some sort of crisis, which wasn't far from the truth. But the case was becoming murkier and heavier with each new discovery. Before she could change her mind, Marissa began typing out an email.

Hi Jeannie!

I hope you're hanging in there! It's been a roller coaster—some days are good, others are brutal.

I'm trying to pass the time with a new investigative piece. It's a weird story about an unsolved murder in the San Gabriel Valley . . .

Three weeks into the quarantine, Jeannie was going out of her mind like everyone else when she clicked the email in her inbox, subject line: Cold Case.

On Wednesday, April 8, 2020, 11:07:49 A.M. PDT, Marissa wrote:

Hi Jeannie!

I hope you're hanging in there! It's been a roller coaster—some days are good, others are brutal.

I'm trying to pass the time with a new investigative piece. It's a weird story about an unsolved murder in the San Gabriel Valley. The gist is, a couple was last seen on 5/28/05. Family members reported them missing on 6/1/05. On 7/7/05, the couple's car was spotted at the bottom of a ravine off the Angeles National Highway. Detectives deemed it an accident until the following month when one of the adult children contested the 2001 will. I spoke with a reporter who wrote a story about the disappearance in 2005. He said he doesn't recall much about the case except that family members were originally eager to get the story out to the press and then, suddenly, they stopped talking, which he found bizarre. I reached out to all four of the adult children and none of them responded.

Anyway, I was chatting with Eileen last night and I

wondered whether you would be interested in collaborating on this. It's been a challenge to track down documents in the quarantine, but I'm actually starting to
make some progress. The process might be more enjoy-
able and productive with someone else and I thought of
you.

Jeannie was thrown. Not by the out-of-the-blue invitation to
investigate an unsolved double homicide so much as the phrase
"the couple's car was spotted at the bottom of a ravine." It sent
her mind racing into the past.

Two traumatic losses had helped to shape the Jeannie of
2020, twin tragedies that had altered the trajectory of her life.
Both were sudden, accidental deaths of people she was close to.
The first one struck in her junior year at UCLA. Jeannie had
been born and raised in the San Fernando Valley, north of Los
Angeles, in a neighborhood of tract houses built on land for-
merly planted with orange groves. She was fifth-generation An-
geleno, her mother a homemaker and PTA volunteer, while her
father, who had served in Korea and considered a career in the
U.S. Army, worked a union job at a local General Motors plant.
Both parents were determined to create a healthy and happy childhood for Jeannie and her younger brother.

It was the 1970s and she lived in the kind of neighborhood
where kids walked in and out of friends' houses without knocking. Every day after school, Jeannie would climb the tree in her
yard to see if her best friend's family station wagon was in their
driveway so she could dash down the street to play. Her friend
was one of eight children, and Jeannie was drawn to the casual
chaos of their household, so different from her own warm but
orderly family life. She considered them eight surrogate siblings,
but especially her best friend and the freckle-faced middle son
four years younger than her, who also loved surfing.

They had remained close into her college years. Two days

after spending an afternoon at the beach together, Jeannie received a phone call from her brother, who was crying. The freckle-faced middle son was dead, the passenger in a car that had gone over a cliff into a ravine where he drowned in the river below. Jeannie hung up the phone, put a blanket over her head, and screamed. The worst moment was standing at his door the way she had a thousand times before and seeing the look in his mother's eyes. That was the moment Jeannie's childhood truly ended.

Though she still thought of the boy often, she hadn't considered the accident itself as she used to, imagining the unimaginable, picturing what it would be like to go over the edge of the road like that, tumbling down with such shattering force. His death changed her. It cracked her faith in a higher power or a greater plan. She felt vulnerable knowing that anything could happen at any time, but this realization also set her free to live large while she could.

Since childhood, she'd been immersed in books and dreaming of adventure—her favorite movie had been *Swiss Family Robinson,* and she liked the idea of living off the beaten path. Her rational, cautious side was there to balance her, so she did actually look before leaping, never wanting to cause her parents the pain she'd so recently seen. Her new outlook on life took her to Costa Rica after graduation, surfing and backpacking with friends. She continued to travel, sometimes with friends, sometimes on her own, funding her adventures with gig work in Los Angeles, nannying and waitressing. With school loans catching up to her, she fell into the Wild West of dot-com start-ups, where she basically lived out of the warehouse she worked in, napping under a desk she herself had built, and learning a lot by doing a little bit of everything for the company.

Between the travel and the start-ups, she learned to be resourceful and to think quickly on her feet. She also discovered she had a knack for out-of-the-box thinking and judicious risk-taking. Her friend group moved into a three-bedroom ocean-view apartment blocks from the beach in a funky area of Santa Monica once called Dogtown by the surfer/skater crowd. For most of the next decade, Jeannie and friends cycled in and out of the apartment as people changed jobs or enrolled in grad school.

Jeannie had only ever considered dating men until she met a woman at work who had a sense of humor so similar to an ex-boyfriend of hers that she thought of fixing the two of them up—until one night after work when the woman kissed Jeannie. She felt confused and intrigued, but also concerned: How would dating a woman affect the camaraderie and closeness of her other female friendships? She sat with this for more than a year, eventually telling her friends, one by one, each conversation a little less frightening than the last. She found herself with a cadre of supportive and willing wingwomen.

She was at a gay bar one night when a woman whose wit would prove as sharp as her cheekbones pressed a flyer into her hand for a punk band named Yank. Tamara was a homebody who loved entertainment, especially horror movies and true crime, and was hell-bent on becoming a TV writer, which they both knew could take years. Jeannie shifted her career from international development to domestic public policy and worked on issues like redistricting and campaign finance. Her report on redistricting was used to successfully lobby the state legislature to enact a law, and this achievement felt meaningful. Still, if they wanted to someday own a house and have a family, something had to give. This is how Jeannie ended up at an entertainment company. Within the year, she created a research and analytics department from scratch, and over the next decade she enjoyed leading her team in discovering new and interesting consumer insights.

Tamara's writing career finally took off, and they could afford their next move. They found a donor—after what she refers to as "the most difficult online shopping ever"—and, after some fragile years with several false starts, welcomed their one and only child.

With Tamara working long hours, most weekends, and many out-of-town location shoots, Jeannie juggled motherhood, her career, and household duties. In the back of her mind, she wondered if she was doing her child a disservice by not providing the safety and stability Jeannie had enjoyed growing up with a stay-at-home mom. A good friend came to town ahead of relocating there, and Jeannie was so overextended she had to pass on getting together with him. Back in New York City, the friend texted her not to worry, that he would be in L.A. for good soon and was excited that they would be seeing more of each other. Hours after sending that text, the friend died in a shocking accidental fall. Again, Jeannie's life priorities underwent a thorough reassessment. A few months later, with Tamara's support, Jeannie quit her job.

There was plenty of volunteer work to keep her busy at their co-op preschool, and Jeannie also started a nonprofit with an economics professor she had met through work. This venture kept her résumé from getting stale, but her heart wasn't in it. Most of her friends were working, and their occasional questions about what she was doing with all her time off stung. When their child started elementary school, she put her research and planning skills to good use solving all manner of child-related concerns. Although that was satisfying, it was also a very narrow use of her attention, and she wondered if she could step back into the broader world that she used to inhabit so easily and with such curiosity.

At their new school, Jeannie and Tamara were "assigned" to another couple, veteran parents with a boy in the same class. These were Eileen and her husband. Eileen and Jeannie hit it off right away—which was how it came to be that in early 2020, Jeannie confessed to Eileen her desire to bring her professional life full circle, harking back to her earliest career goals and her time writing freelance surfing articles. Pursuing a new career as an investigative journalist was a crazy dream, something she hadn't even shared with Tamara yet. Eileen said, "You have to meet my friend Marissa!"

Jeannie and Marissa bonded authentically at their lunch at Lulu, downloading their former professional lives and sharing a love of adventure, travel, and good books. The conversation was effortless and unusually frank, with both women expressing struggles with their identities in this phase of stay-at-home mothering, missing the independence and intellectual stimulation they had so valued prior to having children. While both loved being parents, they recognized and commiserated over the restrictions that parenthood had placed on their lives. They both felt they had reached another *Now what?* moment.

Jeannie left their lunch feeling that Marissa was real and grounded, as well as being warm and inviting, with her big smile and soft speech. Jeannie valued integrity and felt the same from Marissa. Collaborating with her on an article sounded like an interesting challenge, as well as something productive to do rather than doomscrolling and obsessively watching the news— but two unsolved murders with a family angle? Did Marissa think she could actually solve this cold case? Had she any experience doing criminal investigative work? Jeannie certainly had none. Still, she was flattered, and immediately replied.

On April 8, 2020, at 1:26 P.M. PDT, Jeannie wrote:

Hi Marissa,

A rollercoaster sounds about right. I once was stuck on a sailboat for 6 weeks (my own damn doing) and this reminds me of that experience—minus the seasickness and all the free time to read.

I would love to work with you on this! You know, of course, that I'm a neophyte and won't pretend to know what the hell I'm doing. But I would be glad to focus on something worthwhile.

Let me know how you would like to proceed.

Thank you for thinking of me (and I'll thank Eileen too).

Best,
Jeannie

Jeannie looked up some newspaper articles about the disappearance and snooped on a few Facebook pages that night, but she didn't read too deeply, wanting to keep an open mind. Marissa got back to her the next day.

On Thursday, April 9, 2020, 1:50:22 P.M. PDT, Marissa wrote:

Great! This is new for me too so we'll learn together. Do you have any time to chat today and I can give you the latest? I can create a google drive to share info, too.

At the time, Jeannie had no inkling that this cordial email exchange with someone she barely knew would alter the course of her life.

As stressful and strange as the early days of Covid lockdown were, Zoom meetings and remote work and schooling hadn't kicked in yet, so there was still a staycation vibe amid the pandemic terror and uncertainty. No carpools, no nonessential errands, no workers coming to the house. Life had become a schizophrenic mix of apocalyptic dread and mandatory vacation—a snow day for an invisible storm that nobody knew when or even whether it would end.

Jeannie read half of the 110-page Pacific Heritage Bank & Trust lawsuit on her iPad that night while drinking a dry martini in a hot bath. (The quarantine did offer a *few* consolations.) The narrative of Joel Watkins's disappearance and the scope of his company's fraud was compelling.

But upon further review, Jeannie's initial excitement began to fade. With his financial crimes so obvious, and the bank clearly on to Joel's desperate scheme, there were only two options: prison or suicide. It seemed clear to Jeannie that Joel Watkins, either with or without his wife's consent, had taken the latter way out.

The next day, Jeannie used a now defunct aggregating site for professional contacts to pull together a list of employees at Wattkins LED from the company's inception until its shuttering in June 2005. She used LinkedIn to assemble contact information for all known former employees and dutifully entered them into a spreadsheet for easy reference. But her heart wasn't in it. She felt terrible about having to disappoint Marissa. She dreaded their next conversation, not wanting to burst Marissa's balloon by telling her that there likely was no case to investigate.

"So," said Marissa, in her lilting SoCal voice, before Jeannie could say anything, "I talked to the homicide detective investigating the case."

"I'm sorry—you what?"

In the many weeks since Marissa first viewed the captivating footage of the SUV being lifted from the ravine, her interest in the case had crossed over from mere curiosity to minor obsession. But despite her best efforts, Marissa had come to an impasse on gathering intel about the Watkins family. Every new piece of information led only to more questions, never any answers. *Why did son Andrew stop practicing accounting? What were his employment responsibilities at Wattkins LED? Joel and Angela's son-in-law Greg Medina had a lengthy list of court actions against him, and was deeply in debt—did he stand to gain from* *his wife's parents' deaths? Who else, if anyone, knew about the factoring fraud going on at Joel Watkins's company?*

Working first out of her kitchen, then her bedroom, then off a broad coffee table set before her favorite chair in her living room, Marissa felt herself going a little stir-crazy. But who wasn't? That's when it occurred to her: Everyone else in the state was also stuck at home. She looked up the detective's name from the 2005 newspaper articles: Raymond Fonseca. She spread out all her research on the table in front of her, ran through the facts of the case in her head a few times in preparation, then dialed the telephone number she had found for him.

She was nervous—actually, scared—but also thrilled. She couldn't explain why, but she had an inexplicable sense of confidence that Detective Fonseca would be receptive to her outreach.

He was anything but.

"Who are you?" he barked. "Why are you calling my home?"

He sounded agitated and legitimately angry at her. All the blood drained from Marissa's face. While she had felt from the start that she was getting involved in something she had no right to, in that moment she was overcome with shame. Was she acting out of a sense of entitlement? Privilege? The last thing she wanted was to be disrespectful.

She shook off the fear and channeled all of her energy into persuading him to hear her out. After a few preliminaries meant to jog his memory about the case, she began spitting out some of the information she had found. The bank lawsuit, the factoring invoices, the uncooperative adult children of the victims. How she thought it was suspicious that the son, Andrew, had moved all the way across the country immediately after his parents' estate probate closed. She expected him to hang up on her at any moment.

"Why are you interested in this case?" he asked, still annoyed. "Is this for some podcast or tabloid or something?"

She answered honestly. "I don't know why I am so compelled

to investigate this case." She explained her tissue-thin personal connection to the crash site—having camped and explored near there in her youth—and how her interest in the deaths and the family had ballooned from there. "I'm studying journalism, and I know that if this cold case were to be solved, it would make for a terrific article. But really, above all else, I just want to know who killed Joel and Angela Watkins, and why."

There followed a long pause, to the point where she wondered if he had finally hung up. "Well," he said, "I want to know too."

He went on to say that it had been the most frustrating case of his career. Seizing upon what felt like an opening, Marissa brought up how bizarre it seemed to her that the family had withdrawn their cooperation with the press and the police after their parents' disappearance.

"Bizarre, no," he said. "Suspicious, yes." He said that Andrew Watkins was the primary family contact, and the first of them to clam up after making some conflicting statements. About the Watkinses' son-in-law, daughter Marie's husband, Greg Medina, he said he was "a complicated character."

"Does that mean he was a suspect?" Marissa asked.

"I'm not telling you that."

"What were Andrew's conflicting statements about?"

"I'm not getting into that with you either."

"But it was definitely murder?" she asked.

"It was two murders."

It felt like her heart hit a double beat. "How do you know?"

"I can't share that."

For a moment, Marissa thought that maybe he wanted her to ask yes-or-no questions. "Was their car forced off the road?" she asked. "Were they murdered before they went over into the canyon?"

"I can't share that."

"But it was not a murder-suicide?"

"It was not," he said. "The Watkinses died at the hands of someone else."

Later, she would wonder whether Detective Fonseca was being intentionally ambiguous, or whether his wording reflected the fact that he himself still did not know what really happened. In the moment, she plunged ahead, keeping him talking. "Why were you unable to solve the case?"

"There were reasons," he said. "I'm retired now, as of last year. The Watkins case is one of very few pieces of unfinished business from my career. And I don't mind telling you, it haunts me to this day."

"What's the status of the case now?" she asked.

"I was the lead investigator," he said. "With my retirement, the case has officially gone cold."

Marissa felt a tingle in the back of her neck at these words. "What does it take for a cold case to become active again?"

"I suppose the Watkins case could be reopened if a compelling new lead or some substantial additional information developed," he said. He didn't sound very hopeful, but his tone had changed completely since the unfortunate start to their conversation. He seemed impressed with all that Marissa had learned on her own, to the point where she thought he might be subtly inviting her to look deeper into the murders, encouraging her to take up his torch. Only later would she realize how wrong she was on this point—that not only was no one going to hand them a torch, but they were going to have to grab it themselves.

She apologized again for calling him at home and asked if she could keep in touch with him via text. Detective Fonseca gave her his cellphone number, which, to Marissa, felt like a win.

It was a bit of an out-of-body experience," Marissa told Jeannie. "After I hung up and snapped back into reality, I thought, 'Who the hell do I think I am?'"

Jeannie was flat-out amazed. "I cannot believe you cold-called a homicide detective."

"It was a little crazy," said Marissa, laughing. "I don't know what came over me. Sometimes I do impulsive things. I really thought he'd be happy to hear from me. He burst my bubble real quick. He definitely kept me at arm's length throughout, but he didn't call me an idiot or tell me to go away."

"On the contrary!"

"Like, it's still settling in—that I talked to a homicide detective. I'm not used to dealing with a personality like that. It was unreal. But very real."

Jeannie's head was swimming. She looked over the notes she had scribbled down. "Definitely murder, he said. You realize that means the killer or killers are still out there somewhere. Maybe close by. Maybe their name is known to us already."

"Family members," said Marissa.

What had always been a possibility now seemed like a probability. "I wonder what prevented him from ever solving it," said Jeannie. "Like, was it for a lack of conclusive evidence? Does he know who did it, but he couldn't prove it? Or did he never get close enough to the truth?"

"All I know is that he said it was a career case for him. He's retired, but it seems he remains the detective of record, since no one else is working on it. After I got off with him and settled myself down, I reached out to the Los Angeles County Sheriff's Department for their records regarding this case."

Jeannie told Marissa about the spreadsheet of former employees she had begun compiling.

"That's amazing," said Marissa, excited. "Do you want to split it up and start making calls?"

"You're the cold-caller," said Jeannie. "How about you do that, and I'll dig deeper on the accountant son and the shifty son-in-law."

"Great! Let's circle back in a few days and compare. Detective Fonseca said that new information could jump-start the investigation—so let's give him some."

Jeannie hung up in a daze. Instead of lowering the boom on Marissa and dashing her dreams, Jeannie found herself inspired by Marissa's having taken such a great leap in calling the homicide detective. Now it was Jeannie's turn to impress. Just like that, she was back on the case.

Since quarantine began Marissa had found herself sleeping later and later. With no school drop-off, an eight-thirty wake-up became the norm. She couldn't tell whether it was mild depression setting in or a convenient way to avoid the tedious sameness of the days.

Between Brian, the girls, and their dog, Cecil, Marissa's house seemed to be shrinking fast. The case became her respite, though she found it nearly impossible to shut the door on everything else when she wanted to focus on it. Her living room setup was too exposed for telephone calls. *Mom, open this. Mom, the Wi-Fi's slow. Mom, Cecil's throwing up.* The bathroom door had a lock on it, but that was the first place anyone would look for her, so she took most of her calls about the case in her bedroom, sitting cross-legged on the floor of her closet with the door closed.

Marissa reached out to former employees of Wattkins LED via email and LinkedIn messaging. She wrote that she was a journalist working on an article about the unsolved murders of Joel and Angela Watkins and alluded to being in contact with the police. It wasn't a dishonest approach, just a little embellished.

Few responded. A woman named Patti Chenton, who had worked in sales at Wattkins LED, was the first. Because of Patti's earnest and generous nature, her insight into the early days of Joel Watkins's company, her evident affection for her former boss, and her undimmed curiosity about what happened, this early call was one of the most productive interviews of the entire case. Marissa taped the conversation, with Patti's permission, and later transcribed it:

> I joined Wattkins LED in August of 1995. Joel started making a lot of money pretty quickly since there was very little competition in the lighting industry at that time. We went from a four-million-dollar company to a ten-million-dollar company within twelve months and we built a pretty nice business there. Joel was spending money like crazy. He liked to get things from Europe and he and Angela would go on trips, and he became very much like he felt he'd arrived, that kind of thing. We used to joke about it amongst ourselves. I mean, we all liked him, we all loved Joel, but we knew that we were really the ones that were making him successful.
>
> But coming into 1998, things started getting weird. Joel had hired a new manager to come in, and they started going out drinking in the afternoon and, you know, discussing what to do with the company and this and that or whatever, and kind of leaving me out of it. The son, Andrew, came in too, and it was kind of a boys' club, and I was worried about losing my footing in the company.

Marissa had a list of questions for Patti. Foremost among them were questions regarding Andrew Watkins's relationship with his father and his authority to make decisions in the company. She also wanted to know more about Angela Watkins.

> At the time when I worked there, Joel always talked about Andrew as, you know, being this great accountant and whatever. But Joel made all the money decisions. My cousin Hal stayed on after I left, and he did the payroll,

so I don't know what Andrew's duties were. Didn't he shut down the business, and then move away very quick after it all happened?

Angela, the mother, was very interesting. She was, from what I remember, very, very beautiful. Not stunningly beautiful in the sense of gorgeous makeup and hair and that type of thing. She was half Chinese, or Asian, sorry, and a very natural, naturally beautiful woman. And she would not ever go in the sun, to the point where Joel would tell us when they would drive in the car, she would wear gloves and a hat to protect her skin. She had very beautiful porcelain skin, and Joel was really proud of her. And we had a Christmas party one time where Angela came, and she just sat there like a doll. I mean, she really was not very social. She smiled a lot. And Joel used to say that she's just a wonderful housekeeper. She cleans one room a day, so the house is [always] clean. It was just the most bizarre thing to me.

We had a great team back then and it was a blast. One of the funnest jobs I ever had. But he was just so bizarre in certain ways.

Yeah. I always questioned Andrew. Maybe Andrew helped his dad, maybe murder-suicide? Because I think that the company was in Angela's name, and that if he went down, she would go to jail.

Marissa clarified that Joel and Angela were listed as co-owners, each with signature rights to the company. "It does seem a little bit strange that both of them happened to go down like this," she observed, to which Patti replied,

You see, I think that there's definitely something to that, that Joel could not stand beautiful porcelain Angela going to jail. And this is just a theory we threw around, that either Joel and Angela took some drugs, killed themselves, or he killed Angela first and then he drank the potion or whatever, and put a brick on the gas pedal and went over the cliff. Or Joel went to Andrew and said, "We're in trouble. There's no way your mom and I can go to jail, and we will go to jail. Will you help me?" But we always thought it was very weird that Andrew left town so quickly. It's all weird. I just know that something was shady, and Joel was in deep in something.

Do you know who Dennis Ladd is? Okay, well, unfortunately Dennis Ladd is the person who probably knows the most about everything, and he died a month ago. He was very sick. Joel and Dennis were close, Dennis did the books, and I knew Dennis a little later in life, and he never said too much, but I always felt Dennis knew a lot more than he was letting on.

I do know about the last time Dennis talked to Joel. Joel had gone into the office on a Saturday right before he disappeared, and he called Dennis, and he was in a panic. He said, "Dennis, I'm in trouble," and Dennis said, "Don't worry about it, don't do anything, we're gonna fix this." I don't know what he meant by that, but this is what Dennis told me. He said, "I made an appointment with him to go to lunch on Monday, telling him to calm down, go enjoy the weekend, don't worry about it." So anyway, Dennis went to lunch on Monday, and Joel never showed up. I believe, if I've got my days right, he went missing between that Saturday phone call and the Monday.

Patti would continue to be helpful, checking in from time to time and answering Marissa's occasional queries. More than that, her avid interest in the unsolved murders so many years after the fact, coupled with her sincere hope for a resolution, gave Marissa a jolt of confidence. *Maybe I can do this,* she thought.

Marissa had learned about California wiretap laws in her journalism courses, and for legal purposes she made certain to have each interviewee state their name and that they understood they were being recorded at the start of each conversation. Marissa shared the audio file of her talk with Patti Chenton with Jeannie, who listened to it twice. Both agreed that they liked Patti, who was gossipy and real. That was one of the things they missed about working, the social camaraderie of office friends— something that, in time, they would develop with each other.

"So, it seems that Joel was liked," summarized Marissa. "Money was rolling in, the company was growing, and then Andrew came in and things started to change? I don't want to read too much into that."

"No, I got that too," said Jeannie. "And, of course, Dennis, the accountant, who maybe knew where the bodies were buried— not literally—died just a month ago. Perfect timing. What about her take on Angela?"

"Super interesting. She's the one we know the least about."

"I wonder how much Angela knew about the fraud, if anything, and when?"

Over the next few days, Jeannie pulled files on Andrew Watkins and Greg Medina from the website of the California Secretary of State. She pulled multiple corporate filings for Greg Medina's many businesses. Medina Industries. Medina Technology. GXM Engineering. Companies started and closed from the mid-1990s through to the present day—all of them having to do with manufacturing and engineering, but none, so far as Jeannie could tell, involved with anything related to the lighting products that Wattkins LED brokered and installed.

"Let me start with Andrew," Jeannie said to Marissa, catching her up on the phone during a rare spare moment in the middle of another day of lockdown. Tamara was working in a remote writers' room from a detached home office, while Jeannie was always in earshot of their seven-year-old, who was attending Zoom school while curled up in a blanket with Oliver, the family's three-legged Bengal cat. The progressive school's philosophy was "Learn from Play," which did not translate at all to independent homeschooling. It fell to Jeannie to bridge the gap, playing math and word games together, and later quitting for the day to go on a bike ride together around the vacant UCLA campus. Suddenly Jeannie was a combination substitute teacher and end-times recreation counselor. Only at night could she reliably sit at her desk in the bedroom and get some detective work done—once she stopped herself from fatalistic surfing of the internet kind.

"He moved to South Carolina in 2007, married, and bought the house he currently lives in."

Marissa said, "I can't find anything on him in South Carolina."

"There's next to nothing. I don't even know what his occupation is out there. He's not a CPA again, I know that. From what I could scrape off the internet, I found nothing nefarious in his professional life prior to his parents' disappearance. In South Carolina, he's kind of a ghost, whereas his time in California was filled with all these civil cases."

"Like civil suits? Or creditor-type stuff?"

"Both. He has a deep, troubled financial history in the civil records, from what I found, and I bet there's more that I can't get. Case after case." She paused. "Have you ever been sued? Even once? I haven't."

"I can't even imagine," said Marissa. "Have all these cases been settled, or are they still open? Were they settled after the murders?"

"Some were still outstanding and only settled as recently as 2018. Mostly real estate–related things. Like, petition to curb for arbitration, enter a judgment and award. He's always the defendant. And yet it doesn't seem like their standard of living ever took a huge hit. Andrew was living well while being in significant debt. There's something here, right?"

"Just after he closes the company, all these creditors come forward and say they're owed, never mind the bank and his father's American Express card, and he jumps in front of them and makes a claim for one hundred and twenty thousand dollars?"

Jeannie said, "There is a lot going on with this family."

Marissa laughed. "Makes mine look sane."

"And then Greg Medina, daughter Marie's husband? Also with a ton of financial issues, including right around the time of the murders. He has all these other businesses and a trail of judgments and liens and whatnot that makes Andrew's case history look modest. But, zeroing in on the first half of 2005 when all this happened, six months prior to the deaths, it looks like he had some connection with Wattkins LED that started around the beginning of that year and, naturally, ended with its dissolution. I can't find out what the relationship was, because it doesn't appear professional, in that his company had nothing to do with lighting or importing. It could be a coincidence, but there are unpaid invoices and returned checks and so on. It looks to me like he would have been desperate for cash around that time. And so somehow his and his father-in-law's businesses become entangled."

Marissa said, "I wonder how he got along with Joel and Angela. You know, in-law relationships."

"That would be good to know. And I'm still kind of looking for a Chinese connection in this. With the importing, and Joel having launched the business maybe, allegedly, using contacts on Angela's side of the family? I don't know, it just seems that he could have gotten in over his head with money owed to overseas people who were the wrong people to owe money to?"

"There's so much. There's *too* much. Speaking of which—I want to run something by you. Two other women—moms, we have kids in the same grade—and I were talking about the Watkins murders, and each of them, separately, asked if they could help."

Jeannie was surprised but tried not to let on. "Oh. Yes, sure. Of course."

"Only if you're okay with it. I thought putting some more eyes and ears on this would help."

"Great," said Jeannie. "Yes."

"I'm talking to another Wattkins LED employee tomorrow, Patti's cousin Hal, so if you think of any other questions I should ask him, let me know. And then I'll connect the four of us."

Hanging up, Jeannie felt a pang of self-reproach. *Am I not doing enough?* She liked Marissa a lot and felt that they were connecting. At the same time, having more women on this case could certainly help. There was a chance it could also derail their progress with personality conflicts and promised contributions that never materialized—but she trusted that Marissa was as good a judge of character as she appeared to be. Hopefully it would all work out.

The bowling night fundraiser was one of the last "normal" things Samira did before the world shut down. No one knew what was coming. Had she known, Samira would have skipped the potentially infectious event and missed out on one of the most profound connections of her life.

After having already made meaningful friendships within her older daughter's school community, Samira was now trying to do the same at her younger daughter's school. But when only eight other parents showed up that night, she wondered whether the effort was even worth it. But when Marissa—whom Samira knew from school activities but only by sight—pivoted from discussing second grade curriculum and Covid fears to an obscure cold case that she had become obsessed with, Samira leaned right in. Her fascination with true crime ran deep. In eighth grade, she had done a book report on *Helter Skelter: The True Story of the Manson Murders,* and upon learning what a forensic psychologist was, wanted to become one. She had always been drawn to puzzles and wanting to understand what made people tick—so when the bowling began and they divided into two foursomes, she knew she wanted to team up with Marissa and Nicole. That night for the first time she really got to know both of them—and liked them immediately. She was relieved that they were not "precious" moms, but friendly, open, and easy to connect with.

"If you ever want help researching this for your article," Samira told Marissa, "let me know."

Samira woke up the next day thinking about the case. The vanishing, the car crash, a double murder, financial improprieties—all of it compelling. But what gripped her most was the family at the heart of the crime. From a young age, she had always asked the same question: *What makes people do the things they do?*

In many ways Samira's childhood had been typical. But life is layered and complex, and so are family dynamics. The defining event of her young life came at age nine when her biological father remarried, started a new family, and cut off all contact with her and her sister. Blindsided and completely devastated, she struggled to understand how a parent could so easily walk away. Though her mother got married to a wonderful man—whom Samira calls Dad to this day—nothing could fully fill the hole left behind. The abandonment left scars: a lingering fear of never being enough, a wariness of people's true intentions, and a deep need to decipher human behavior.

Samira refused to let this hurtful experience define her. She threw herself into high school, excelling in sports, theater, clubs, and academics. Socially and academically, she thrived. College brought new challenges. She initially attended Butler University on a promised track scholarship—one that failed to materialize after the coach who recruited her left the school. Unable to afford the tuition, Samira transferred to IUPUI, a public research university offering degrees from both Indiana University and Purdue University. She put herself through school by working two jobs and graduated with a psychology degree. And through it all, the same question persisted: *What makes people do the things they do?*

During college, Samira reached out to her biological father in a heartfelt letter asking him that very question. His response was brief and inadequate—falling far short of the emotional connection and closure she was looking for. She was deeply disappointed, but it was then she decided it was time to truly let him go.

Years later, out of the blue, he called her. When he told her that he was proud of her, Samira said, "How can you possibly be proud of me? You don't even know me. You have no idea what kind of person I am, what kind of mother I am." Rejecting his hollow approval turned out to be one of her own proudest moments.

Samira and her husband, Ward, had met at age fifteen in high school, and they became best friends. Ward was popular and smart like Samira, and in him she found a kindred spirit. His family dynamic was very different from hers, yet they both held the same role in their families—that of the "responsible, dependable" child, the one no one had to worry about. Despite their attending different colleges, their bond deepened. Samira would vet his potential girlfriends for him, and when a football player broke her heart, Ward, who was gallant but nowhere near the size of a college football player, offered to beat him up.

After graduation, they, along with another longtime friend, become roommates as they tried to figure out how to make their way in the world. One night a few months in, each of them wound up back at the apartment with their respective dates. Ward was downstairs watching TV with his when he heard Samira upstairs laughing with hers. In that moment, he realized he was in love with Samira. He held off confessing his feelings for her as long as he could, until one day, much to Samira's surprise, he declared his love. They had a long talk, during which she put on her psych major hat and talked him down, convincing him that this was a straightforward case of emotional transference. Her greatest worry was that Ward's confession of love threatened to blow up their friendship, which was so important to her. By night's end, he agreed that she was right. It was a passing impulse—never mind.

The next morning, he greeted her in the kitchen with more certainty than ever. "Nope," he said, "you're wrong. I love you, and I bet you love me too."

It took Samira a few months to admit she felt the same. It turned out everyone else around them—friends, family, neighbors—had seen it. Samira was hesitant because she was most afraid of losing her best friend. And she had always assumed she would marry someone who was Black like herself. Clearly, she had to let that go, because she now knew she and Ward were forever.

Her first job after graduating was as a therapeutic foster care caseworker. Her caseload included children with developmental and physical special needs, as well as those emerging from profoundly abusive and traumatic backgrounds. She was entrusted with the critical responsibilities of monitoring and supervising court-ordered family visits, conducting thorough home studies to assess potential foster families, and performing regular home visits to ensure that existing foster homes remained compliant and safe. It was a demanding role for someone in her early twenties, and she witnessed some of the most challenging aspects of human behavior and the impact they have on children, to the point that she was reluctant to have children of her own. Once she and Ward had saved enough money, they packed up their lives and moved to California, seeking bigger opportunities. They had no jobs lined up and no place to live, but once they got there they never looked back. Samira took a job as a receptionist at a start-up and soon bluffed her way into a project management job, which ultimately led to a successful career in digital advertising.

Samira loved her work, and it became her identity. Seventy-hour weeks were no problem, even welcomed. Digital advertising was new and hot at the time, and she felt fulfilled, challenged, and appreciated. Ward worked similarly ridiculous hours at his job in the technology sector, and in 2010, he embarked upon a start-up with friends, adding to his heavy workload by commandeering the dining room table on nights and weekends. That venture, an employment website company, eventually took over his professional life, and he quit his "day job" to become its chief design officer.

Ironically, only when doctors told Samira she might not be able to have children on her own did she realize how much she wanted them. Years of fertility struggles and multiple heartbreaking miscarriages followed before she finally got the family she wanted. Samira had her first daughter at age thirty-three. She returned to work six months later, cried on that first day back, then got on with it. At thirty-nine, she had her second daughter. Six months later she again returned to work, but this time the daily crying went on for months. Samira was on track for a vice president position. Though balancing the demands of a busy career with family life could at times be overwhelming, leaving that career, a job Samira loved and in which she thrived as a leader, was a difficult choice. In the end, her desire to be home with her two beautiful children was greater than her desire to be at work. And, as she says, it wasn't like she was curing cancer.

Samira was a crafty person and loved to cook, so she envisioned making costumes and preparing gourmet meals. A few years in, she admitted a difficult truth to herself: Maybe this wasn't enough for her. She was a connected and engaged mother, but while she very much enjoyed and cherished the time with her kids, she knew she was not a hundred percent fulfilled, and she felt guilty that so much of her identity was still caught up in being a working woman. At the time, she thought it was just her.

She redoubled her efforts, throwing herself into more activities, including taking on a two-year commitment in her daughters' school's PTA. That role was largely administrative, dealing with budgets, and actually quite stressful—all of which was right up her alley. Samira had been more involved socially with her older daughter's friends' parents than those of her younger daughter, which felt like a disservice. Having come to full-time stay-at-home mothering a little later in the game than most, Samira had missed out on the formative moms' groups and baby classes where relationships were formed.

By the time Samira talked to Ward about going back to work, a few years in, the start-up company he had co-founded was truly taking off. He suggested she take a little more time to figure out what she wanted her next chapter to look like.

When Covid hit, Samira took lockdown seriously, assiduously cleaning produce in a vinegar-water bath outside her house before transferring her grocery purchases from their packaging into her own sterile containers. Once Zoom school was up and running, she felt it was essential that she function as a co-teacher to both daughters, especially her second grader. Zoom school begat Zoom dance classes and even Zoom soccer. She had received a sewing machine as a present the previous year but had never taken it out of the box. Now she set up the machine and taught herself to make masks. Samira had herself and her family tested regularly as a precaution. She didn't want to get the virus from anyone, and she didn't want to give it to anyone either.

These were some of the forces working on Samira when she received a text from Marissa a day or two after the bowling alley fundraiser:

Marissa: Hey were you serious about helping with research?

The answer was hell yes, and Marissa forwarded her the bank affidavit in order to get Samira's thoughts. Samira was excited, not only because true crime was her binge but also because it was something to *do*. Something she could use her brain for that was an escape from Zoom school and the ever darkening news and Covid.

Samira took copious notes and started making lists. Knowns

and unknowns. Questions to be asked, contradictions to be re-solved. She packed it all into a document and emailed it to Marissa—and immediately after she'd hit Send, wondered if she had overstepped. Maybe she would come off looking like a kook.

Marissa responded almost immediately, sending her a link to the Google drive containing all the case files and interviews to date.

Okaaay, thought Samira, riding the adrenaline. *Maybe I've found my people.*

There were two newly recorded interviews on the Google drive. The first was with Hal Durban, Patti Chenton's cousin, who had worked for Joel Watkins longer than she had. He did the company's payroll, so this was their first insider's perspective on Joel's financial practices. Just by the sound of Hal's voice, Samira could tell that he was one of those people who loved to dish, even if the gossip was fifteen years old.

> *As a normal person, Joel Watkins was really good. I think he had a kind heart. As a businessman, he was hor-rible. I think he grew too fast. When I first started there, we were in a small office, and he was making really good money, we all were. He decided to lease a new place and this place was probably a good four to five times the size and the rent. And then he started hiring just these abso-lute jokers or just people who didn't necessarily have experience. He would be at a restaurant and talk to the waitress and then the waitress would start working for us as a salesperson. When we went to the new office, he wanted to hire people to fill the space rather than hire people he needed. So it was kind of ass-backwards in my perception, because he didn't have the accounts to sus-*

tain that many people, but he needed to perceive that he had this huge business and his head just got really big after that. Really, really big.

The son was a trip. Here's some background on him that you probably could use. Andrew was an accountant, and I use that term loosely. I think he was at one of the larger firms and something happened and he left. Draw your own conclusions, but going to work for his dad was not a step up. So Joel gave him an office and put him on the payroll, which was ridiculous. He didn't do much of anything other than use his office to do day-trading.

As a person, no, I didn't like him at all. I thought he was smarmy and completely stuck-up and very egotistical. He walked around with a very arrogant air as if he was so much better than everybody else. Making big bucks and really not doing anything.

At the end for me, I'll be honest, there were certain things I did not want to do. Having to do with finances. I was not comfortable doing them. Joel was trying to get a personal loan, and stuff came to me to verify, and I didn't want to put my signature on it. He seemed to commingle his stuff, his business and personal. I remember him having a separate checking account that nobody had access to at all. I never even reconciled it, never saw it at all. But he would move money into it.

Hal went on to talk about a CPA who came in once a week, with whom he'd had a disagreement about how to book certain invoices and expenses. Soon after that, Joel told Hal he was letting him go. Hal said that at the time he assumed it was because business was slow, but after the fraud allegations came out, he remembered his dustup with the CPA and wondered if that was why Joel sent him packing.

When he first went missing, I heard about it on the news. I think my partner was watching TV and said, Oh my gosh, isn't that, I think your boss was on TV. *And I turned it on, and they had it, he and Angela's face on there. And oh my God, it was so weird. That's really, that's unbelievable. I remember talking to Patti, you know, and I'll be honest, we were both kind of morbidly curious. So we called the office to see, like, who answers or who's still there and kind of like what's going on. And we got the recording that they had shut the business down.*

No one had reported him dead. *I said this to the detectives, maybe six, seven months after they found them, they came to my work to question me and just get some background. I said something's not right because nobody would shut a company down that quick if they didn't know what was happening. And frankly, I know Joel well enough to know if somebody did that to him, and if he came back, he would have been so pissed knowing that everything he built was lost or accounts gone and all that stuff. Yeah. He would not have been happy about that at all, no way.*

I remembered that they liked to go driving, and I said, Well, maybe they flew off the road, *because he drank, you know, Joel would drink.* Maybe they flew off the side of the road. *I heard on the radio that they had found two bodies, and they didn't say who it was, but I kind of knew, weirdly. And it turned out it was them.*

The other thing I remember when the detectives came was that there was some speculation where the bodies were found outside the car. I asked him, Can you tell me if they were wearing their seatbelts? *And he said,* Why? *And I said,* Well, I've been in the car a zillion times with Joel. And I know he always put a seatbelt on. *It was the first thing he did. He was totally that kind of guy who would always do it. He says,* No, they were not wearing their seatbelts. *And I said,* Well, that's a really interesting fact because Joel would have always put a seatbelt on. *So that's a little weird. I don't know if that came out.*

Honestly, part of me is like, okay, well, if it was a murder-suicide, if Joel just felt like he was at the end of his rope and he didn't want Angela to go down with him, not go to jail, then that's the case. But it sounds to me that it's more complicated than that. He loved Angela so much that I can't see him doing anything to her. He just wouldn't have, he couldn't do it. Angela was fifty-one percent owner of the company. She owned a higher percentage so that we could get tax credit for being a female-owned company. I know, a little shady, but that was Joel. So if Joel went down, she would have gone down too.

The trickiest part of breaking down these firsthand accounts was separating office gossip from office fact. People's reminiscences were naturally colored by the tragic deaths that followed, and certain incidents loomed larger in their recollection many years later. The second interviewee provided more background on Joel and Andrew, as well as a seemingly revelatory and insightful account of an office conflict that was, however, later contradicted by other accounts, illustrating how people remember the same things differently and underscoring the fact that every person is the hero of their own story. Because Samira had no idea what facts were both accurate and pertinent to the case moving ahead, she took copious notes and added them to the growing Google drive, including suggestions for next steps. She felt lucky to have a project separate from everything else going on inside and outside her house. Real life had become too real. It was a pleasure to turn her attention to an unsolved double murder.

*N*icole had nearly skipped the bowling night fundraiser. Not because of Covid fear, but because she was dog tired after another long day of work and mothering—and because she was a terrible bowler. She decided to attend at the last minute, and when she saw the sparse turnout, she immediately regretted it. She knew Marissa but not well, having been with her at group lunches from time to time. Their daughters were in the same grade but weren't friendly yet, though that would change. They got to chatting, and soon Marissa mentioned the murder case she had been looking into.

"Oh my God," Nicole said, "tell me *everything*."

She was fascinated but felt no compulsion to look into the matter personally; she wanted someone else to solve the case so she could find out which family member did it and why.

Their conversation that night led Nicole and Marissa to begin talking on the phone after Covid descended, connecting on many levels, including complaining about their spouses. Some nights they would talk for two and a half hours. Nobody talks on the phone for that long, but during Covid you did. She has zero memory of the specifics of what they discussed, only that the conversations were effortless, and after hanging up, Nicole was always left thinking, "I really like her." Lots of moms she met were nice, and it was fine. This connection felt like more.

A few weeks later, during a socially distanced walk on a closed beach with Marissa, Samira, and a few other moms, Nicole thought to ask, "Hey, whatever happened to that cold case you were talking about?" Marissa told her she was actively investigating it, and that Samira was in on the case as well, along with a third mom named Jeannie whom Nicole didn't know.

"Well, I want in too!" said Nicole, in a predictable burst of FOMO. She was the last to join the effort, but of the four of them, Nicole was the best suited to be an investigator.

Nicole grew up far from the Westside of Los Angeles, in a log cabin on a dirt road in a town of fifteen hundred people in rural western Massachusetts. Nicole and her younger sister were free-range children, and she loved it. Playdates were spent exploring the woods, building huts out of sticks, getting lost and getting dirty. Her parents were hippie lawyers out of step with the conservative 1980s, her father working in private practice, her mother affiliated with the University of Massachusetts Amherst working for Student Legal Services and representing their town. Activism was in her family's blood. Nicole attended her first protest march at age five, advocating for a nuclear-free zone. Secretly she wished for a typical television commercial mom who would greet her with freshly baked cookies after school, but she was proud to have two working parents, and as soon as she was old enough, she went to work herself, progressing from babysitting to waiting tables.

A theater kid in high school, she yearned to live in a big city and went on to major in communications at American University in Washington, D.C. She never envisioned herself as the kind of young woman who would pledge a sorority, and then it happened. The fun part of college came easily—but the work did not. She was later diagnosed with ADHD, which explained her habit of leaving homework until the very last minute. While her assignments were sometimes late, her work ethic was never in question. The moment she arrived in D.C., she hit the ground running, seizing every political internship she could find.

Nicole was home in the early fall of 1999, packing for a semester abroad in Italy, when she learned her mother had been diagnosed with breast cancer. Nicole's mother insisted that she go to Rome as planned, as a semester abroad in London had changed her life years before. When Nicole returned home in December, her mother was bald from chemotherapy, but the treatment had been a success. Her margins were clear. It looked as though she had beaten cancer.

When Nicole first saw the job listing for a "political opposition research worker," she had to ask around to learn what that was. Oppo research, as it is now known, appealed to Nicole's set-the-world-right activism as well as her inquisitive nature, and she had a great interview with a prestigious firm in D.C., but in the end she was passed over for the job. After some other near-miss job opportunities, she had to take what she could get, which was a job with a law firm that handled evictions. Her mother, having thought that Nicole would be working on protecting the rights of tenants rather than landlords, was appalled. Nicole knew she was working on the wrong side, but she also needed to eat. Mercifully, a few months later, the opposition research firm called her back and offered her another position.

She began work in the 2002 election cycle. Looking back now, she is amazed at how young she and her colleagues were, just a bunch of kids working in a bullpen, mainlining coffee, living on ramen and popcorn, working ridiculously long hours. The job involved a lot of budget travel in the pre-broadband internet days, back when research meant legwork.

After a few healthy years, in 2002 Nicole's mother began suffering headaches and joint pain. She reluctantly returned to her doctor, and the diagnosis was grim. The cancer had returned and was spreading throughout her body. Unable to face this bleak news, Nicole shoved it aside and threw herself deeper into her work, spending several months in Topeka, Kansas, as research director for a gubernatorial campaign. It took her boss ordering her to take time off to be with her mother to make Nicole see that her coping mechanism was not a healthy one.

In 2004, while serving as research director for the League of Conservation Voters, an environmental group, she found herself in Boston attending the 2004 Democratic National Convention. The highlight of the convention turned out to be its keynote speaker, a little-known state senator from Illinois named Barack Obama, whose landmark speech launched his national political career. At a party afterward in Downtown Crossing, a friend introduced Nicole to Paul, who had been Howard Dean's political director. Something about him intrigued her. They spent the entire night talking and crossed paths a few times throughout the remainder of the week. The connection wasn't immediate. Paul was from New Jersey, but he lived a political operative's nomadic lifestyle, carrying everything he owned with him in a small blue suitcase. Nicole had sworn to friends that she would never date anyone in politics. She and Paul stayed in touch while she worked on the New York City mayoral campaign. He moved to D.C., and after the campaign, Nicole returned there and they began dating. Eventually she got what she considered her dream job with the Democratic Congressional Campaign Committee, moving up to research director and managing a large staff expected to churn out research for dozens of House races. Paul was by then working on John Edwards's ill-fated presidential campaign, and he purchased a car for Nicole so she could visit him in North Carolina. Tragically, their engagement coincided with a serious downturn in her mother's health, and four months before their wedding in 2008, Nicole's mother succumbed to cancer.

In 2011, both Nicole and Paul had hit a wall with politics, which they had come to see as, in Nicole's words, "a soul-sucking blood sport." Paul took a job in finance, and they decided it was time to start a family. Getting pregnant was easy. The move to Los Angeles was not. Relocating from an apartment in D.C. to a house in L.A. was a complete do-over as well as a culture shock. Nicole tried to look upon it as an adventure, but she knew a sum total of two people in California. "Don't worry," Paul told her, "the baby will be your friend," which they later laughed about as something only a parent-to-be would say.

Nicole was an anxious new mom. Her firstborn daughter was not an easy baby, but asking for help felt like a sign of failure. She would have given anything to be able to pick up the phone and call her mother. Becoming a mom without having her own to turn to was the hardest part. She remembers sitting on the floor after trying and failing to calm her daughter, feeling alone and sad, just wanting her mom. It was several months before she found other families with children of similar ages and she and the baby found a good rhythm.

Her mother's cancer diagnosis prompted Nicole to undergo genetic testing herself. The results showed that she had inherited a harmful change in BRCA2, known as the breast cancer gene. More than 60 percent of women with this variant develop breast cancer during their lifetime, and they are more likely to do so at younger ages. She felt she was walking around with a loaded weapon. The normal course of action at the time was undergoing tests and examinations every six months. At every appointment, the testing detected some abnormality that threatened to upend her life. Nicole realized she could not go on living six months at a time. She was clear about not wanting her children to lose their mother the way she had lost hers. When her daughter was fifteen months old, Nicole underwent a double mastectomy. At that time, the procedure was considered aggressive, though it is much more common now. Between Nicole's second and third surgeries, Angelina Jolie went public with her decision to undergo the same procedure, leading to increased awareness. It was another trauma early in her new life in Los Angeles, but Nicole knew she had made the right decision for herself and for her children and grandchildren. After the surgery, Nicole and Paul decided it was time to try for a second child—and they became pregnant right away. Ten weeks later, Nicole miscarried. Heartbroken, they kept trying, only to experience a series of early losses. Finally, after what felt like an eternity, they were rewarded with the joyful arrival of their son. Her mothering experience with her second was the opposite of what it had been with her first—this time she was a calm mother with an easy baby and plenty of support.

Unlike the other three women, Nicole never stopped working. After some false starts post-politics, she met a *New York Times* reporter at a cooking school class, which led her to put her professional experience to work in freelance nonfiction book research. She worked on a fascinating project about Silk Road, the online narcotics and weapons black market site shut down by the FBI, then on a political biography by a well-known journalist at *Vanity Fair*. Both books became bestsellers, and these detail-oriented jobs led later to work providing research for a drama series that aired on Apple TV+. No one in politics ever said thank you. They only noticed when you screwed up. Now, for the first time in Nicole's professional life, she felt that her talent was recognized and appreciated. At the same time, in the back of her head, she understood that she was assisting others in achieving their ambitions, not her own. She thought to herself, *What is my ambition?*

Then Covid hit, and everything fell apart. She was home alone with her kids, including a preschool son now, with no help, trying to ensure that their young lives wouldn't become permanently derailed. Never before had she felt anxiety at that level. Never before had she felt less connected to anyone, including her family. Her first Covid purchase was a Roomba, which got more use spinning her rambunctious son around the house than it did cleaning her floors. She got scammed trying to buy massive bottles of hand sanitizer from Canada, and she purchased various highly recommended homeschooling supplies, all of which remain unopened in a closet. Like everyone else, she was desperate for something to make her days go by faster—something to quicken her pulse.

Taking on more research didn't seem all that appealing at first. Nicole started off way behind the others. But she was impressed at how much Marissa, Jeannie, and Samira, as amateur researchers, had already uncovered, and the more she read, the more interviews she listened to, the more she felt herself being drawn into this family and workplace mystery. The opportunity to right a wrong—to bring closure to the unsolved murders of Joel and Angela Watkins—appealed to the activist in her. She had gotten into politics because she wanted to do something that truly mattered—and that mattered to her.

As with pledging a sorority, or falling in love with someone working in politics, Nicole had never imagined herself being a stay-at-home mom. But now *every* mom across the country was a stay-at-home mom. Every mom out there was doing the thankless task of mothering in a bunker. She needed something that was her own. She needed to connect. At the same time, she thought it would be a great lesson if her kids could see her pursuing a passion. Experience had taught her that one never knows where an investigation might eventually lead—but she never expected it to lead to a whole new life for herself.

At the moment, she was still trying to sort out who was who—so many names!—and what was the father-son dynamic between Joel and Andrew. Marissa had spoken to Nina Stengle, who highlighted some of the shenanigans going on back in the early 2000s:

When I first started working there, it was a really great place to be. We were busy. Sales were booming. Then Andrew showed up and then there was like all this other stuff going on.

I knew Andrew when he came in to be, I guess, the company accountant. He was supposed to do new business development. He was very cold. He wasn't rude with me, but he was, you know, Good morning, Good morning. *That's it. I thought he was kind of a cold fish, myself. There was a lot of time spent on speculation of who was doing what with the boss's son.*

I met Angela once at a Christmas party. There was a girl called Mariela that was referred in. Joel liked to hire some of the girls who worked at the local restaurant, and when Mariela came in, she didn't really have the skill set to do what she was hired to do. But I did notice that Mariela was very hands on. She's a touchy, feely kind of person, and I could tell that his wife wasn't happy that Mariela was so familiar with Joel. But that was Mariela, though. She was very much like that with all the guys. Like, There goes Mariela.

When Joel and Angela went missing, it was like, Oh my gosh. *I was on the* Valley Sun *website, where people were making comments about things, and it was like,* Did they run off with the money? *It was kind of a joke, like, yeah, Joel and Angela are in Mexico somewhere, you know, sipping margaritas and enjoying the free life. But after they found their car, and I'm sure that everybody said this, my first thought went to Andrew. Because he had the most to gain from this. Once Joel was gone, all of Joel's debts were gone. But Andrew would be able to collect from the estate still.*

I remember I had lunch with Dennis Ladd a few years ago, and by the time I got there, already he'd had like two, three glasses of wine. Dennis liked to drink. One thing is I remember asking him what he thought happened to Joel. And it was just one of those weird moments, you know, where people give you a weird look.

He just looked at me with this weird look. He said, like, Who knows? *but that weird look told me he probably knew something.*

As the interviews continued to give color and context to the environment inside Wattkins LED, they also provided insight into Detective Fonseca's investigation and who and what he was focusing on—giving Nicole a broader sense of law enforcement's thinking at that time. Maya DiNardo was another good friend of the late Dennis Ladd's, and she set the record straight on some of her co-workers' accusations:

At some point, I think around 2003ish, the projects were just kind of drying up. Customers were getting better deals from bigger firms. It came to, like, we were getting outclassed. Joel really, really tried his best to keep everybody on as long as possible. I remember the day that he laid me off, he was in tears about it. He was crying. I adore Joel because he was very professional, very serious, but he was so sweet and he cared about every single one of his employees. And I was like, Hey, it's okay. *I wanted to console him.*

I didn't hear anything about the company until a couple years later when my ex-husband called me at night and said, Oh my God, turn on the TV, there's a story about your old boss. *I cried when I found out that Joel passed away. I was very upset about that.*

Sometime afterwards, I came home from work one day and went to open my screen door and a business card fell. It was from a detective in the L.A. County Sheriff's Department. For the life of me, I couldn't understand what was going on. So I called him in the morning and he said, Yes, we're looking into the death of Joel and Angela Watkins. *I said,* I don't know how I can help, I haven't seen or heard from him for years. *And then he started asking about if I knew anybody who would want to harm Joel. If I knew anything suspicious about any of his business dealings.* What was my relationship with Andrew? *And I was like,* I don't understand, there's other people that have been there longer. *Like, Andrew Watkins was a country club guy with frosted tips in his hair. Like, he was that guy.*

I know Joel and Andrew didn't have that great a relationship. They were always kind of like at each other's throats. About work and the way that Andrew would handle things. They would get into arguments, there would be pretty heated yelling matches, then doors would slam, and it would just be awkward for all of us. The rumor was that Andrew was a spoiled brat and he had been a corporate accountant before this, but something happened and his father gave him a job.

He would get to the office at nine-thirty, ten, and he would leave for an extended lunch, come back after a couple of glasses of wine, then shut his door for the afternoon and leave at three-thirty. Joel was completely the opposite. That man, Monday through Saturday he was at the office, six days a week, pulling in to the parking garage at five-thirty, six. He would go down the street to the YMCA, work out, take a shower, and he would be at his desk no later than seven. Every day.

I had no knowledge of financial stuff or anything that happened on that end. I went in there, I did my work, I did my job, and I went home because I had kids to take care of. But Dennis told me that Joel has *questionable business transactions going on with questionable people. And that he was kind of cooking his books. He was taking out loans with different banks and differ-*

ent individuals and using falsified invoices to get security for those loans. I don't know how true that is. When I heard that timeline of events in the disappearance, I got weirded out by it, because why would Andrew shutter this man's business after not being around for three days? Like, this is your dad's whole life.

Was Andrew Watkins every office worker's number one suspect because he had been Detective Fonseca's number one suspect? Certainly, one or more interviews with a homicide detective about a double murder would color someone's perspective on the case. Memories, like bone and cartilage, harden over time.

Along with this developing cast of characters, a new name kept popping up. Ben Dealer was a former friend and business partner of Joel's, with whom he had had a falling-out. Strangely, Ben Dealer operated out of an office in the same building as Wattkins LED, and apparently was a competitor. Maya DiNardo continued:

Ben Dealer? Okay, that guy, he predated me. Now that name is kind of triggering like a lot of stuff going on. Stocky guy, goatee, dark hair. They had a very contentious relationship, Joel and Ben. They worked in the same building but weren't talking to each other. There was bad blood. They could not get into the same elevator together. Because then it was just all like, you know, mother-effer this, and cocksucker that. Shit-talking like guys talk, bluster. But no one ever explained their backstory to me.

I remember talking to Dennis soon after they first went missing. He gave me two scenarios. Joel either faked his death and ran away with the money to Mexico, and that proved false when they were found. Or, he said,

I don't want to say this, because I don't want to believe it, but maybe Andrew had something to do with it. *A theory was that his brakes were tampered with or something mechanically with his car. The sheriff's detective said the same thing. It's all very weird and suspicious to me how things went down after the fact.*

We have to talk about the frosted tips.

Oh. My. God.

He's clearly guilty!

Everyone laughed: Samira in her kitchen, chopping vegetables; Nicole with her kids running back and forth behind her and occasionally mugging for the laptop camera; Jeannie in Tamara's office, after writers' room hours; Marissa in her closet with the background blurred out.

Marissa had begun their first virtual meeting as a foursome by making introductions. For all four women, it was their first Zoom call ever. Jeannie was uncomfortable with the distracting new medium—eyes darting from the screen to her camera—and felt a little self-conscious. Never mind that they were about to discuss a murder investigation. A lot of firsts. Would they prove to be a good mix? Would this endeavor continue beyond this initial call? They were all in uncharted territory.

Marissa had brought them all together; now she felt the need to persuade them that this was a thing worth doing. A childhood friend of hers who put a lot of faith in astrology once informed Marissa that she had been born on the "Day of Persuasion." Marissa did have a gift for persuasion, a talent that had served her well. She put it to good use now. More than anything else, she was seeking community. Something told her that these three women, like her, had stories to tell that were forged out of life's challenges. She sensed that they were like-minded gritty souls.

In conducting information-blind interviews by asking

strangers to recall people and incidents from fifteen years ago, they had cast a wide net. After dumping their haul into their shared Google drive, now came the sorting. What they knew versus what they didn't know. In talking about the interviews and documents, they quickly reached consensus on a number of issues.

First, Andrew Watkins was a shit. An accountant who did very little accounting, an entitled jerkoff mooching off his father, who got drunk at every lunch—and frosted the tips of his hair. Clearly, he was a bad character, and shutting down his father's company so quickly without knowing—or admitting to knowing—what had happened to his missing parents was suspicious in the extreme.

Second, they knew next to nothing about the other three siblings, older daughter Marie and younger twin daughters Carrie and Lily.

Third, Joel Watkins was beloved, hardworking, and devoted to his wife, Angela, but was also a distant boss who exploited his workers, and oh yes, someone who committed massive financial fraud.

It was impossible to say for sure who was a bad guy and who wasn't. They needed more insight into the family, and more intel on the later years of Wattkins LED, specifically toward the end, around 2004 and 2005, when things went bad.

They bemoaned the death of Dennis Ladd as much as the people who had known and liked him. Had they only started a few months earlier, when he was still alive, Dennis might have answered many of their questions. He must have been interviewed by the detectives in the past. Had he shared with them the incriminating scenarios he'd discussed with friends and coworkers? Or had he been more circumspect, trying to protect his good friend Joel? Dennis would not have been candid about Joel's financial mismanagement if he himself had had any concern about being implicated in that very same scheme.

Everyone had something to contribute. Marissa went first, putting on her forensic accounting hat for the first time in years. "When the bank went into the accounts to see what was going on, there was less than fifty thousand dollars left. Joel owed the bank basically one million dollars. There were other accounts too, and some of them were private, so tracking down the money trail will be challenging, as will figuring out where it was sourced from and who was actually signing off on these things. Also, in the months before the disappearance, when he was already in this trouble, Joel requested a loan from another funding network for five hundred thousand dollars. Presumably it was Joel—I think it was probably Joel—but could it have been Andrew? Or somebody else? We need to know for sure."

Jeannie agreed with everyone about Andrew Watkins's character, but she was concerned about bias distorting their analysis: both selection bias, excluding from suspicion anyone who was not a Watkins family member, and confirmation bias, pursuing a predetermined suspect or outcome. And was the amount of money to be inherited worth killing for? She reminded them to keep an open mind about everybody and everything. With that said, she shared what she had learned about Marie's husband, Joel and Angela's son-in-law, Greg Medina.

She had put together a timeline of Greg's lawsuits and bankruptcies, beginning before his in-laws' disappearance and continuing well afterward. A manufacturing company Greg ran for most of the 1990s filed for bankruptcy in 1999 with zero assets and more than half a million dollars in debt. He racked up lawsuit after lawsuit, dragged to court again and again by both individuals and various companies. In 2002, he purchased a house for $800,000 with a $640,000 mortgage—while he was being sued for $250,000, $15,000, and $115,000 in simultaneous but separate cases. The company he was running at the time neglected to pay its taxes and was suspended from doing business in the state of California. In the first three months of 2003, Greg and Marie refinanced their house three times, for $700,000, $805,000, and, in a private transaction—for which Greg was sued the following year—in the amount of $200,000. How was any of this even possible?

"It's mind-boggling," said Jeannie.

In 2004, American Express sued Greg for $30,000 in unpaid credit card charges. US Bank did the same for $12,000. Greg and Marie had federal and state liens on their property totaling $400,000. He was hit with a $100,000 judgment against him, and US Bank purchased his house in what appeared to be a foreclosure. In 2005, the year of his in-laws' disappearance, he was being sued for $605,000 and was summoned to court to pay the $100,000 judgment he had reneged on the previous year.

"And that's just what I've found so far," said Jeannie. "It's clear he had a staggering amount of debt and was desperate for cash."

Both Andrew and his brother-in-law, Greg, looked like prime suspects. Marissa acknowledged that she had made a major mistake early on, which she now admitted to the others. Assuming that the family would be as eager as she was to see the mystery of Joel's and Angela's murders solved, Marissa had reached out to the Watkins children directly, including Greg, before knowing any of the facts in front of them now. She shuddered to think how misguided and presumptuous she'd been. None of them ever responded to her, but it was a rookie blunder she hoped wouldn't come back to haunt the investigation.

Samira worried about their safety, asking if everyone was using their regular email address in correspondence. Jeannie explained that she had started using an old email account of hers, changing her name on it to just her initials, after having the late-night thought *What if the family got involved with a crime syndicate for loans?* "I am physically the strongest person in my household," Jeannie said, "which is not saying much. As with

Marissa approaching the family, we really don't know what we don't know—yet."

Ever the opposition researcher, Nicole pointed out to them that the people they were approaching, if they were smart, were googling them as well, to make sure they were who they said they were. After some discussion, the four agreed to change their LinkedIn profile professions to "Investigative Journalist." Nicole also warned them to tread carefully when it came to offering information, since they did not know who might be talking to whom behind the scenes.

Nicole's career had familiarized her with a wealth of resources beyond widely known content sites such as Spokeo, Newspapers.com, the Internet Archive, and the Wayback Machine. Through her work, she had a subscription to LexisNexis, the data analytics company with the world's largest electronic database for legal and public records information. Most helpfully, Nicole's skill set and depth of knowledge gave them the assurance that if they could not uncover some piece of information, chances were that it was not available or did not exist, which saved them from wasting time and effort.

The biggest difference between opposition research and investigative research was that with oppo work you never wanted to tip your hand to the person or entity you were researching. You didn't want them mounting a defense strategy. The need for stealth meant that in-person interviews were exceedingly rare, though Nicole's more recent endeavor in book research involved a lot of one-on-ones with people, and here was a chance to further hone her interviewing skills. But first, building upon Jeannie's impressive work, Nicole offered to start looking more deeply into Greg Medina's personal and professional affairs.

Of all the unanswered questions about this case—and they were adding to the list daily—the circumstances surrounding the fateful crash intrigued them most. One key piece of information

Marissa had recently gotten her hands on was the video that inspired her to begin this investigation—the B-roll news footage of the Skyhook helicopter extricating the wrecked Ford Explorer from the ravine in the Angeles National Forest, with its haunting image of the vehicle twirling slowly at the end of the massive straps. The women carefully reviewed the daylight footage, which was exactly as Marissa had remembered it, examining the dangling vehicle and the surrounding topography for clues as to the exact location of the crash.

Marissa had driven up and down Angeles Crest Highway several times, scouting landmark hills and rocky outcroppings from the video clip, trying to guess where the SUV went off the road. Jeannie had used Google Earth to narrow down the likeliest spot. Together, they had zeroed in on a bend in the road with a gravelly turnout along a section of the state route where there were no guardrails. In the years since the Watkinses' deaths, at least three other vehicles had gone over the edge at that same location, two drunken driving incidents and one presumed suicide.

Newspaper articles at the time mentioned that the car had been discovered by a "hiker." This was curious, because there were no hiking trails anywhere down that deep ravine, the remote canyon below being difficult to access on foot. Identifying and locating the person who had found the Watkinses' 2000 Ford Explorer was added to their list, along with the question of why the vehicle had been left to rust in the canyon for more than a year before being recovered.

A few former employees of Wattkins LED claimed that the detectives told them that Joel's and Angela's bodies had been found outside the vehicle. If confirmed, this fact, and the insight into Joel Watkins's use of seatbelts, seemed critically important. It had been an incredibly violent plummet down six hundred feet of sheer rock face. Brake tampering seemed to them a tough sell. How could anyone messing with the brakes determine exactly when and where they would fail and the vehicle would go out of control? They had to know why and how police had belatedly come to the conclusion that it was murder as opposed to accident or suicide. Second- and thirdhand accounts were helpful in outlining the picture, but they wouldn't be able to get anywhere without firsthand knowledge of these details.

Before they ended their first call, Marissa played two short employee interviews she had conducted earlier that day. The first, with a pleasant-sounding woman named Inez Gonzalez, hit many of the same notes as the interviews with other workers in the predominantly female office staff. Joel Watkins was "the nicest man," and "everybody was like a family to him. I honestly cannot tell you anything negative about him because he was always really respectful and good to me." The women agreed that, while people generally tend to speak well of the dead, Joel had clearly inspired a lot of loyalty among his former employees— even as they admitted, like Inez, to hearing about Joel's "getting loans from people he shouldn't be dealing with." About Angela, Inez said, "He was very much in love with his wife. Maybe it was one of those things where he turned around and looked at his wife, and they held hands and he drove over."

The new information Inez provided concerned the mysterious Ben Dealer.

I made the mistake of working for Ben Dealer after I had my daughter and went back to work. Ben Dealer was a snake. He would always go around saying he was in the CIA and I call bullshit on that. I don't think he was. One time he left and said he was on a special assignment. Meanwhile, the girl running our office payroll calls me in and says, "Inez, we don't have any money to pay our contractors, and payroll has to be met this Friday." And I went into a total panic. We tried everything and couldn't get ahold of him. Later, when he came back—after I had convinced my poor husband to help us cover payroll, because my reputation was on the line—Ben told us, Oh, sorry. I was on a special mission. *With a straight face. In the meantime, some girl he was supposed to meet had called the office from the airport of whatever island he was at, saying he was supposed to pick her up, and he's late, and where is he?—like we're his answering service. Which just confirmed that his whole story was bullshit. I was livid.*

Marissa told her that she had confirmed that Ben Dealer had indeed never been a CIA agent, as he'd claimed.

"I knew it! I freaking knew it. My husband said, 'Inez, an active CIA agent will never say he's a CIA agent.' My husband being six three, and Ben being nothing but five two. It took Ben a year to pay my husband back. He's lucky he did."

Then Marissa told her something else the team had learned: Ben Dealer now had a criminal record after being convicted of robbing a toy store at gunpoint in 2014.

"Shut up!" Inez exclaimed. "Get out of here! I cannot wait to tell my husband."

They laughed at Inez's triumphant glee, but also agreed that Ben Dealer was bad news and perhaps still highly unstable, and not someone they wished to contact if they could help it.

Marissa had one more call to share, having reached Mariela Sanchez, whose name had come up before. "She was the 'handsy' one with Joel," said Samira, "who Angela supposedly didn't care for."

"This conversation got really awkward," said Marissa. "It started off fine."

Mariela, in her Spanish accent, said of Joel, "He was very, very generous, a kindhearted man, but most of the time his door was closed." About Andrew Watkins: "I didn't have much interaction with him. Their dynamic was odd. More like strangers than father and son." About Angela Watkins: "They would have a Christmas gathering and that's when Angela would come. I only talked to her a couple of times. I found her to be very sweet, very caring, a very lovely lady. All into her family. She loved her grandson, and the fact that he will never see his grandparents again or know them is heartbreaking to me."

When they got to this part of the recording, Marissa covered her eyes. The other three heard her apologetically and stumblingly say: "Mariela, I'm sorry to ask you this, it's not my place, but we've heard from other people we've spoken to who've said that they thought or they heard that you and Joel . . . that you two might've had an affair at some point?"

The pause was long, the other three women leaning in toward their screens so as not to miss Mariela's response.

"Wow," Mariela said. She wasn't defensive and she wasn't angry. "Honestly, that is so disgusting to me, because when I was working there, I was going out with this gorgeous Black man and everybody knew it. I'm Puerto Rican, he was Black Puerto Rican, and he would come to the office, so I don't know why she would say that. You don't have to tell me who it was. I know."

The others reacted open-mouthed but remained silent until the recording finished.

Mariela ended the interview by saying, "Like I told the detectives, it would not surprise me if Andrew had something to do with it. Either he hired somebody, or, I don't know, but I can imagine one day turning on the TV and seeing Andrew in the news being handcuffed and being taken away because he murdered his parents. Am I a hundred percent certain that it was Andrew? I would probably say ninety-five percent."

Marissa was still cringing from bringing up the suspected affair, but the others reassured her that she'd had to do it. Marissa was grateful Mariela didn't go off on her, which would have been her right.

There was lots to look into, lots more to come. Their first

group Zoom felt seamless and productive, energizing. They divided up responsibilities before signing off, each one eager to do
her part. Marissa had a few more ex-employee interviews scheduled in the coming days and would share whatever she learned.
She had also requested Joel's and Angela's autopsy reports,
which were publicly available records. The virus that had dis-
rupted every facet of their lives also delayed the Los Angeles
County Medical Examiner's Office's response time, but she
hoped the reports would arrive soon and that they would be in
some way revelatory.

The likeliest scenario, though still an assumption, was that
Joel and Angela were killed inside the SUV, or killed elsewhere
and their bodies placed in the SUV, which was then sent over the
cliff. If so, two main outstanding questions remained: Where had
they been murdered—and by whom?

THE LIGHTBULB

*B*y virtue of being the first state in the nation to issue a stay-at-home order, California had largely avoided the nightmarish scenes witnessed in places like New York City, where refrigerated trailers served as makeshift morgues and workers wearing hazmat suits buried coffins in mass graves. Nicole recalled early mornings when the fog blanketed the Southern California mountains and she rose before anyone else in the house to make a fresh pot of coffee, adding almond milk and mixing it just right, eager to enjoy a few peaceful moments of solitude before the usual havoc ensued. She sat down to launch the *New York Times* website, as was her routine—and was confronted with the most awful headlines. Hospitals overwhelmed, spiking nursing home deaths, unemployment rate skyrocketing. There was no place to hide from it all. Los Angeles's perennially congested multilane freeways stood empty and eerily silent. Disneyland, the Staples Center, and the Santa Monica Pier were all closed indefinitely. It was as though every single public location in the state had been shut down for the filming of a movie that would never be made. All of this was unthinkable just eight weeks before.

Word began to filter in via Facebook of friends contracting the virus, requests for prayers for parents and family members who had been hospitalized, invitations to Zoom funerals. Samira checked in daily with her mother and stepfather via FaceTime, and Nicole with her father, while Marissa and Jeannie made sidewalk visits to their parents, their kids blowing masked kisses to grandparents waving from behind windows. Everything was weird. Nothing was certain. It did feel apocalyptic. The president had absurdly claimed that the country would be back to normal by Easter, which had come and gone three weeks before. The number of new cases continued to surge, with no end in sight, and any hope of a vaccine was still many months away. The situation was easy to obsess over.

Coping mechanisms ranged from compulsively baking sourdough bread to bingeing *Tiger King* to hosting Zoom happy hours. Brian dyed Marissa's roots, and she cut his hair, and their marriage survived. Jeannie and Tamara discussed entering into a "pod" arrangement with another family with a same-age child, which they would begin by mid-May. Nicole juggled her paid research employment with her unpaid and unappreciated Zoom school monitoring and childcare. She and the kids made Paul an "office" with a folding chair and a backdrop of random research books for his Zoom look, but just as Nicole was not meant to be a stay-at-home mom, Paul was not meant to be a work-at-home dad. After coming out to quiet them all down for the tenth time, they both agreed it was better for him to return to his empty office building with a pack of masks and a container of bleach.

Jigsaw puzzles were a popular diversion during lockdown, and that's what the case felt like to them, a thousand-piece jigsaw puzzle without an image as a guide. They had framed out most of the edges, and some of the interior picture was beginning to come into view. There were pieces they had acquired but could not find a place for yet, and some extra pieces that were contradictory or red herrings. Of course, actual jigsaw puzzles offered stress relief and a satisfying sense of control in the gradual progress toward an achievable solution. Their puzzle still had many missing pieces—who knew how many—and there was no guarantee of completion. But at least they felt a sense of progress.

The emerging portrait of Joel Watkins was notably contradictory. He had engendered a great deal of affection from his employees while being described as distant and difficult to know. He was described as a fatherly type in the way he helped and encouraged his staff, yet most workers spoke to the tension in the office resulting from his actual relationship with his son. Was Joel a stand-up guy who, for reasons yet unknown, perhaps desperation, crossed over into major financial fraud in the last few years of his life? Samira, for one, was convinced he was the kind of duplicitous person who would show one face to employees and another to his son and closer associates.

One large piece of the puzzle fitted into place when Marissa finally spoke to someone who had been employed at Wattkins LED right up until the May 2005 disappearance of Joel Watkins. Oliver Croce was one of the first employees Marissa had reached out to, recommended to her as a good resource by the reporter who had first filed stories on the Watkinses' disappearance. All Marissa had been able to find at the time was an old AOL email address and a now defunct landline. Nicole had since turned up a current cellphone number.

By now, the team had developed a boilerplate list of questions for Joel's former employees and co-workers. *How long was your term of employment? What was Joel Watkins like as a person and a boss? What can you tell me about the firm's business practices? Did you ever have concerns about marijuana-related criminal elements? Can you speak to Andrew Watkins's character and his relationship with his father? Did you know Joel's son-in-law, Greg Medina? When was the last time you saw or spoke to Joel? How did you find out about the disappearance? What do you think happened?*

"This is like going back down memory lane," said Oliver, an affable man, recently retired, the father of four adult children. Marissa's conversation with him lasted nearly two hours. Oliver was a slow talker, but also helpfully thoughtful.

Oliver had worked at Wattkins LED from 1998 until the day

the company closed down. He described Joel Watkins as an "interesting fellow" who was "never super close to people" but who had treated Oliver well. Oliver's background in lighting technology made him a core member of the team, which, along with his no-nonsense, no-drama temperament, was likely the reason he was one of only four full-time employees still in the office at the very end.

Oliver said that Joel once mentioned that he had served in the military in an intelligence capacity, which explained Wattkins LED's tax status as a veteran-owned business. As many before Oliver had said, Joel was "not a big drinker." Joel was often flirtatious in a complimentary way toward women in the office, which, Oliver made clear, was not entirely inappropriate for the time but "wouldn't fly in 2020."

He described Andrew Watkins as a good-looking sort who had been brought into the company after Oliver started there. He was an accountant, but Joel had his own CPA who handled business matters. Andrew managed the account managers, but basically he was the typical boss's son, and his job description was never clearly defined. Andrew routinely left the office before everyone else, something the other employees grumbled about behind his back. "He drank more than some people did," said Oliver, but he had no recollection of any drug problems. Oliver recalled that Joel and his son had "clashes and disagreements," though Oliver was not as put off by this as some other employees were. He and Andrew were "not friends."

Son-in-law Greg Medina was in and out of the office near the end. Oliver had some chitchat with him but nothing more than that, though Greg was one of the people who helped close up shop after the disappearance.

Angela was known to him primarily through holiday parties, though those had tailed off in later years. He thought she might have had some health issues but did not believe she was seriously ill. He had seen Joel's daughters from afar but never interacted with any of them.

Oliver had not heard that Dennis Ladd had passed away, and he was deeply affected by the news. Marissa apologized for being the one to tell him. Oliver said Dennis was a suave ladies' man, "fun and a real gem." He and Joel had worked together closely, and it had been a great disappointment to Oliver when Dennis left the company.

The only thing Oliver knew about Ben Dealer was that "Joel hated his guts." They had worked together in the past and had some kind of falling-out. Oliver could not remember what Ben's company did, only that they were not direct competitors with Wattkins LED.

Business started falling off in 2002 or 2003, but Oliver remained busy until the end, picking up former employees' clients and installs after each wave of layoffs. They were "a boutique company that couldn't compete with the big boys," the companies that constructed, sold, and distributed their own lighting products. Wattkins LED was getting outpriced at the same time their suppliers were being acquired by international competitors. There was no longer a need for a middleman, which is what Joel's company was. At the end, the only employees in the office with Joel were Andrew, Oliver, and an office manager named Bonnie Salazar.

Bonnie was someone Marissa had been trying to contact for as long as she had been trying to reach Oliver. She had worked for Greg Medina briefly after Wattkins LED closed down, whereas Oliver moved on to another firm. Marissa was confident they had up-to-date contact information for her, but Bonnie refused to respond. Marissa hoped Oliver might provide an introduction, but he had no current contact with Bonnie either, and in fact struggled to remember her name.

But Oliver remembered very clearly the last time he had spoken to Joel. Oliver was a groomsman in a Reno wedding that weekend, so he'd requested that Friday off from work. At the end of the day on Thursday, Joel's door was closed, as was customary. Having already cleared the vacation day with Joel, Oliver called out to him, "I'm heading out now," and Joel responded with something like, "Okay, then," through the door. Completely routine. That was the last time they spoke.

Monday morning, Joel, who was always the first one to arrive, wasn't there. Concern grew throughout the day as Joel missed the lunch appointment with his banker. Oliver remembered Andrew's saying "Maybe he went hunting," because Joel often went on trips down to Mexico with two friends who were retired firefighters. At some point, he heard Andrew place a call to the gym down the street, and they reported that Joel hadn't been in that morning. Andrew seemed "perplexed." By day's end, all three of them were concerned. Not being able to reach Joel was unprecedented.

Oliver did not have a clear recollection of the next few days, other than "It was an awful time." At some point, he was told— "I think Bonnie and Andrew told me"—that they couldn't keep the doors open any longer because Joel was the only one who could sign checks. Oliver cleared out his belongings ahead of the shutdown. He was never compensated for six weeks of lost vacation time. Oliver never spoke with Andrew Watkins after that Friday, and he was unaware of any funeral service after the bodies were found.

*i*Message 5/8/20, 8:55 p.m.

Marissa: Look what came!

She attached an image of the top sheet of the autopsy report dated July 12, 2005. "JOHN DOE LATER IDENTIFIED AS WATKINS, JOEL"

Samira: Wha?!!

Jeannie: Wow.

Nicole: I'm impressed that our bureaucracy works so efficiently even in these times!

Barely able to contain her excitement, Marissa plopped down on the floor next to the mail slot and ripped open the envelope.

The official cause of death was listed as "Undetermined." Photographs of the corpses were redacted from the public version of the autopsy, but the report included annotated posterior and anterior diagrams of the body. Arrows drawn indicated "mummified skin," "pelvis skeletonized," and "skin absent." The body had been found in "an obvious state of decomposition."

The examination notes were extensive, much of it in shorthand and difficult for a lay person to parse. One note that caught Marissa's eye read, "There is no obvious evidence of antemortem fracture of the larynx or hyoid bone." They knew from true crime documentaries that a fractured hyoid bone could indicate strangulation or choking, which was apparently not the case here.

The examiner's handwritten notes beneath the "Undetermined" designation stated that the then John Doe had broken ribs, a detached left arm, a fragmented spine, and a detached head. At first she thought that meant that the body had been dismembered, but Joel Watkins's corpse had lain out in the open for more than four weeks, and nature and its animals likely had done what they do. He had been wearing a short-sleeved shirt, jeans, white socks, and brown loafers.

Angela's autopsy report was similar, though her body had been better preserved, as Joel's corpse apparently had been more exposed to the sun and other elements. She had been found lying in the fetal position, dressed in a brown cardigan sweater over a white shirt and beige bra, black jeans, black underwear, and tennis shoes.

Then Marissa read the words "abandoned vehicle found nearby."

She had already uploaded the files to the team's Google drive, but this was too big to hold back for that night's Zoom.

Marissa: Bodies were found outside the car!

Samira: Placed or thrown?

Nicole: Amazing!!! Shocked!!!

There was more. The parking brake had been set and no airbags had been deployed. Had the Explorer's engine even been running at the time it went over?

The toxicology test for alcohol was negative, and no cocaine, barbiturates, amphetamines, methamphetamines, morphine, codeine, or phencyclidine were detected.

A separate document entitled "Investigator's Narrative" provided more details. A Nature Conservancy group testing water quality at the bottom of the ravine had discovered the abandoned Ford Explorer. The bodies had been located approximately three hundred feet above the vehicle.

The report concluded, "Foul play is not suspected." Not at that point, anyway.

Normally, their every-other-night Zoom calls began casually, discussing kids and spouses and venting about the day's travails, the four of them trying to make sense of the pandemic quarantine and this case. That night's Zoom was different. It began with an intensity and an urgency that were sustained throughout the entire call.

"The airbags had not deployed," said Marissa. "and the Explorer was found in Park. Not in Drive, not even in Neutral. It makes almost no sense."

Jeannie said, "We should contact a mechanic and find out whether the force of impact could cause the gear to shift."

"Was anyone even behind the wheel?" said Nicole.

"Maybe whoever did this turned off the engine for fear of fire or explosion," said Samira. "Which would mean their primary concern was not making the crash look like an accident, but making sure that the car would not be discovered." This made sense to everyone. "If not for the water quality people," continued Samira, "Joel and Angela and their car could have sat down there for years without being found. I'm going to track down somebody from that Nature Conservancy group."

Jeannie brought up a comparable crash from 2018, a horrible incident in which a married couple with a history of child abuse drove a GMC Yukon off a hundred-foot cliff on the Northern California coast, killing themselves and their six adopted children. Officials determined it was a murder-suicide and not a tragic accident because the vehicle's airbag-deploying computer indicated that the Yukon had been intentionally driven off the cliff at full throttle. The seven bodies recovered (one child was presumed to have washed away) all had broken necks.

Jeannie said, "The Watkinses' crash would presumably have been more of a violent roll and bounce, not a straight drop. The bodies being discovered outside the car, three hundred feet above where it came to rest, seems to explain all the seatbelt questions the detectives were asking, though it's unlikely that airbag computer technology existed in a 2000 vehicle."

"Adding it to the list," said Samira.

Marissa returned to one of her earlier scenarios. "Joel and Angela could have been alive when the car went over—unconscious or drugged—but what chance was there of them surviving the crash and crawling out of the wrecked vehicle under their own power? Slim to none. It's much more likely that their bodies—probably unbuckled—were thrown from the vehicle during its descent."

"Are we dealing with dumb criminals?" asked Nicole. "Maybe the fact that the airbags didn't deploy is the evidence that convinced detectives this was a double homicide?"

They added questions to their ever growing list: *Were the car keys found—and if so, where? Were any cellphones recovered—and if so, why weren't they used to locate the crash site? What personal effects were found in and around the Watkinses' car, such as Angela's purse or Joel's wallet?*

As ever, each new revelation spun off more questions to be answered—but the autopsy report revelations had given them a boost they'd sorely needed. The detail that would stay most vividly with the four women was the haunting image of Angela

Watkins's corpse lying curled up on the side of the ravine in the fetal position.

Marissa awoke the next morning unable to shake the idea that Joel and Angela may have survived the crash. That would explain Joel's putting the Explorer in Park. She imagined them trying to ascend the steep ravine—able to climb only some three hundred feet back up toward the road before succumbing to their injuries. This dire scenario did not explain why the airbags did not deploy—but the thought of their surviving for some length of time at the bottom of the ravine plagued her to the extent that she felt compelled to text Detective Fonseca.

> Marissa: Question 🙏 . . . Is the idea that this was a murder suicide (at Joel's hands) still a possibility in your mind?

He responded immediately and definitively.

Raymond Fonseca: No

Whatever evidence he had, it was apparently conclusive. Marissa sent a screenshot of the exchange to the team, to which Jeannie replied, "That is one direct man."

Nicole produced better, more recent contacts for many of Greg Medina's ex-partners, former employees, and lawsuit complainants. Each person told a similar story of being wronged by a man who came off as friendly and optimistic but who never delivered on his promises or fulfilled his responsibilities. One former employee who reported him to the California Division of Labor Standards Enforcement—the labor board—said that he had worked for Greg for three to four months without pay. He said Greg was always trying to scrape together money to meet payroll, while at the same time taking his wife on trips to Las Vegas. People were afraid to sue Greg for fear of a countersuit that could bankrupt them. Greg, who obviously knew his way around the legal system, kept changing the names and addresses of his businesses in order to evade scrutiny. "This guy is a snake," the person said. He also claimed that Greg's wife, Marie, had to have known exactly what was going on.

This opened up a deeper conversation among the four women. Joel and Angela having an equally shady son and son-in-law stretched the concepts of bad luck and coincidence to the breaking point. And then there was the daughter Marie. How did she partner up with a huckster and a tax cheat like Greg? Samira theorized that the Watkinses' family dynamic was such that the men were the decision makers and the women became accustomed to that, and comfortable with it so long as it sustained the lifestyle they enjoyed. Entitled men and dependent, deliberately oblivious women was an arrangement as old as time, and yet none of the women could themselves conceive of being so willfully ignorant. Entrusting one's security to an untrustworthy partner was as sure a recipe for victimhood as has ever existed.

Jeannie speculated that growing up with parents modeling this arrangement, while at the same time being raised alongside a dominating brother—the spoiled, privileged, layabout Andrew—might have caused Marie to internalize this dynamic and allow another narcissist such as Greg to enter her life. Nicole pointed out that the many, many business associates Andrew and Greg had wronged were across-the-board good people who were left with loads of bad debt and, in some cases, utter financial ruin.

Marissa contacted a man who had direct knowledge of Greg Medina during the time of Joel and Angela's disappearance. Herschel Wensinck had been employed by Greg right up until

June 2005. The team located him through a lawsuit Herschel had filed against Greg seeking recovery of unpaid wages. In anticipation of his legal action, Herschel had taken copious notes during the late stages of his employment with Greg and had preserved copies of paychecks, bank notices, and other documents. Reached by phone, Herschel seemed overwhelmed deciding what was best to share with Marissa, who offered to go to his house, sift through his notes, and scan the relevant documents herself.

The others thought Marissa was crazy. They insisted on going with her, but Marissa told them it wasn't necessary. Even if Herschel was sketchy, Covid meant that Marissa would not be entering his house. She texted the others his address "in case I'm murdered," with a sarcastic shrug emoji—emblematic of their gallows humor—and drove out to Glendale.

Herschel Wensinck was exactly the oddball Marissa expected him to be, a small, anxious man with a silvery beard spilling from beneath his cloth mask. He remained in his front doorway, having set out a thick folder of legal documents and his personal journals for her on his front lawn. He could not have been more eager to help, and Marissa found an old kids' blanket in her trunk and set up shop on his sidewalk, using a scanning app on her phone to copy his files and notes.

It was a gold mine. Page after page of neatly handwritten entries recounting Herschel's daily interactions with Greg Medina, presented sequentially by date with exact dollar amounts, hours worked, and related conversations. At the end of a two-and-a-half-page, step-by-step accounting of bounced paychecks, promised direct deposits, and NSF notices from overdrawn accounts, Herschel recorded that in late April 2005, one month before the Watkinses' disappearance, Greg had claimed "the money was not there because his father-in-law who does the payroll through his company Wattkins LED was shorted $100,000 from some other customer, which screwed up everyone's payroll." The next day, Greg handed Herschel $500 cash "to get me through the weekend." Over the next month, there followed a series of broken promises, until finally Herschel realized that Greg was attempting to push him into quitting so that he could use that excuse not to pay him. This made Herschel all the more determined to hang on for dear life.

In his entry for May 30, 2005—the Monday after the weekend of Greg's in-laws' disappearance—Herschel arrived for work promptly at nine. His paycheck, which had for some reason been drawn on Wattkins LED's account, had bounced over the weekend. Herschel discovered Greg asleep in his office, having apparently spent the night there. Upon waking, Greg told Herschel he was too busy to talk and said he should redeposit the check. Herschel did so, and the check cleared.

There was still the matter of his other outstanding paychecks. Herschel called Greg at two o'clock the next day, Tuesday—day two of Joel and Angela's disappearance—but Greg's secretary informed him that Greg was out on a "personal matter" and would not be back that day.

After a series of unanswered calls the next day, Wednesday, June 1, Greg finally "called me back after eleven A.M. and told me his father-in-law had been kidnapped and him and his wife have been missing the last three days. He would try to get me my money tomorrow and to call around ten and he should have a check waiting for me."

At ten o'clock Thursday morning, Herschel was told to come in at three that afternoon to pick up the check. He did as instructed. There was no one in the shop.

Later that night, Nicole emerged from her house with a bottle of Casamigos and a stack of paper cups. The team gathered in beach chairs in Nicole's driveway, eager to discuss the day's developments and to unwind.

"They were 'kidnapped,'" said Samira. "Greg Medina said that. At the time when no one knew where they were or what had happened—weeks before they were found."

"It gets better," said Marissa. "Herschel said Greg continued to use his father-in-law's disappearance as an excuse not to pay him. At one point he said that Greg said to him, 'Who knows? Maybe they drove off the Angeles Crest Highway.'"

"Super dirty," said Samira. "Super fishy."

They talked about the paycheck made out to Herschel from Wattkins LED. Greg had never officially been employed by Joel, as far as they could tell, but he was clearly a party to the fraud. "Herschel also said that Greg and Andrew were close. He said Andrew was cold, seemed like a dick."

Herschel had eventually won his lawsuit, recovering unpaid wages, but the experience with Greg had really messed him up, both financially and emotionally. He told Marissa that the detectives had shown great interest in his journal entries, and in fact had subpoenaed them and even asked Herschel to take a lie detector test to attest that everything in them was truthful. Herschel's understanding was that his notes were part of the evidence prosecutors eventually placed before a grand jury—but ultimately the grand jury did not find sufficient evidence to file an indictment against Greg Medina and Andrew Watkins.

Nicole had news. Greg's multitudinous legal issues had continued right up to the present day. His mother had passed away in 2016, leaving behind a substantial estate, but her will explicitly excluded Greg from the inheritance, stating that the mother had given Greg enough money during his lifetime and he would get nothing more. Greg filed a claim against the trust regardless, and his petition was currently making its way through the courts.

As they digested this new information, the front door opened and Nicole's young son ran up behind her.

"Mom! Can I get some water?" he whined.

"Give me a minute. Mom is working—I'll be right there."

He scampered back into the house.

She widened her eyes in annoyance and raised her paper cup of tequila in a mock *Cheers* to the other women. "To never getting a break," she said.

Minutes later, the boy came running out again, this time carrying a glass of water. Knowing he was much too small to reach the kitchen cabinets, Nicole was confused, but impressed with his independence.

"Whoa! Way to go! How did you get the water?"

"My sister helped me!" he said.

Nicole was charmed that her daughter would do such a kind thing for her little brother, and all the other women were duly impressed.

"She got the water from the toilet," her son added, before running back inside, Nicole sprinting after him.

Marissa felt she had developed a rapport with Detective Fonseca via text, though he remained steadfast in refusing to share any privileged information regarding the case. She texted him about her rendezvous with Herschel Wensinck, knowing now that Fonseca had considered Herschel's journals to be important enough evidence to warrant grand jury consideration. She clued him in on Greg Medina's current probate case, of which the detective had been unaware.

> **Detective Fonseca: So you understand now why Greg is suspicious in the investigation.**

Marissa read this twice. This text literally contained more insight than the retired homicide detective had shared with Marissa in all the weeks since she had first contacted him. This emboldened her to take a run at him with the team's working theory. She cleared it with the others, then texted him the team's thoughts.

> Marissa: I see how Greg inappropriately used Wattkins LED funds and helped (along with others) to create phony invoices to pull money from their line of credit. When the line was coming due in June, meaning the fraudulent activity would inevitably come to light, the Watkinses disappeared. Their deaths wiped free all of the company debt (it was only in Angela and Joel's name), but left the estate and properties to the next of kin (some of whom were in severe financial trouble). It doesn't look good for Greg or Andrew.

> Marissa: Am I on the right track?

She realized only after she had pressed Send that if their theory was wrong, Fonseca would likely lose interest in communicating, dashing her hopes of getting hold of the police files. Three pulsating dots on her phone indicated that the retired homicide detective was typing. She stared at her screen in anticipation.

> Detective Fonseca: 💡

Marissa's fingers flew as she took a screenshot and shared it with the text chain.

> Nicole: Oh. My. God.

> Samira: A 💡?

> Nicole: This is major.

Nicole: This is huge.

Marissa: I'm going to push him. Should I ask the car questions?

Samira: Yes!

They had a list already prepared. Marissa switched back to her text chain with Detective Fonseca.

Marissa: In regard to the scene of the car wreck . . . a few questions . . . Were the keys in the ignition? Were there any other personal items of note in there? Was Angela's phone in the car? And was Joel's cell phone found at his office?

More dancing ellipses. The suspense was killing her.

Detective Fonseca: None of which I can tell you at this point due to the integrity of the investigation.

She went back to the team texts, sharing the new screenshot.

Marissa: He shot me down.

Samira: It is progress though

Nicole: Think he would meet with us in person?

Marissa: I think, if we have something to give him? Maybe yes

That one lightbulb emoji was galvanizing.

Jeannie kept pulling up the image, reveling in how far the team had come without access to any police files. Nothing like this had ever happened in her life. It felt surreal.

She felt a major shift in her mindset. After years of dedicating her life to mothering her child, a job she loved and embraced with her whole being, she realized that during that time she had lost touch with a key piece of her identity. Being a mother was addictive in so many ways—expanding her love to levels she hadn't known possible—but it also left little room for her personal passions. As the team continued to make real progress toward actually solving the case, she could feel herself reconnecting to the adventurous, scrappy woman she had been before her child was born.

The team keyed in on Greg Medina, reaching out to any and all of his past business connections they could find. Those who responded shared similar tales of promises broken and fraudulent deceit. One interview stood out. This person was unusually defensive, voicing unambiguous support for Greg before quickly getting off the call. Marissa noted this in their files but didn't think much more about it.

The next day was a typical Covid Wednesday. School sessions for both girls in the morning, Marissa having her online grocery order placed in the trunk of her car by masked and gloved Gelson's employees, a morning walk with Cecil while mindfully crossing the street to avoid contact with other pedestrians, online yoga. The girls came up for air at lunchtime, and Marissa was in the process of fixing them jelly sandwiches, knowing how particular they were about the jelly-to-bread ratio, the girls complaining about the hike Marissa was making them join her on later that afternoon, when Marissa's cellphone rang. While the number was unfamiliar, the area code was local, so, gooey knife in hand, she answered.

It was a man's voice, speaking quickly, harshly, insistent. "Who is this?"

Marissa, immediately put off, said, "Who is *this*?"

"This is Greg Medina. Why are you digging around into my past?"

Marissa froze, breathless. One of the two main suspects in a double murder case was on the line. Greg Medina was talking to her in her kitchen. A sudden pealing in her ears made it difficult to hear.

She stared at the jelly-smeared knife, heart pounding. "Oh—hi," she said, instinctively tuning her voice up an octave or so to sound friendly and nonthreatening.

It didn't work. "I asked what you are doing digging into my past," he said, his voice rising.

"I'm an investigative journalist. I'm just trying to, um, resolve a situation. . . ."

"Wait," he said, after a pause. "Is this about my in-laws?"

"Yes—yes, it is." She turned away from the girls, feeling them watching her, attuned to their mother's alarm and wondering what was happening.

His attitude softened just a bit. "Yeah, they never gave us the answer to that—to what happened. I'd really like to know too."

Marissa kept up her chipper voice, her mind racing, playing innocent and a bit naïve. Based on their findings to date, she strongly suspected that Greg Medina didn't take women seriously. "Oh—great," she said. "That's great. If you're interested, I'd love to talk to you."

"Oh, I don't know about that," Greg said, his tone again shifting.

"I'd love to get your thoughts on your parents-in-law and what you think might have happened."

Now he was the uncomfortable one, fumbling his words, a complete one-eighty from the angry tone in which he'd begun the conversation. "I'd—I have to talk to my family about that, because they'd . . . I'd have to get back to you."

"Sure, sure, I understand that. But just speaking generally, what do you think really happened to them?"

"Yeah, let me . . . I'll get back to you."

The line went dead.

By now, Brian had drifted into the kitchen. He could tell something was wrong by the pitch of Marissa's voice and the defensive way she was gripping the gooey knife. She could not hide her shock, her initial fear returning.

"Who was that?" he asked.

Marissa put the knife down on the cutting board. Her hand was shaking. She told him.

"He called you on your phone?" said Brian. "One of the guys you think is"—here he lowered his voice for the girls, but not low enough—"*a murderer?*"

Marissa reasoned that he must have gotten her number from someone she had recently spoken with—the man who had vouched for Greg, who Marissa would later discover had been a groomsman in Greg's wedding.

Seeing how shaken Marissa was made Brian more agitated. "If he has your phone number, he can get our address, right? That's what you've been doing this whole time."

"I know, I know." Marissa was gripping the kitchen island, half apologizing, half reeling from the call. "I never thought he was going to call."

Brian said, "You've been using your own phone."

"Holy shit," she said, realizing her huge mistake.

"Is this the guy with all the lawsuits?"

Marissa nodded. Brian was right, but he wasn't making this any better. "I should get a burner phone. How do I get a burner phone?"

Her older daughter was already looking it up. "They're on Amazon," she said.

When she had recovered somewhat, and the frenetic energy in her house had settled down, Marissa texted the others.

**Marissa: You are never going to believe who called me!!
I'm shaking!**

The women were rattled, as were their spouses. Safety had always been the primary concern of Samira's husband, Ward, especially as the team pursued the theory that the killer or killers were still out there somewhere. Why was she willing to take on such a huge risk doing something no one had asked her to do? One of the main suspects now knew that Samira's team was on to him. What was his next move?

They all agreed to cover their tracks better, both in real life and online, and pledged never to go anywhere alone. Herschel Wensinck had proved to be a harmless eccentric, but Marissa promised not to take any chances like that again. Once she recovered from the shock of the call, Marissa viewed it as another indication of their progress. Something was happening with the investigation. She had turned over the wrong rock this time, but what they were doing had succeeded in heating up a fifteen-year-old cold case. Things were happening. Marissa had been struck most by the abrupt shift in dynamic from Marissa stammering to answer Greg's questions to him backpedaling from Marissa's inquiries and hanging up: the accuser becoming the accused.

Marissa used her burner phone for everything case-related after that, but she always kept her personal phone at hand, both hoping and fearing Greg Medina would follow through with his pledge to call her back. She was of two minds, wanting dearly to hear his version of the murders and financial fraud—though it was sure to be self-serving and evasive—but also eager to avoid interaction with a known conman, litigious liar, and potential murderer. Still, she had a sneaking suspicion that she would hear from Greg Medina again.

The *alarming* *phone* *call* *from* *one* *of* *their* *chief* *suspects* *also* made the team reassess their progress, and they determined that they had done about as much as they could do while operating on the periphery of the case. The flow of new information into the investigation had slowed to a trickle. Interviews with employees and associates of Joel and Andrew Watkins and Greg Medina had become largely repetitive, confirming and reconfirming many things they had learned but rarely turning over new ground. Marissa's request for the Los Angeles County Sheriff's Department police files on the Watkins case had been denied. At the same time, though never explicitly, Detective Fonseca's texts continued to encourage Marissa (his only point of contact with the team) to press on with their investigation—while still refusing to share any actual police evidence. "Case integrity" was his annoying mantra.

Unexpectedly, Medina's phone call shifted things just a bit, as, like Marissa, Detective Fonseca viewed it as a sign that the investigation was gaining traction.

Detective Fonseca: At some point, we need to sit down and discuss your direction, objectives, and intentions. I would like to see what you have as well.

Marissa: Anything specifically?

Detective Fonseca: I have all the information. Just want to know where you're going.

He was being cagey, as always, but this seemed like an opening. Marissa consulted the team and they agreed. *Let's go for it.* Samira helped assemble a succinct overview in hopes of impressing him and perhaps moving the needle beyond a light-bulb emoji.

Marissa: We are still gathering a lot of content, but our research leads us to this general story. Andrew Watkins and Greg Medina (with possible involvement from others) found themselves in increasingly distressing financial trouble from 2002–2005. Andrew and Greg got involved in a business entity together, at least on paper. They (and others) falsified invoices through their company to funnel money from the Pacific Heritage Bank & Trust line of credit. Meanwhile, Joel was getting increasingly stressed about the situation. He found other sources of loans and increased his line of credit. Joel was scheduled to meet with the bank officer at Pacific Heritage to discuss the unpaid receivables and knew he was in big trouble. We presume he discussed this distress with Andrew (& maybe Greg). They, worried that they might be "found out" and realizing their family estate may be at risk, did the only thing they could to wipe out the enormous Wattkins LED debt (and the record of their fraudulent behavior)—orchestrated the deaths of Joel & Angela (the only responsible parties for the debt). The estate was left clean and they walked away with life insurance, family assets, and some properties.

Marissa: Would you say that lines up? Any areas that I'm way off?

Detective Fonseca: Yes it lines up very well on the financial side. From the outside, it looks fairly complete.

Detective Fonseca: Just curious. You've said "we" on a few occasions regarding your investigation. Who are you working with and what is their relationship to you or the investigation? I was under the impression that you were a solo independent reporter.

Marissa: Three other women. One is a seasoned researcher. The other two are novice investigative journalists like me. Given the density of content, I wanted more minds in this

Detective Fonseca: At some point when we meet, can they be a part of the meeting?

There it was. Marissa took a screenshot of the exchange and forwarded it to the team with two exploding head emojis.

Samira: Game changer!!!

Nicole: OMG

Jeannie: Yes! Ok. Man, this is big.

Marissa: Now I'm nervous. He wants to meet us all soon!

Samira: Excited! We have to prepare

Nicole: This is a dream

They had gotten what they wanted; now they had to produce. They logged as many Zoom hours as they could over the next several days, cramming for this presentation, determined to impress him. This was a job interview and a make-or-break career presentation all in one.

By this point, Samira was spending all of her free time on the case, much of it coming at the expense of sleep, researching late into the night. She treated it like a job, a job she wanted to do. Nerding out on details, doing deep dives. Not just the scandalous stuff, but educating herself about 2000 Ford Explorers, poring through the social media contacts of every person involved, building out bubble charts of interconnectivity. She was vigilant for any overlaps that might reveal unknown friendships and hidden alliances. Falling down a rabbit hole is easy when you are chasing an actual rabbit—or two. Whereas her daily existence had devolved into a blur of chaos and uncertainty thanks to Covid, here was a pursuit offering a unique opportunity to bring order to disorder.

They selected the most Covid-safe location they could think of: a public park. The four women arrived separately and early, carrying folders and notebooks, with an air of excitement and tension. Not only was this their first meeting with Detective Fonseca, but this was Jeannie's first in-person meeting with Samira and Nicole. The park had walking trails and benches not far from the street entrance, and they set up around a picnic bench away from masked children playing in a fenced playground under the watchful eyes of their parents. Covid-cautious Jeannie brought her own folding chair and sat back from the rest, wearing a mask. Samira was also masked; Marissa and Nicole were not. After long hours chatting and bonding over Zoom and text, gathering as a foursome for the first time made everything vividly real. They were waiting to meet a homicide detective about a murder case. After a few pleasantries, anxiety took over, and none of them said much as they watched the park entrance.

Marissa's fantasy was that Detective Fonseca would arrive pushing a dolly stacked with banker's boxes brimming with case files and evidence. That he'd listen to what they had to say and substantiate it with corroborating information, or else point out things they'd overlooked and helpfully guide them in the right direction. They had put in so much work, and were so sincere in their efforts, she was certain that they would be rewarded here, that he would take them into his confidence and supercharge their investigation by sharing privileged police information.

About five minutes after the agreed-to meeting time, a tall man entered the park and walked toward the bench area.

"There he is," said Nicole. "That's got to be him."

The man carried a slim notebook tucked under his arm—nothing else. Marissa's initial thought was, *Fuck*. Her expectations had been so unreasonably high. Still, she forced a smile. Maybe the documents were in the trunk of his car. Maybe he was just being cautious, wanting to size them up first.

He wore dark slacks and a button-up short-sleeved shirt, appeared to be in his early sixties yet had almost no gray in his hair, and looked trim and athletic, like a college-level coach. He wore a cloth mask, which he pulled down as he approached them, his cop-like manner difficult to read.

Marissa introduced herself and made the Covid-awkward introductions. No fist or elbow taps, just nods and waves. Marissa thanked him for coming. Samira could feel him evaluating them, scrutinizing their intent: Were they seriously committed to finding the murderers of Joel and Angela Watkins? Or was this a passing hobby?

Raymond Fonseca opened by reiterating what this case meant to him. That he had been unable to close it and prosecute those responsible before his retirement still rankled him. The conversation was not recorded, but each woman recalled it vividly.

The team ran through their findings—laying out everything from the financials, to the dramatic family dynamics, to the provocative witness interviews. Detective Fonseca barely reacted to their presentation, save for an occasional corroborative nod, each one of which the team eagerly noted.

Greg Medina was having grave financial trouble in the month

leading up to Joel and Angela's disappearance and was unable to make payroll. *Nod.*

Angela's body was found in the fetal position. *Nod.*

Joel had made a call to his longtime friend and confidant Dennis Ladd on the afternoon of his disappearance saying "I'm in trouble." *Nod.*

These were some of the things they had uncovered that were not part of the public record. They revealed at least one fact new to him: that Greg and Marie were currently separated. But Fonseca's cop-perfect poker face remained difficult to read.

They tried a different tactic, throwing caution to the wind and shooting him questions. Samira jumped in with "What was it about the crash site that told you it wasn't a suicide case?"

"I can't tell you that," he said.

She asked if there was any possibility that modern advances in DNA evidence and genealogical tracing could prove useful here.

"I can't tell you that."

He wasn't at all rude, he just wasn't helpful. When pressed, he always came back to "maintaining the integrity of the case." Understanding his perspective did not make it any less frustrating. The man before them held the answers to so many of the questions they were currently working so hard to find.

"But are we on the right track?" asked Nicole.

"A lot of what you have said here tracks with what I know," Fonseca answered, choosing his words carefully.

They realized this was going to be a one-way street. His attitude was, *You are helping me, I am not helping you.* There would be no opening of the murder file, no partnership. No real guidance at all. At the same time, he did not tell them to stop. He didn't say that their hypotheses were way off. He didn't shake his head and walk away.

"Let's keep talking," he said at the end.

Marissa made one final request, on their behalf as well as on behalf of their spouses: Could they run some things by him from time to time with regard to their personal safety? "Can you at least advise us, don't talk to this person, or that it's okay to talk to that person?"

He made a face as if this seemingly simple request put him in a difficult position. "I'll do what I can," he said.

Not wanting to lose the moment, Marissa quickly asked his opinion about Angela's sister, Gwen. Angela Watkins was still very much an enigma to them, almost a blank slate. They needed to learn more but had learned the hard way to be apprehensive about approaching family members. "Do you think she might be receptive to having a conversation with us?"

To their surprise, Fonseca nodded. "Gwen and her husband are good people," he said.

Marissa pushed a little more. "What about the younger Watkins daughter who lives locally, Carrie?"

Fonseca was more reluctant to answer this one, responding with just a shrug.

Samira said, "Obviously, daughter Marie is off the table, but if we were to reach out to Carrie, what do you think? Would you vouch for us and our intentions?"

"She has my phone number" was all Fonseca said.

He parted with a warning. "The further you get into this, the more careful you need to become. Burner phones and house alarms are all well and good, but understand what you are doing here and where it could lead. If something scares you, trust your instincts. Information is not authority. Being right about something doesn't make you safe. In fact, it makes you dangerous. There's a legal line you have to walk, too, because you are civilians. I think you've encountered some of the pitfalls already. Nothing's worth getting hurt over. There's no shame in taking care of yourselves first. No shame in walking away from trouble before it's too late. Somebody killed Mr. and Mrs. Watkins, probably to guarantee their silence. You need to proceed accordingly."

Then he said goodbye and walked back to his car.

Afterward, the four women sat around the picnic bench unsure what to do. They were chilled by his parting words, and disappointed by his lack of candor and cooperation, yet they felt a sense of exhilaration now that it was over.

He'd listened to them. He'd respected them. He hadn't given them everything they'd hoped he would, but he'd heard them out and he'd engaged. This was validating in itself. The hour-long meeting had felt three times as long. They were drained and they were hungry. They were also out of their houses without kids for once.

They regrouped at a Mexican food place Marissa knew of nearby, sitting along the sidewalk curb with six feet of space between them, eating tacos and recharging. This was Jeannie's first opportunity to get to know the others in person. They commiserated about how hard it was during lockdown, having gone from stay-at-home moms to shelter-in-place moms. Zoom was a pale substitute for sitting curbside eating street tacos and drinking Mexican Cokes.

"So," said Nicole, finally coming around to the postmortem on the meeting. "What do we think?"

"He impressed me," said Jeannie. "And he frustrated me."

Everyone concurred. They also agreed that they had never talked to a hardened personality like his. They were dealing with someone for whom there was no equivalent in their circle. Marissa's disappointment ran deeper. "We delivered and he didn't. I feel like we have made huge strides, and he's still stonewalling us. What's it going to take?" Later, she would admit to being naïve at best, privileged at worst, in expecting Detective Fonseca to open his investigation to them.

They agreed on one thing they had learned: They didn't need Detective Fonseca's validation after all. He could have made their path ahead easier, but adversity also yielded results. They were going to keep moving forward on their own. Though the meeting hadn't played out exactly as they had hoped, they emerged from it more dedicated than ever to cracking the case.

THE CLIENT

With what would have been her mom's seventy-first birthday approaching, Nicole was feeling particularly nostalgic. There remained this hole in her life where her mother should have been, and she wondered what her mother would have thought about Nicole's investigating this case. She knew her mother would have loved that she was doing it altruistically, pro bono, and doubly so that she was partnered with three other women on the project. Nicole's thoughts also turned toward someone else who had lost her mother too young: Carrie Watkins. Approaching a family member was a huge step for the team, and they had no idea how their interview request would be received. Nicole tried to put herself in Carrie's shoes. How would she react to four strangers offering to insert themselves into her personal life? People acting with the best intentions can still make a bad situation worse. They had no right to be doing what they were doing. None of this was their business. All they could offer was their interest and their time. If they came across as dilettantes, the family could cut off communication altogether or even request that they stop investigating.

They all felt this was a risk they had to take. In early June, Marissa sent Carrie Watkins a respectful email at her office and waited for a response. Days passed, and they assumed she was a no. According to Fonseca, she had turned down offers from true crime television shows like *Dateline* and *48 Hours* that wanted to feature her parents' story, so they weren't offended or surprised. No one would have blamed her for ignoring their request. But then:

Marissa: CARRIE CALLED! 😬 😬 😬 😬

Jeannie: Whoa!!! Deep breaths!

Jeannie: I'm sure she's nervous too . . .

Marissa received a voicemail from a private number: *Hello, this is Carrie Watkins. Raymond Fonseca gave me your number and said you and a small group of investigative journalists have taken an interest in my parents' deaths. My preference would be to meet in person rather than over the phone.*

The women were elated. It was a huge opportunity, and at the same time it seemed to them like the ultimate you-have-only-one-chance-to-make-a-good-impression moment. After some texting back and forth, Marissa set the meeting for a Sunday afternoon in Carrie Watkins's backyard. The women obsessed over compiling a comprehensive but not overly long list of questions.

Carrie Watkins lived in Normandie Heights in north Pasadena, which, even with reduced Covid traffic, was a trek from the Westside. Since they were all making another rare foray outside their home bubbles, it made sense to make an afternoon of it—but not for tacos this time. Instead, they did something they had talked about doing almost since the beginning. They caravanned to Paradise Canyon to view Joel and Angela's home on Shadow Peak Road.

They parked a few houses down and walked, masked, along the curb to the Watkinses' address from fifteen years earlier. They had zillowed the hell out of it over the past few months, but seeing it now, they were struck by how ordinary the house looked. The faux-stucco siding was beige, the tiled roof cinnamon brown. The driveway was a half circle, a two-car garage extending from the left side of the house, double doors facing the crest of the driveway for direct access. The garden inside the arc of the driveway and the landscaping on either side showed none of the care that Angela was known for. Golf ball–sized oranges hung from an unshaped tree, nondescript greenery sprouting up around a flat stump. A single crane-like crimson-and-apricot bird-of-paradise plant rose above thick-leaved lower plantings, perhaps a perennial planted by Angela that had survived her. It was a hot summer day, the sun beating down. Jeannie pictured Angela in her wide-brimmed sun hat and elbow-length gloves, pruning and planting, while Joel tended to the grass and mulch.

The team had contacted the current owners, who had purchased it from the Watkinses' estate, but they were not receptive to answering questions about the transaction or allowing them to take a look inside. Did that stop Marissa from walking up the driveway to the wide front door and ringing the bell? It did not. When no one answered, she went up on her toes to peer in the window, looking back at the others with a shrug. Instead of giving up like a normal person, she wandered over to the right side of the house to get a look at the backyard.

"What is she doing?" Jeannie said. "She's crazy."

Samira looked up and down the quiet street. It was very still, yet she felt watched. "You know somebody on this street is already reporting us on Nextdoor."

Jeannie said, "Maybe we look like realtors."

Samira watched Marissa fearlessly knocking on doors and jiggling gates. Samira felt very conspicuous standing out in the road. Black residents made up less than one percent of the population in that community.

"Do you think it happened here?" said Jeannie. "Maybe in that garage?"

Joel and Angela's murders predated Ring and Nest cameras and even most traffic cameras. Not that surveillance made the world much safer. Murder could still happen anywhere, even on a street lined with houses with an average value of $2.5 million. But it was more difficult to get away with now.

There was one other thing to do before meeting Carrie Watkins, something that had become a pressing issue during and after their park rendezvous with Detective Fonseca, having to do with the lack of public restrooms in the time of Covid. Leading up to this meeting, they joked via text about taking along one of their children's old travel potties, the way they used to when their kids were little. As the meeting grew nearer, it became less of a joke and more of a logistical reality. Nicole was especially concerned, so Samira, whose youngest never had to go to the bathroom before leaving the house for a pandemic road trip but absolutely had to pee like she hadn't peed in days once there was no possible place to stop, recommended a funnel-shaped rubber device called a GoGirl. It came highly rated with customer recommendations calling it "a game-changer," a "Mardi Gras and Burning Man must-have," and "a female hiker's best friend." "Don't Take Life Sitting Down" was the GoGirl motto.

They pulled in at a nearby park and Nicole hopped out of her car. "I'm going for it!" she said with a laugh, marching into the trees. She reemerged a few minutes later having peed all over her legs. Samira dug out some baby wipes from her center console and tossed them to Nicole. It occurred to them that this was an obstacle that male investigators never had to face.

All cleaned up, game faces and masks on, they parked outside Carrie Watkins's tidy tract home and walked together to the front door. Nothing any of them had encountered in their lives prepared them for this task. The solemnity of what they were about to do settled over them. This was another *What are we doing?* moment. Agreeing to meet with them was a great leap of faith on her part, and now it was on them to prove they were up to the task.

Carrie answered the door wearing a thin casual sweater over leggings. She was very attractive, and she introduced her similarly good-looking husband, Henry, who was friendly but initially more suspicious of the women than his wife. Carrie thanked them for coming, and she and Henry led them around the house into the backyard. Chairs had been arranged on a patio of ornately patterned stonework under the shade of a wide blue umbrella. They sat at appropriate distances and removed their masks, beginning with some small talk about managing kids in lockdown and the weird summer everyone was having. Nicole and Carrie connected on the travails of managing at-home work with at-home mothering. Her youngest was closest in age to Carrie's only.

Carrie was polite but reserved and chose her words carefully. She told them that she appreciated their interest in her parents' murders but wished to go slowly at first. The women assured her that they would proceed at whatever pace she desired, and that they could only imagine all that she had gone through since her parents' disappearance. Samira assured her that as women with extended families themselves, the last thing they wanted was to create any more distress for her and her siblings.

"No need to concern yourself about that," said Carrie. "This thing caused the disintegration of my relationship with my brother and older sister a long time ago." Carrie was still in touch and close with her twin sister, Lily, who had moved to Indiana a year or so before their parents' disappearance. At the time they went missing, she had been pregnant with her first child and on bed rest, unable to travel. "All the damage has already been done. I cannot anticipate anything coming out of this that could further injure it. You may reaffirm suspicions I have, or this may lead to some new revelation, but the worst you could do would be to reopen wounds that have never fully healed."

As they talked, Carrie let her guard down by degrees. She

was candid about never having moved on emotionally from what had happened to her parents. Not a day had gone by in the past fifteen years when she didn't wonder how they had spent their final hours.

Seeing how desperate Carrie was for answers helped to put the team's own interest in the case into proper perspective. The murders of this woman's parents had left a gaping hole in her life. Nicole, still thinking of her own mother, could not imagine losing both parents at the same time.

"As grateful as I am for your interest in this case," Carrie told them, "I don't understand your motives yet. I would like to build up trust, and I'm happy to start answering any questions you have."

Samira had come prepared with their list of questions in her notebook, but it suddenly seemed like the wrong approach. They had no business quizzing this woman.

"Maybe," said Samira, "you could just tell us your story. What happened in the hours and days after you found out your parents were missing."

She nodded. "Okay. What do you want to hear?"

"Absolutely everything," said Samira.

Carrie settled into her chair, gave her permission to be recorded, and began.

On Monday, May 30, 2005, a hot day in late spring, Carrie received a call from her brother, Andrew, around four o'clock. They did not speak regularly, but Carrie recognized a note of distress in his voice, which was very much out of character. Andrew was a brash, calculating person who normally radiated confidence and self-control. He said their father had not shown up for work that day and had missed a lunch meeting without any notice. Calls to his cellphone were going straight to voicemail, which was highly unusual, given that their father was tied to his phone. More alarmingly, there was no answer on their parents' home telephone.

Carrie told him she would swing by their parents' house to check on them. On the drive to La Cañada Flintridge, it occurred to her that Andrew's office was closer to their parents, and that it would have made a lot more sense for him to check on them. But with her anxiety rising, this incongruity left her mind as soon as it came.

The house on Shadow Peak Road, elevated against the foothills and canyons of the San Gabriel Mountains behind it, appeared serene as always. She parked and hurried up the driveway to the front door, ringing the bell without answer, the door locked. She had come straight from her office and did not have a key.

No sound came from inside. She wasn't sure what to do next. Her parents were particular about security, locking doors, arming the alarm. She didn't want to trip it and set it screaming, but then again, maybe that wasn't the worst thing, either. If dispatched, the police would have to do a wellness check. She walked to a side door that connected to the two-car garage and tried the knob.

It turned and the door opened. No warning tone from the alarm.

She entered cautiously, calling out ahead, "Mom? Dad? It's Carrie! Hello?" She looked into the garage, switching on the light. Her mother's Mercedes-Benz was parked in its usual spot, but her father's Ford Explorer was gone. This came as a relief. Maybe they were out somewhere.

She moved into the house, still calling out to them. The stillness seemed pronounced. At first glance, everything looked as it should. Her mother, a bit of a recluse, was fastidious about housecleaning. Carrie saw visible vacuum lines in the carpet and noticed that the countertops were spotless. In the dining area, all the chairs were pushed in to the table except one, angled out.

Next to it, a vacuum cleaner lay on its side on the floor, still plugged in to the wall. It was a small thing, but Carrie knew her mother well enough to know that she would never have left the house without putting the vacuum away in the closet and arranging the chairs neatly.

"Mom!" she called out. "Dad!"

Growing more nervous as she moved upstairs, worried about what she might find, Carrie checked each room, finding nothing out of place. She hadn't been up to the second floor since her parents moved into the house two years before—Carrie herself had never lived there—but she noticed no obvious red flags.

She settled herself down by thinking of the simplest explanation for their absence. Her dad's car was gone. Maybe they'd left on an impromptu vacation? Maybe her father surprised her mother and they packed up quickly and drove off in the Explorer? It was highly unlikely that they wouldn't let anyone know, especially if her father was going to miss work. Carrie realized that it had been about two weeks since she'd last spoken to her parents.

Her next thought was that they'd met with an accident— maybe something serious.

Carrie called her husband and briefed him on the situation, telling him she was heading home to start calling area hospitals. She scribbled a note and left it by the kitchen phone, asking her parents to call, then exited through the same side door, leaving it as it had been, unlocked. She checked in with Andrew and updated him. Andrew said he would start calling hospitals too, and they divided up the list.

At nine-thirty that night, after no word from her parents and having checked with every hospital within twenty miles, Carrie placed a call to the Pasadena police and officially filed missing persons reports on her mother and father. She returned to her parents' home with a Sheriff's Department detective named Adam

Cully. Carrie went around turning on lights in the dark, still house. This time she pulled open drawers and cabinets, not knowing what she was looking for, but it seemed the thing to do. Inside a drawer in a small table in the hallway, she discovered a zippered bank deposit bag containing $14,000 in cash. She showed it to the detective, who recommended she return it to the drawer.

The next day, Tuesday, there was still no contact from either parent. Late in the afternoon, the three locally residing siblings, Marie, Andrew, and Carrie, along with Marie's husband, Greg, and Carrie's husband, Henry, met at the house on Shadow Peak Road. Carrie was too distraught to notice, but Henry remembered thinking that the other three were acting strangely. Marie in particular was a shell of herself. When they left the house, Marie took her mother's pillow and a necklace that Angela had said many times that she always wanted Marie to have. It was as though Marie already knew they were never coming home.

Wednesday, Andrew informed Carrie that he would be shutting down their father's company. He said that the business had been failing and there was significant debt exposure, and the only person who could sign for things was their father. Since Andrew had been working there for the past several years, Carrie trusted his word at the time. Much later, she realized that this course of action matched a disturbing pattern of her siblings and her brother-in-law acting as though they already knew their parents were dead.

On Friday, Carrie helped Andrew and Greg and the office manager, plus her aunt Gwen and uncle Bill, clear out the office. Carrie was still very much in a fog, but one thing that stood out to her was how distraught Andrew was acting. Earlier in the week, she had put it down to distress on the order of what she herself was experiencing, but as that day went on, she began to see that her brother was not sad or bereft but scared. Only after the doors were locked and the moving van loaded, shuttering the company their father had built, did Andrew return to his arrogant self.

Soon Carrie learned about a bank lawsuit filed against her father and her father's company, alleging that between half a million and one million dollars had been fraudulently invoiced and was gone. Her parents' financial fortuncs had fluctuated throughout Carrie's adult life, but allegations of criminal activity were completely inconsistent with the father she knew. Opening her parents' mail, she was shocked to learn that they were in serious credit card debt as well—several hundred thousand dollars' worth. The idea that her parents had committed suicide, once unthinkable, started to seem like a possibility. Detective Cully suspected that her parents had fled the country, which Carrie knew was totally antithetical to their characters.

She spoke daily with the Sheriff's Department over the next five weeks while Andrew retreated from the family and the world. He seemed unmotivated and did not assist with the search. More and more, he spoke about his parents in the past tense. Carrie also learned that during this time Andrew visited their grandparents, Angela's parents, asking for $100,000 he claimed he had lent to Joel months before the disappearance.

One day Carrie received a letter from a lawyer she did not know, an estate attorney, informing her that Andrew had met with him for a consultation about the possibility of distributing his parents' estate funds without proof of death. Disturbed by this request, the attorney had declined to advise Andrew, and was alarmed enough to write to Carrie to alert her to her brother's actions, which he felt were unethical given the uncertainty surrounding her parents' fates.

Five weeks after their disappearance, Carrie received a late-night phone call from Detective Cully. Her parents' Ford Explorer had been located at the bottom of a deep ravine off the Angeles Crest Highway, and two decomposed bodies had been recovered near the wreck. It appeared to be a terrible car accident. Carrie was devastated but the news was not unexpected. Part of her was relieved to have an answer at last.

A few days after dental records confirmed their parents' identities, Andrew, acting as executor of their estate, withdrew $125,000 from it as repayment of his unrecorded "loan." Her suspicions well aroused by this point, and unable to persuade Andrew to hold off or provide proof of said loan, Carrie hired a lawyer who filed an objection in probate court, forcing the siblings into mediation. This was the beginning of the unraveling of their relationship.

Months later, the new detective on the case, Homicide Detective Raymond Fonseca, met with Carrie and Henry, Marie and Greg, and Andrew at the Crescenta Valley Sheriff's Station to update them on the investigation. It was there that Fonseca informed them that their parents' automobile wreck was not an accident or a suicide but in fact a double homicide. He showed them photographs of the road and talked about the trajectory of the SUV, saying that a vehicle approaching the curve from either direction on Angeles Crest Highway would have driven off the road at an angle, whereas their parents' Explorer had dropped straight down over the edge, as though it had been rolled or pushed into the ravine.

Carrie recalled a strange tension in the room as she and her siblings realized they were not there for an update but to take part in what was more akin to a *Law & Order*–type gathering, in which the detective assembles suspects in a room and shares certain pieces of information with them in order to gauge their reactions.

Detective Fonseca suggested that the quickest way to move forward was for each sibling and spouse to take a lie detector test. Carrie was amenable, but Andrew lost it at this moment, becoming startlingly angry, his voice rising indignantly. "How dare you bring us in here under the guise of discussing our parents' deaths to give us a lie detector test!" He refused outright, and that meeting at the sheriff's station turned out to be the end of Carrie's relationship with her siblings.

Carrie became emotional at times in the retelling, her pain reflected in her face. Otherwise, she spoke almost as if in a trance, as though all this had happened as recently as last month and not fifteen years ago. Clearly, she had been over and over the sequence of those days many times since then, reliving and still affected by this foundational event in her life.

Nicole was the first to speak. "So, he never took it?"

"The lie detector test?" said Carrie. "No, he never did."

"Did you?"

"We did, Henry and I. We both passed, of course."

Marissa said, "Do you remember what questions they asked?"

Carrie looked to Henry for help remembering. "Biographical things," she said, "you know, to get a baseline for truthful responses. The big ones were 'Did you have anything to do with your parents' murder?' and 'Do you know who murdered your parents?'"

"What about Greg Medina?" asked Marissa. "Did he take it?"

"Greg took it," Carrie said. "He passed."

"He passed?" said Samira, before she could stop herself.

"I was shocked too," admitted Carrie.

Henry said, "But her sister failed it."

"Marie failed it twice," added Carrie. "I don't know if she asked to retake it or if they wanted her to or what. We weren't communicating at the time. Still aren't."

The team glanced at one another. This was confounding, and they would have a lot to talk about later. But they didn't want to squander their audience with Joel and Angela's daughter. They felt they were connecting on a personal level, in a way that would never have been possible in the company of police detectives. Now it was their turn to share some of what they had learned.

They outlined the factoring fraud scheme, and Carrie was shocked to learn that Andrew and Greg had a shared interest in two of the companies involved. When Marissa told Carrie that Herschel Wensinck had said Andrew and Greg sometimes went ATV'ing together, Carrie shook her head in disbelief. "I didn't know they had any kind of relationship like that," she said. "No idea."

Marissa went on to tell Carrie about the phone call she had received from Greg, demanding to know why she was looking into his background. Carrie was aghast at first, but then she thought it through.

"He can definitely be threatening," she said. "Greg's shady. He always tries to play off that he's the smartest guy in the room. Always trying to bend the rules, always looking for an edge." She turned to Henry and said, "Remember, early on, that first Friday, he came up to us and told us that he'd had a dream about my parents?" Carrie turned back to the team. "He said that he saw that they were alive. 'It was so clear,' he said then. Like he was trying to convince us. Who says something like that? It was totally, totally bizarre."

As to Andrew, Carrie held back little. She said Andrew could be charming when he wanted something and had a way of making people feel special. As a child, she had looked up to her older brother, but as they grew into adulthood, Carrie recognized that Andrew was emotionless and manipulative. They were in contact now only about estate matters, nothing else, and strictly via email. Carrie refuted the team's speculation that there might be something nefarious behind Andrew's not being a CPA anymore. "He probably let his license lapse because keeping it up involves taking classes and spending money and he was working in the private sector now. He didn't need it, and I don't think he wanted to work that hard. That's when he moved away from accounting and started working for my dad."

Nicole asked why the family stopped cooperating with the Sheriff's Department and the press. "Andrew made some conflicting statements, I remember," Carrie said, unable to recall any specifics. "Once the bank sued, he said he was concerned about making any comments publicly, for fear that we could be personally sued. I didn't care. I never gave up. The detectives were convinced they had run off to Mexico with the money, which I knew wasn't true."

Carrie also cleared up some questions about her mother's health.

"My mom had a heart attack in 1999, which she recovered from, but it scared her. Her own mother had died of a heart attack. She didn't want to be alone with her grandson for fear she might suffer another and be unable to care for him. This made her more reclusive, and nowadays I would say she was probably a bit depressed. But she was in okay health physically. They both were."

Samira asked, "Were any personal effects of hers recovered from the crash site?"

"I don't think so."

"Maybe a purse, a cellphone?"

"My mom didn't own a cellphone."

"Your father had one."

"He had two. One we found at the house. I think Andrew found the other one in his office, still charging."

Samira was writing all this down. "Two phones and he didn't take either one with him?"

"Even in 2005, it seemed odd. We also found an empty tequila bottle in my father's office. My dad had given up drinking some years before, or so we thought. Then, when I got his credit card bills, I saw that he was hitting a bar near his office pretty regularly toward the end."

Jeannie said, "You don't still have copies of his credit card statements, do you?"

"I do," said Carrie. "I have his phones, I have everything. I saved it all."

"The police must have searched your parents' house for evidence," said Marissa.

"They definitely fingerprinted and looked for blood. But that was all later, weeks afterward, after we had been through the house several times looking for things. And then there was the fourteen thousand dollars in cash in the hallway table drawer. That was never explained to me."

"They searched the other car, the Mercedes?"

"I don't know," she said, thinking back. "I don't think so. It was a lease, and I turned it back in to the dealership sometime after they were found, but before it was known they were murdered. But that's another thing. Her Mercedes had a flat tire. And there was dirt, like soil, on the floor of the garage near the driver's side door. If you knew my mother, you would understand, there's no way she would have left it that way."

The meeting had gone longer than anybody had anticipated, closing in on two hours. It was draining for all of them, but none more so than Carrie. They wanted to leave her with something other than dredged-up memories from the worst period in her life. They told her how everyone they had spoken to had wonderful things to say about Joel, and that those people who knew Angela spoke of her love for her family. With very few exceptions, Joel's employees and associates had revered him and all expressed hope that his family would finally get answers.

Carrie thanked them for that. "I'll be candid with you all," she said. "I didn't know what this was going to be, exactly, but you're going at this just as I hoped you would. You asked all the questions I wanted you to ask. I don't know why you feel compelled to put so much of your own time and energy into solving my parents' murders . . . but I suppose if you were to ask me why I'm choosing to trust you, I wouldn't have a satisfactory answer either. I guess we're all looking for answers." She thought a moment, fighting emotion, summoning strength to speak. "I believe my brother and maybe my brother-in-law had something to do with my parents' deaths. Either they did it, or they had someone else do it, and they let my dad take the fall for all of the fraud. I believe they know what happened. Part of me doesn't want to reopen this chapter of my life. But a bigger part wants closure. That's all I've ever wanted. That's why I'm going to help you in any way I can."

The team were overwhelmed. What had in the beginning felt like a challenging puzzle they wished to solve had now become very real, with an actual victim sitting before them. They had never expected to become this emotionally invested in the deaths of two people they'd never met. As they stood to leave, Carrie asked them to go on ahead, saying she would meet them out front. She headed into her house through the patio door holding hands with Henry.

The four women walked around the side of the house without a word. They waited there a few moments until the screen door squeaked open, Henry holding it for Carrie, who emerged carrying a printer paper box containing a stack of documents and a few freezer-size Ziploc bags. "These are the papers I kept," she said, "my parents' bills, some notes I took, phone numbers—copies I made a long time ago. And these—these are my dad's phones."

The team realized to their amazement that she was offering these items to them. Samira accepted the box from her, unable to speak.

"I don't know if you can get them working," Carrie continued. "Maybe there's something in there."

Her demonstration of trust in them was staggering. Taken aback by Carrie's gesture of faith, the women promised they would be in touch.

There was no going straight home after that. They had to talk, and they knew instantly where they needed to go. It was in the opposite direction from home, but that didn't matter.

They pulled off and parked on the turnout where Joel and Angela's car had gone over the side of Angeles Crest Highway. They stepped over the dirt and scrub along the roadside, venturing several yards to the berm, as near to the edge as they could safely go.

Cars slowed approaching the curve, passing four women wearing masks and sunglasses in the late-day sun. It was a solemn moment. Angela and Joel were becoming more real to them every day. Their investigation had reached yet another new phase.

The drop-off ahead of them was so sudden and sheer, they could not see more than halfway down the ravine, never mind to the bottom.

"Straight down," Jeannie said, feeling a shiver as she pictured it. "Just rolled off the edge here and dropped into oblivion."

Marissa stepped back to face the others. "Guys," she said. "What just happened?"

It seemed dreamlike. They were now in possession of actual physical evidence, entrusted to them by the dead couple's daughter. Their euphoria at this fact was offset by the overbearing weight of responsibility.

Nicole brought out the box. She was looking through the papers; she couldn't wait to dig in. "These are Carrie's contemporaneous notes from the days after the disappearance. An emergency contact sheet, the Mercedes-Benz lease agreement. Credit card statements. Oh my God."

Samira held the sealed bag containing two black flip phones. "If we can get these working—contacts, call logs . . ."

They rattled off some of the major revelations from the meeting in a rush. *Greg Medina passed the polygraph?*

"Of course he did," said Jeannie. "Total narcissist."

But Marie failed it?

"Twice!" said Nicole.

"You know how they use the lie detector," said Samira. "It's as much a threat as a tool. To see who squirms and who doesn't. Andrew Watkins certainly squirmed."

" 'Borderline emotionless and manipulative,' Carrie said," added Jeannie. "Her own brother. And the sister taking the pillow and the necklace out of the house? Marie *knew* her parents were dead. No wonder she flunked the lie detector test."

"Twice!" cried Nicole again, this time resulting in a faint canyon echo.

"I really like Carrie," said Jeannie.

"You all realize," said Samira, "there is no turning back now."

"Here's my takeaway," said Jeannie. "The police overlooked things early, because they'd decided Joel and Angela had skipped town. Mistakes were made. Like the Mercedes not being impounded. There were stones left unturned. I think that means there's space for us to find out some things they overlooked."

"We've got all this new intel here," said Nicole. "Fresh leads."

Samira agreed. "We have a lot to do. Starting with inventorying this haul."

Marissa said, daunted but invigorated, "It is so critical we get this right."

It was clear to all of them that they had crossed another line. They were responsible to someone else now, no longer doing this just for themselves. They couldn't barge into this woman's life and ask for her trust and not deliver. They had to see this through now, and it freaked them out a little—but it was also exciting.

For so many of their days and nights since the Covid lockdown, they had felt as if they were on autopilot, making sandwiches and setting up Zoom school and disinfecting everything in sight. Now, this moment, at the site of the crime, holding a box full of evidence given to them by the victims' daughter, they felt wildly alive. By all rights, they shouldn't have been doing any of this— and yet Carrie Watkins was their client now. They had to solve this case for her.

*Putting a face to the victim whose life was shattered by the mur-*ders inspired them all to push harder. With this incredible new evidence in hand, and bolstered by their revelatory meeting with Carrie Watkins and her faith in them and their investigation, the team dug in—even as the hour-to-hour challenges of lockdown life persisted.

At six years old, Nicole's son was the youngest of the team's children, and keeping her little "Dennis the Menace" focused and in front of his laptop throughout the school day was a constant battle. She worried about all the nonacademic developmental learning children acquire in traditional schooling, including socialization and group skills; these were his formative years, and they could not be replaced. On top of that, Nicole and Paul had begun to suspect that he had ADHD, and while this gave a name to the challenges he was facing, she worried constantly about the effect the Covid lockdown would have on his future. Nicole bared her heart about all this to Marissa, spending hours on the phone with her, so grateful to have someone to whom she could entrust her deepest, most personal anxieties.

School, thankfully, was winding down as summer approached. Nicole especially looked forward to not dealing with homeschooling, but instead of having more free time to devote to the case, she realized to her horror that once school ended she would have to keep her kids occupied all day, every day, through-out the hot Covid summer.

Outdoor playdates were risky but socially essential. Maris-sa's youngest and Nicole's oldest began getting together to sit separately and play Roblox, and over time, as it had with their mothers, a strong friendship bloomed.

Personal connections were essential in this new, dystopic world of plastic barriers and arrowed aisles and touchless QR codes. The number of confirmed COVID-19 cases in the United States had surpassed two million, and many people feared that the world as they knew it had changed forever.

Summer arrived and free time became a commodity more pre-cious than toilet paper, but the first order of business was to go through the new evidence.

According to Carrie's timeline, on the Saturday before the Saturday her parents went missing, May 21, 2005, her father had disclosed "all details of business and financial situation" to her mother. This was a private conversation, so there was no way to know exactly what information was exchanged or whether it went so far as to include the criminally fraudulent invoices. Daughter Marie was the one who had reported this conversa-tion to Carrie, claiming that Angela had called her the day after "so upset about their business and financial situation that she couldn't talk about it." Greg claimed that Joel had spoken with him that same Sunday and said, "Angela is very upset about [the] disclosure of [our] business and financial situation." The only corroboration of this conversation, aside from the statements of the married couple Marie and Greg, came from Angela's father, Terry, who told Carrie that he had received a telephone call from Angela that same Sunday in which she had asked him for a $400,000 loan. He had declined, saying to Angela, "I'm not going to let you throw good money on bad money. If you need money, sell the house." Apparently Carrie's grandfather had lent Joel and Angela money in the past.

Then, Marie claimed that on the day before the disappearance, Angela had called her in the morning to say that Joel was "having problems with new antidepressants" and was "forgetful and clumsy." Greg claimed to have received a call that same day from Joel, who said, in Greg's retelling, "the new medication is affecting him and that he almost ran two people off the road."

> Samira: Oh hell no. This totally reads as a set-up to make a case for an accident!

Joel had visited a doctor in early May, according to his credit card statement, which recorded a $35 co-pay. Given the amount of fraud Joel was committing, he certainly had good reason to be suffering from anxiety. But his reported remark that he "almost ran two people off the road" struck them all as prescient in the extreme.

The credit card statement gave them a window into Joel's activities and mindset in the weeks leading up to his disappearance.

> Nicole: Keg and Cask. EVERY day

> Samira: Multiple times a day

> Nicole: Remember brewpubs? All the rage in my dating days

The Keg and Cask brewpub had been located in Pasadena near Wattkins LED's office. Of the seventy-two transactions on Joel's platinum business Visa card on his April/May 2005 statement, thirty-four—almost half—were charges at Keg and Cask. Not only had Joel resumed drinking, unbeknownst to his daughter Carrie—he was drinking a lot, and frequently, if not always, alone. This was a man under a lot of pressure and seemingly losing control. They wondered what finally pushed him off the wagon—and what else he might have been hiding.

It was surreal to hold Joel Watkins's old Cingular flip phones in their own hands. The devices opened to reveal actual, tactile keypads. Neither phone held a charge any longer, but thanks to eBay that problem was easily remedied. Marissa ordered two new batteries for $14 each. They would ship in a few days' time.

Samira had tracked down the Nature Conservancy group that discovered and reported the wreckage of the Watkinses' 2000 Ford Explorer at the bottom of the ravine. She had been trading messages with a woman named Mollie. Eager to call her back, Samira returned from some errand with her youngest trailing behind her. The entire car ride had been a slew of random yet profound questions.

"How many stars are in the sky? Where do we go after we die?"

Samira remained patient, giving the simplest and best answers she could. She needed a brief reprieve from parenting, and the case was foremost in her mind. She opened her laptop to review her notes ahead of the call, and was only half paying attention to her daughter's chatter.

"Mom. Mom. Mom!"

"Yes, what do you need?"

Cocking her head and furrowing her brow, her daughter said, "I get that half of your DNA is in me because I was inside your body, but how did Daddy's DNA get inside your body? I know it can't just crawl into your stomach."

Samira stared at her daughter, thrown, trying to contextualize her question. Her youngest had been fascinated by her older sister's recent journey through puberty.

"I guess we're going to have a conversation about that, honey," she said. "But first Mommy—" Her daughter interrupted:

"It's okay, Mommy, I know you need time to research an age-appropriate way to explain it to me," and with that she turned and ran out of the room. Samira, stunned but amused, took a beat and went back to case business.

Samira reached Mollie, who seemed nervous and awkward on the phone. She was uncomfortable with having Samira record the conversation, but Samira's initial suspicion faded once she understood the source of Mollie's anxiety: She thought she had done something wrong. *I'm so sorry I waited so long to report the wreckage, but at the time I didn't know it was associated with a missing persons report.*

Samira reassured her that everything was fine, that all she wanted was for Mollie to describe the wreck. Mollie said that her team did monthly surveys of canyon waterways, taking samples, measuring erosion, and counting fish. She had been carrying the team's gear when she saw the vehicle above her, beyond a large tree. It was upright, but from the condition of the sides and hood, it was evident that it had rolled over many times down the side of the ravine. She looked inside the broken windows and saw no bodies in the vehicle. She scribbled down the license plate number and continued with the survey. Two days later, she was going through her field notes when she came across her notation and remembered the vehicle.

The "monthly surveys" part excited Samira. Mollie said that they always surveyed the same route, and that she was confident that she would have seen the Watkinses' SUV if it had been there previously. If Joel and Angela disappeared five weeks before they were found, and the Explorer hadn't been there four weeks before that, then where had it been? Where had Joel and Angela been? Had they been held somewhere else for a period of time, alive or dead, after their disappearance? This was a wild new wrinkle. Mollie promised Samira she would look up the date of their previous survey and get back to her soon.

Then Mollie ghosted Samira, not returning follow-up texts

or phone calls. More than a week later, Samira was walking her dog, Roxy, in her neighborhood when her burner phone rang. "I'm so sorry!" Mollie explained. "I meant to get right back to you but I dropped my phone in a fish tank." Unfortunately, due to funding restraints at the time, the most recent survey prior to her discovering the wreckage had been performed three months before. Another nothingburger. The timeline remained unimproved.

The flurry of activity continued. While lockdown meant that everyone was available to talk if you could reach them, the team were surprised that so many people actually *wanted* to help them. The women's manner helped, consistently polite yet firmly inquisitive. Each used an almost identical approach line to hook their targets. *Hi, my name is Marissa (Nicole, Jeannie, Samira), I'm an investigative journalist working on a cold case.* These simple words brought a bit of adrenaline into people's long and bleak quarantine days.

Neither Samira nor Jeannie enjoyed cold-calling people. Jeannie had to psych herself up for her calls, and if a phone number turned out to have been reassigned or was no longer in use, she experienced both disappointment and relief. Over time, she got better at it. Most people truly wanted to help, and she learned that open-ended questions allowed people to start talking, which often led them into areas Jeannie had not considered. People like to tell their story. She focused on making people feel comfortable, not interrupting them, and clearing up any questions she might have at the end of the conversation.

Interestingly, not one person the team spoke to ever asked the name of the newspaper, magazine, or website they wrote for.

The morning the Los Angeles County courts reopened for limited business, Marissa awoke fighting a case of nerves. She and Nicole had made plans to drive downtown to make a records request in the Superior Court Probate Department for a copy of the will of Joel H. Watkins. What Marissa hadn't told Brian was that they'd decided to drive together. He was so paranoid about Covid that she felt terrible about deceiving him, but after she'd picked up Nicole and realized what a luxury it was to be in a car with someone outside her family, laughing and listening to music, her feelings of guilt were forgotten. The masked clerks behind the newly installed Plexiglas windows were still getting back up to speed, and building occupancy was restricted to a handful of people at any one time. Since their time was limited—as always, they needed to get back home for their kids—they bailed out and returned even earlier the following morning, again breaking Covid rules by riding together.

The document they received had been revised and executed in 1999, leaving Joel and Angela's estate to the Watkins Family Trust, with son Andrew as executor. The will was not notarized, which struck Samira as odd, as she and Ward had recently drawn up their will and signed it in the presence of a notary public. The Watkinses' will had been witnessed by two people: Dennis Ladd, Joel's longtime friend—no surprise—and a woman whose name was unfamiliar to them: Mariana Méndez. The document listed her address, and while Marissa drove them back, Nicole did a simple Google search that turned up Mariana, now going by her maiden name, Veloso, living in Pasadena. Marissa called and left her usual approach message.

Mariana Veloso called back the next day. She was an older woman who could not have been sweeter, though her English was very poor and Marissa's Spanish was conversational at best. Mariana had been Angela Watkins's housekeeper for six years, from 1998 through 2004, and she exuded nothing but love and admiration for her former employer. "They were so, so good to me. I wanted to speak English and Angela helped me. She was like an angel. She was beautiful inside and outside."

Mariana started work for them in the house that Joel and

Angela had "lost," as she put it, then at the apartment they rented afterward, and later at the house on Shadow Peak Road. She kept house for them there for approximately one year until Angela told her they couldn't afford to pay her any longer.

"I wanted to clean for free," said Mariana. "She called me her friend. She came to visit me a few times, at the holidays. She always gave me advice, relationship advice. After she died, I took her advice and finally left my husband. She was so beautiful."

Marissa was thrilled to finally speak with someone who had known Angela personally. From everything they'd heard, even from daughter Carrie, Angela did not leave the house much, and almost never alone.

"She liked to be home," said Mariana. "I never saw her with anyone. She went to sleep early. She said, 'I have this skin because I always sleep eight hours.'"

Marissa asked her about Joel and Angela's relationship.

"Joel was so kind. 'I'm proud of you,' he told me. They had a very good marriage. Before, when he used to drink, I think it was not so good."

"Did you ever see the Watkins children?" Marissa asked. "Would they come around often?"

"No, they never come around when I was there. She talked of her older daughter and her grandson often. She was so proud."

"What about the other children?"

"She didn't talk about them much, that I remember."

"What about her daughter's husband, Greg?"

"She did not like Greg. She said he was not a good man, he didn't take care of Marie. No money."

Mariana had been hurt that no one in the family reached out to her after Angela passed away, having been a part of their mother's life for so many years. After Mariana stopped working for Angela, they would occasionally leave flowers on each other's doorstep as a gesture of their enduring friendship. When Mariana realized she hadn't heard from Angela for some time, and couldn't reach her by telephone, she left flowers at the front door on Christmas Eve 2005. When she heard back nothing, she returned a few weeks later and saw the flowers still lying there, all dried up and untouched. Worried, Mariana left a note in the door, saying that she hadn't heard from Angela and was concerned. Several days later, she received a call from Marie Watkins, telling Mariana that Angela had passed away.

"She said they were driving and they went down," Mariana recalled.

"Joel and Angela were driving and they went down?"

"Went off the road and died together."

Mariana was so upset at the news that Marie invited her for a visit. In late January or early February 2006, Mariana went to the house Marie and Greg were living in at that time, and Mariana said she was "shocked." Angela and Joel had always lived so well, even in harder times, even in their apartment, that she was scandalized by how "simple" Marie and Greg's townhouse was. They had very few possessions and the house was unkempt. It seemed to Mariana that they had very little money.

When Marissa asked her about having witnessed the Watkinses' will, Mariana became confused. Assuming this was due to the language barrier, Marissa texted her a copy of her signature on the document. When the text came through, Mariana gasped. "I never signed that. That's not my signature."

Marissa clarified this with growing excitement. This felt huge. The housekeeper had no reason to lie. If the will was indeed fraudulent, the person who had the most to gain was its executor: Andrew Watkins.

The team contacted a probate attorney, who offered his consultation for free. He informed them that the State of California did not require wills to be notarized, but did require witnesses to be present. Forging a witness's signature would not automatically render a will null and void, but it could invite contest from other parties.

One night, Nicole's father called her excitedly, the television blaring in the background. An avid MSNBC viewer, he explained that he had just watched a retired medical examiner speak on one of the prime-time shows. "This fellow was very impressive," he said, and he insisted that Nicole send him the autopsy reports on "that thing you're looking into."

This was an out-there request, but Nicole was pleased that her dad had taken an interest in the case, so she dutifully took down the man's name and contacted him via the email listed on his website. He appeared to be quite old but also quite experienced. Nicole explained that her father had seen him on television and she asked if he might be available to consult on a cold case she and three other journalists were investigating. He replied that he would be happy to take a look.

Things went south from there.

Nicole: Just got off the phone with my dad's autopsy expert who yelled at me for five minutes.

Jeannie: What for?

Nicole: I emailed him the autopsy records and he wrote back that he couldn't find them. I sent them again and he called me in a rage

Nicole: OLD MAN COULDN'T FIGURE OUT HOW TO OPEN AN EMAIL ATTACHMENT

Jeannie: Oh, man. The cost of free advice

Nicole: Thanks, dad

He emailed Nicole later—no apology—with his thoughts. While qualifying his opinion due to the unavailability of photographs of the crash site or the bodies, based upon the fact that both bodies were ejected from the vehicle, and considering the distance between where they were recovered and where the vehicle came to rest, it seemed clear to him that the occupants could not have been in the front seats at the time the vehicle went off the road.

Maybe this explained the broken ribs, too. If Joel and Angela had been placed in the vehicle without restraints, the incredible turbulence during the rolling descent into the ravine would have tossed them around violently before they were ejected through the broken windows or the sunroof. It all went to the theory that when Joel and Angela went over the edge, they were dead already.

It wasn't just the autopsy report that raised suspicion. Among the many documents Carrie entrusted to the team's care was her parents' lease agreement for their white Mercedes-Benz M-Class. Samira called the dealership and discovered that the Mercedes had last been serviced two days before Angela and Joel had disappeared. The vehicle had also been washed and the tire pressures had been checked. But days later, when Carrie first arrived at her parents' home after their disappearance, the Mercedes had one flat tire and there was soil on the floor near the driver's side door. This made absolutely no sense. Even more confounding, at the time the service was performed, the odometer mileage was listed at 28,646. Yet when the vehicle was returned to the dealership after their disappearance, a short drive away, the odometer read 28,906 miles. This meant that between Thursday and the following Monday, with the parents presumed to have gone missing on Saturday, not only had the car gotten a flat tire, but it had been driven 260 miles. It didn't track.

One of the team's working theories was that one assailant—say, Andrew Watkins—drove the Explorer containing Joel's and Angela's bodies to the "crash" site, followed by a second assailant—say, Greg Medina—driving the Mercedes. After rolling the Explorer into the ravine, both assailants returned to Shadow Peak Road, garaged the Mercedes, and walked to their own cars. The unpaved turnout on Angeles Crest Highway was rough with soil and loose stones. The right front tire could have been punctured and developed a slow leak, flattening over the course of the next day.

The 2002 Mercedes M-Class had a rudimentary onboard computer recording the rate of acceleration, distance driven, and other measurements, which could be used in accident reconstruction. This seemed like exactly the sort of detail the initial "murder-suicide" investigation might have missed—a significant find, one that could bring them hard data on the vehicle's movement during the weekend in question. But after many calls, Samira's hope of proving that the Watkinses' car had been used in the commission of the crime was dashed: Mercedes-Benz computer data was routinely overwritten every seven years and unrecoverable after that period of time. Another brick wall.

For all the time and effort they were putting into the investigation, the team were getting back so much more, benefits that had nothing to do with the case. This adventure was bonding them. The casework was their through line, but around that these four different personalities had meshed. They referred to themselves as a team, but in Covid parlance, what they had actually done was form a pod. In a time of isolation and dread, they had found a space that was theirs and theirs alone. With one another, they were able to be unguarded and unfiltered. The circumstances of the criminal investigation had allowed them to build a circle of trust and support.

And they could be brutally honest. This was how Samira came to learn that not measuring up to her stay-at-home-mom fantasies of gourmet meals and daily crafts was normal—that she wasn't alone in being unable to live up to her expectations. That finding that "perfect balance" of raising kids and making a home and being a wife was not a mountaintop to be summited but a horizon, admired but never reached. Thanks to the team, Samira was able to shed her guilt and focus on what she could achieve, not on where she felt she fell short.

The women had thoughtful conversations about the pros and cons of raising children with or without religion, recommending books on the subject. They vented about their spouses, the exchanges always ending in laughter. They could be ribald and crass as often as they could be empathetic and deep. The investigation dealt with heavy, grim stuff, yet at the same time it was, for lack of a better word, fun. It was twisted and it was fun. It was scary and it was fun. It was infuriating and it was fun. The contradictory feelings were impossible to explain to an outsider. No one else could have understood what they had found in one another, living through this strange adventure together.

As Nicole had told them from her political opposition research days, there was nothing like the rush you got when you found a game changer.

It was early evening when Marissa texted the team a photograph of one of the Cingular flip phones open, its contact screen illuminated.

Nicole: Omg!

Marissa: Right now my family is not allowing me to dig in—having dinner

Marissa: I'll review tonight but there's A LOT

Samira was desperate to get started and offered to take one of the phones to reduce Marissa's workload. Marissa left the device and the new battery on her doorstep for Samira.

Joel Watkins's personal and business cellphones woke up brightly once the new batteries were inserted and charged. No lock screen or PIN was needed for access, never mind facial or fingerprint recognition. The screen was the size of a business card, the display in color, controlled by the keypad arrow buttons below. Samira had Joel's work phone. She went through everything, comparing and contrasting call logs and contact lists with his personal phone in Marissa's possession.

Texts flew back and forth between them, keeping Nicole and Jeannie in the loop.

> **Marissa:** My call log goes from 12/23-5/12. What's the span on yours Samira?

> **Samira:** Mine goes to a voicemail from Aug 1!!

They were unable to access the voicemails any longer, but they could see the caller's number. For instance, Samira found that Joel and Greg exchanged eleven phone calls on Friday, May 27. Eleven! On Saturday, May 28, the last day anyone had seen or talked to Joel, he'd received a phone call from Greg at 10:30 A.M., followed by a call from his home number, presumably Angela, at 10:59 A.M. That was the last phone call logged on the device.

The work was tedious, but Samira liked tedious. Some names in the contact list were known to them; others weren't, giving them potential new leads. Not every caller was a known contact. There were many more landlines in use in 2005, for people who had since dropped their service or moved. Of course, not every call made or received was important or even pertinent to the investigation.

They received more unexpected insight into Joel Watkins's personality when they discovered that he had set different ringtones for different family members. Joel's ringtone for his daughter Marie was "Sugar, Sugar" by the Archies—a bubblegum pop song, presumably showing affection. Angela's ringtone was "Love Theme from *The Godfather*."

> Samira: This may be the closest we've gotten to the inner-Joel. Is it the Looney Toons theme for Greg?

> Marissa: Interesting that Andrew doesn't have a ringtone

> Samira: They didn't talk much by phone

> Jeannie: Maybe this?

Jeannie texted a link to a YouTube video of the theme from the movie *The Bad Seed*.

They pulled together a new list of names to trace and phone calls to make. Nicole thought it was important that they be transparent with Detective Fonseca, so Marissa texted him an update on their progress.

> Marissa: We had a little more information come in today. Carrie Watkins gave us some phones that belonged to her father. We ordered new batteries and got them working. We are putting together a phone log over the next few days (though I know you have that info).

That was a little dig at the end. With each bit of progress the team made, they grew more resentful of Fonseca. They'd had to rely on a delicate combination of luck and pluck to restore these phones to working order and were now knee-deep in drudge work acquiring cellphone information that Fonseca possessed and was withholding from them. But that didn't stop Marissa from trying. The team contacted an accident reconstruction expert who agreed to consult on the case for free. Marissa asked Fonseca if he would share the original California Highway Patrol accident report with them so they could pass it along. "There is very sensitive and confidential information contained in the CHP report," he replied, "and I can't release that information without compromising the investigation." What made it so sensitive and confidential? It was as though he were dangling evidence in front of them but just out of reach.

On the other end of the gratitude spectrum, they relayed news of the reawakened phones to Carrie Watkins, who could not have been more encouraging. Marissa seized the opportunity to ask if she thought it would be helpful for the team to speak with Angela's sister and Carrie's aunt, Gwen Miller. Carrie said that she had already reached out to Gwen and her husband, Bill, letting them know about the renewed interest in the case, and she thought they would be receptive to an informal interview. Her aunt had an incredible memory, she said, and promised to ask them.

Marissa marveled at the disparity within the Watkins family, with a vein of criminality running through Joel, Andrew, and maybe Marie, and then Carrie and now Angela's sister, who only wanted to help. It was a family of secrets, a fact that resonated with Marissa because of her own family's dysfunction and financial woes. She had always searched for people with a similar experience to hers and never found them. She thought she might have a chance to learn about herself through helping Carrie—by taking care of Carrie the way Marissa had always wanted someone to take care of her.

"One day," she told Carrie, "I'll tell you my story and maybe it will make sense to you why I did this." She understood that some part of her was trying to solve the mysteries in her own family by solving the mysteries in Carrie's.

THE DANGER

The team experienced the same anxieties ahead of talking with Angela's sister, Gwen, and Gwen's husband, Bill, as they had before first meeting Carrie. Talking to people emotionally impacted by the murders was the most intensely personal part of what they were doing, as well as the most stressful. They had no training for an interview such as this, only their own internal sense of propriety and decency. Meeting strangers, asking for their trust, promising them your discretion, and proving your seriousness—it was a delicate situation, and there were any number of ways in which it could go wrong.

They had two major objectives going into the Zoom call. They hoped to add color and shading to their still fuzzy picture of Angela, and they wanted more eyewitness details about Andrew's, Marie's, and Greg's actions in the days following Joel and Angela's disappearance.

Gwen and Bill sat together in a corner of their airy kitchen, a looming presence with their laptop lid camera angled way back. Gwen wore a thin tan cardigan over a white blouse with a small, neat collar. She was warm and with it. In her, the team got a glimpse of what Angela might have looked like had she survived into her late seventies. Bill deferred to his wife's recollections, peering down at the camera through oversized, thin-rimmed eyeglasses, occasionally adding to or seconding her account. They made a wonderful pair, completely compatible, and were open, discursive, and agreeable. Carrie's vouching for them ahead of time had clearly carried a lot of weight.

When they were growing up, said Gwen, Angela was lots of fun. Their parents, father Terry and mother Sheila, were caring and successful, Terry having developed a successful commercial fishing company into a string of profitable restaurants. Later in life, he became quite wealthy. (An older sister of Gwen's and Angela's, Lynn, had died in 1992.) Angela had been bubbly, with a great sense of humor, but for some reason her good cheer faded in her later years.

Gwen regretted that she and her sister had grown apart. They had rarely even spoken on the phone in recent years. Gwen and Bill saw the Watkins family only at weddings and occasional holidays. The last time they had gathered was on Mother's Day, three weeks before the disappearance, when the two couples met in Long Beach for lunch by the ocean. Both Angela and Joel had appeared tense and quiet. Bill confirmed this recollection, remembering that they had remarked on the drive home that it appeared something was bothering both of them.

Gwen described Joel as a "very nice guy" who had courted Angela and was good to her. He had been a computer operator in the service and maintained a military approach in his civilian life: keeping to routines, maintaining his physical fitness. He was ambitious, but he was also quite careless financially and often overextended himself. Gwen was aware that he and Angela periodically borrowed money from Terry, though they always paid it back over time. Joel had been friendly with a couple of firefighters with whom he went on frequent duck hunting trips to Mexico. Gwen thought it odd that Angela had no way to get hold of Joel during these three- or four-day weekends, though Angela seemed to have no issue with that.

The women said nothing in the moment, but this was a bright red flag.

As for Andrew Watkins, Gwen was aware that he seemed to have money, but she wondered where he got it. Even assuming he drew a large salary from Joel's company, he lived beyond his means. He talked a big game as well. He invested in an upscale restaurant in Playa del Rey that closed in less than a year. Gwen believed that, consciously or unconsciously, he was trying to emulate his grandfather Terry's success, but without Terry's patience and foresight.

Gwen and Bill were relieved to have Carrie, Henry, and their young boy still in their lives. Carrie had been through hell, they said, as the fallout from Joel's and Angela's deaths had split the four siblings in two. Gwen had not spoken to Andrew since he relocated to South Carolina, and only once to Marie when Terry was near death. Neither Andrew nor Marie came to Terry's funeral, which to Gwen was the saddest and most unforgivable thing of all.

Terry never recovered from Angela's death. Gwen confirmed that Angela had reached out to him one week before she disappeared, asking to borrow $400,000, an enormous sum. Terry had bridged them the last time they'd lost their home, to the tune of $200,000, evidently with no lessons learned. Angela had told her father that she and Joel were "in a lot of trouble." Terry told them they could move in with him for a time if necessary, but later, in a phone call on that final weekend, Joel had told his father-in-law not to worry, sounding firm and abrupt, saying "I will take care of it." Terry suffered greatly over the five weeks Angela was missing, hoping and praying that his daughter would come knocking on his door. After their bodies were discovered, Terry became furious, convinced that Joel had something to do with it.

Marissa mentioned that some people they had spoken with speculated that Angela and Joel might have been driving to visit Terry that Saturday when they disappeared, but Gwen shot down that theory. Her father told her that he had not been expecting them, and she added that Terry was not the kind of person you dropped in on unannounced.

Bill spoke with Angela on the day of the disappearance. It

was a strange encounter. He answered the telephone that morning, and instead of a typical greeting, Angela blurted out, "Who is this?"

"Angela?" said Bill, placing the voice after a moment. "Angela, it's Bill."

"Bill?" she'd said.

"Yes, Bill. You called me. Is everything all right?"

"Oh," she said, sounding distracted and worried. "I— I found this phone number written in my checkbook, and I didn't recognize it."

"Is something wrong?" Bill asked. "Gwen is out at the moment."

"No," she said, fumbling for words. She began to apologize and then, with a clatter, hung up.

A bizarre conversation, one Bill thought back to often. It was completely out of character for Angela, who was evidently in a disturbed, even frantic state of mind. Had something prompted her to go through their finances for some reason? Joel handled everything having to do with money.

The following Tuesday, Andrew called to tell them that his parents had gone missing. Andrew called again on Thursday to let them know that he had made the decision to close down Joel's company. This was another shock, as the company was a great part of Joel's identity. Andrew said that the business had failed and that he had no choice, but closing the business so quickly struck them as not only rash but almost cruel. Gwen had a difficult time believing that Joel had absconded with funds, despite his prior poor financial decisions. But she knew beyond a doubt that Angela would have had no part in it. She never believed the nonsense about their running away to Mexico together.

Carrie was going to help pack up the office, and Bill and Gwen offered to help too. When they arrived that Friday, the mood was strange. Andrew was intensely focused on clearing everything out of the office quickly, almost as though he was afraid someone was going to show up there, that he would be confronted.

Marie was a mess, crying on and off. She told Gwen that she believed her parents had committed suicide. "I know they are dead," she said.

There was one other person helping to close up shop: the office manager, Bonnie Salazar, a "large, bossy" woman they were meeting for the first time. Bonnie and Greg basically took over, directing everyone on what to take and where to put it. Both Gwen and Bill found it strange that anytime they had a question, they were told "Ask Greg"—not Andrew, who actually worked for the company. After the trucks had all been loaded and the office emptied, Gwen remembered seeing Bonnie sitting on a low brick wall talking to Andrew and Greg, the three of them acting very chummy. Such a sorrowful moment, the closing of the family business, but their attitudes did not reflect it.

Greg said the strangest thing to them before leaving the parking lot. "Joel was my best friend," he said, unprompted. "And I loved Angela." Odd pronouncements, to be sure—but more to the point, he was already speaking of them in the past tense.

One week later, Terry told them that Greg had paid him a visit. At first Greg proposed hiring a private detective to look for Angela and Joel—using Terry's money, of course. Then he claimed that he had lent Joel $100,000 and asked if Terry could pay him back.

Terry did not pay him. Terry had never trusted Greg, and he began wondering what he was up to. Terry's will was carefully worded to provide for Marie only, explicitly excluding her husband.

The team informed Gwen that being excluded from wills was a pattern with Greg.

Joel and Angela had two insurance policies totaling more

than $2 million each. The first policy was used to settle with the firm's creditors, an agreement that Andrew negotiated. The second one was paid out to the four heirs, after Andrew secured a large fee as executor, which Carrie had disputed.

After that, Gwen heard things about Andrew and Greg only secondhand, from occasional contact with Marie. Apparently, Andrew created quite a scene when sheriff's deputies visited his house to seize his computer, to the point where he was placed in handcuffs on the ground in his front yard. When Greg found out he was being investigated, Marie said he had some sort of breakdown. When Gwen offered sympathy, Marie said, "Well, it was really embarrassing." The police were investigating her husband's involvement in the murders of her mother and father—and her reaction was that it was embarrassing? Angela and her daughter were alike in that they seemed emotionally muted, almost expressionless.

Neither Gwen nor Bill believed that Joel was smart enough to pull off the financial fraud scheme on his own. They guessed that he saw dollar signs and gradually, and then perhaps suddenly, got pulled in too deep. Andrew and Greg were cool operators who always thought they were smarter than everyone else. They were devious. Gwen suspected that Joel had realized he was in big trouble and wanted to come clean—and made the mistake of telling that to Andrew and Greg.

So much to process on their later Zoom call, and much of it powerful.

"This family!" said Marissa.

"Greg with new depths of shamelessness," said Nicole, paraphrasing: " 'Oh, by the way, I made a secret hundred-thousand-dollar loan to my mysteriously disappeared father-in-law that no one knows about, Terry, so could you pay me back?' And calling Joel his 'best friend'?"

"That one I kind of believe," said Jeannie. "Maybe he was desperate for a father figure. They talked all the time."

"Not desperate enough not to take financial advantage of the situation," said Samira.

"That I believe too," said Jeannie. "Sickening."

"What about Andrew's computer?" said Samira. "The police were hot on his trail. But they must not have found anything, because he's still walking the streets."

"I can't picture him freaking out so much he had to be hand-cuffed," said Marissa. "Everyone we talk to always portrays him as buttoned down and in control."

"Definitely the reaction of a guilty man," said Samira.

"And the hunting trips south of the border!" said Jeannie. "With no way to get in touch with Joel? Did Angela simply look the other way? What was going on in Mexico?"

Nicole said, "So she found a phone number written down in a checkbook and called it? Introverted Angela? What was she thinking? Another woman? Another man? Her daughter said Joel had come clean about their financial issues the week before, so why be going through the checkbook mere hours before she disappeared?"

"She called Joel on his work cell that morning, too," Samira reminded them. "One or the other was her final phone conversation ever."

"She was in distress," said Jeannie. "It sounds like whatever was happening was coming to a head."

The conversation turned to the odd circumstances surrounding the closing of Wattkins LED's office. Gwen made it sound as if Andrew was scared that day—that he couldn't close the business fast enough. And then there was the Bonnie situation. Bonnie Salazar, the mysterious office manager in the final two years of the company's existence, who had blocked Marissa and Samira after their repeated attempts to contact her via Facebook. None of the telephone numbers they had for her worked.

But Joel's reanimated work cellphone listed her in his contacts at a telephone number different from any of the ones they'd tried. Marissa and Samira dialed it together, knowing it was a long shot but feeling that they should team up on this call.

Bonnie answered. She was pissed. "How did you get this number?" she demanded to know. "Who are you?"

They told her about the "article" they were working on.

"I have no interest in discussing the matter," said Bonnie, her voice hard-edged. "Why are you stalking me?"

"I'm sorry to have made you feel uncomfortable," said Marissa, pushing the sincerity. "We just have some questions about Joel's final days and hoped you could help answer them."

"I called Andrew and he said he had never heard of you people."

Both Marissa and Samira were shaken. She had spoken about them to Andrew Watkins? They were not ready for that.

Marissa recovered enough to press her for details, flattering her. "We understand that Joel told people he thought the world of you."

"He didn't go to the bathroom without telling me first," she said.

"And you worked there until the end. What was your role?"

"Nothing out of the ordinary," Bonnie answered. "I was Joel's admin and receptionist. I enjoyed working there, but I didn't know anything about Joel's personal life."

Interesting, considering they hadn't asked about Joel's personal life. Samira steered the conversation to the last few weeks before the office closed. "Do you remember anything out of the ordinary?"

"I don't know anything," Bonnie snapped. "That was fifteen years ago."

But they kept her talking. The last time she saw Joel Watkins was that Friday. She had returned from a work trip the previous night, and Joel told her there was nothing for her to do and to go home and get a jump on her weekend, which she did. She returned to work on Monday, and the first thing she noticed was that Joel's car wasn't there. Andrew came in around nine. He didn't know where his dad was. Bonnie said she did not remember whether Joel had any appointments scheduled that day, though Marissa and Samira knew that he did, a lunchtime meeting with Dennis Ladd followed by an office meeting with the banker. She said she was concerned about Joel but five o'clock came around and she couldn't do anything other than go home.

Joel did not appear at work on Tuesday either, and Andrew made some calls. According to Bonnie, Andrew left to go to his parents' house that afternoon, which the team knew was not true. She learned on Wednesday that Andrew's parents weren't at home and one of their cars was gone.

She claimed to have no memory of Joel's phone being found inside his office. Whether she was being obstinate or evasive, they couldn't know. She claimed never to have had Joel's cell number, though that was how Marissa had gotten her number. Samira asked about Greg Medina, and Bonnie said that he came into the office once or twice, now and then. Maybe she'd faxed something to the bank for Greg or his company, she couldn't remember. When they shut down the office, she said they moved the office computer server to Greg's business because he had the space.

She didn't believe that Joel's and Angela's deaths should be considered homicides. Their driving off the road made perfect sense to her. As to the factoring fraud, Bonnie said, "I know nothing about that. Joel was a nice man and treated me well. That's why I didn't want to go back and dig all this up."

After ending the call, Marissa and Samira were deeply concerned. When they had first reached out to Bonnie Salazar at the beginning of their investigation, they were still using their personal emails and Facebook accounts. The fact that she had called Andrew scared them. This shadowy murder suspect now very likely had their personal information. He knew they were looking into his involvement in his father's business affairs and his parents' murders.

"She acted like she didn't know him well," said Marissa, "yet she saved his phone number and checked with him? He obviously told her not to talk to us."

"This makes her look super guilty too," said Samira.

"I wonder if he talks to Greg," said Marissa. "I'm so glad he's in South Carolina."

That wasn't far enough away for Samira's comfort—no distance was. Andrew knew about them now, and with that came a dizzying sense of vulnerability. She had believed they were looking into Andrew's and Greg's lives through the safety of a one-way mirror, but now that was no longer the case.

Looking back, they could see other portentous occurrences around the time Bonnie Salazar phoned Andrew Watkins. Little things. Marie took her Facebook profile private. Nicole discovered that Greg had filed a "Petition for Dismissal with Prejudice" to withdraw his contesting his mother's will without judgment, and the timing seemed curious. Jeannie discovered that both Marie and Greg had suppressed their personal information online, making it harder to access their background information on most major search sites.

The picture was becoming clearer. The team felt as if they were crowded inside a darkroom watching an image in a chemical solution gradually appearing. But, also like four people crowded inside a darkroom, they were becoming impatient. The image was still murky. Every win gave them renewed confidence to keep moving forward; each setback steeled their resolve to try harder.

Marissa's obsession kept pulling her back to the crash site. One day she took a drive on Angeles Crest Highway past the turnout, pulling over at another turnout farther along the road. She thought she might get a better vantage point on the ravine's depths, and if she were lucky, maybe even catch a glimpse of the Watkinses' vehicle's final resting place. She found a friendly-looking path and started laterally off the road, moving downward from tree to tree, switching directions back and forth to keep her footing. When her Converse sneakers started to skid, she slid down on her butt until her traction improved. At every turn, she hoped the trees would part below and clear her line of sight, which kept her going even as the terrain became crumblier, steeper, and more treacherous. She kept going until her cellphone rang. She took the call, something unrelated to the case. When she hung up, it was as if a spell had been broken. She turned to look back up at the road somewhere high above her and could no longer see it. The "path" she had followed was a trail of her own making. And she realized that no one—not Brian, not the other women—knew where she was. *What the hell am I doing?* One slip on her woefully impractical Converse sneakers and she could tumble a long, long way down, with little chance of climbing back up. She started to retrace her steps but found she could not make out her own footprints in the dry soil. She worked methodically from tree to tree while maintaining her balance, weaving a new crisscrossing trail back up to the road, her steps growing more frantic as the terrain grew steeper.

She topped out on the state route somehow, a good eighty yards south of her car. She walked up the curling shoulder, the depthless ravine to her right, shaken by her own obsessive behavior. If her phone hadn't rung at that moment, she might have continued down past the point of no return. Desperation was making her do things that were borderline insane.

In July, all four women were watching the HBO documentary based upon *I'll Be Gone in the Dark,* the true crime book written by Michelle McNamara detailing her yearslong investigation of a rapist and serial killer. The book's subtitle was *One Woman's Obsessive Search for the Golden State Killer.* Tragically, the author died before the book's completion from an accidental overdose of Xanax and other drugs she may have relied upon in part to help her cope with the darkness and stress of her investigation, which she researched late into the night while her family slept. The book had been completed after her death by the crime writer Paul Haynes, the investigative journalist Billy Jensen, and McNamara's husband, the comedian and actor Patton Oswalt.

While the case of the Golden State Killer was much broader and more terrifying than the Watkins case, the four women all found the docuseries devastating, Marissa especially. She mourned Michelle McNamara for taking on such a complex and terrifying task alone. Marissa could not imagine attempting this investigation by herself. The loneliness, the stress. Not only was it easier to go through the dark times with like-minded companions, but it made the lighter times better as well. Sharing the emotional load, the highs and lows of the case, the anxieties and the imposter syndrome, and having other women who could meet her right where she was—which was at a place Marissa had never imagined finding herself, on a hunt for a double murderer—was essential.

An opportunity arose for Marissa's family to get away from the Westside for a week, and the chance to get the girls out of the house and into nature was too generous to pass up. It was an invitation to stay at a friend's vacant house in Deer Valley, Utah, north of Salt Lake City. Since reluctantly canceling his business trip at the start of the lockdown, Brian had done a complete one-eighty and was even more Covid-cautious than Marissa now, so he agreed to the ten-hour car trip on the condition that they not stop for food or bathrooms. They packed up the car and followed Interstate 15 north from Los Angeles, through an eerily quiet Las Vegas, clipping the northwestern corner of Arizona and crossing southern and central Utah, with only one tense stop to refuel and one roadside comfort break for humans and Cecil. Their destination was secluded and gorgeous, and they spent the week swimming and hiking and river rafting, and Marissa succeeded in peeling her mind from the case. Well, to some extent. But it was a blissful break.

The others pressed on. Their visit to the house on Shadow Peak Road had piqued their interest in the Watkinses' neighbors at the time of the disappearance. Who knows what they might have seen or heard on the weekend in question? The neighborhood had turned over quite a bit in the aftermath of the 2007–08 financial and housing crisis, and few residents from 2005 remained. Going door to door during Covid was out of the question anyway.

Nicole and Jeannie decided to team up on tracking down neighbors who had moved. Jeannie located the couple who had lived across the street from the Watkinses in 2005. With trepidation, she reached the husband on his landline. He said that he remembered his wife's saying that something odd had happened that night, but he couldn't remember the details. He promised to have her call Jeannie, but it was the husband who called the next day, saying that his wife did not want to talk about it. Jeannie pressed him, but he told her that his wife's mind was made up.

Nicole, at that time, had secured a beach house in Oxnard for a few days. Paul had allowed their son to ride barefoot in the car trip there, and Nicole discovered, when they arrived and unpacked, that he had no shoes. None. And there were no stores open. Another postcard family moment for Nicole. She went from yelling at Paul, to laughing with him five minutes later, to talking to a former neighbor of Joel and Angela Watkins on the phone five minutes after that. The absurdity of life at that time was one of the things that she loved about the case.

This former neighbor turned out to be a retired stuntman named Hank, who had lived a few houses down from the Watkinses on the same side of the street. Hank also claimed to have been a professional safari hunter at one time, and a private investigator. He said he saw the Watkinses only when they were outside gardening and could not recall ever speaking with them. Their privacy made the sudden flurry of activity following the disappearance so surprising. Hank liked to talk, and talk, and talk, unspooling for Nicole a long story about his then wife suffering from clinical depression, which was why they split up and had to move. She wouldn't be any help, he said, but his then sister-in-law had been going through a divorce and had been living with them at the time of the disappearance.

"She's a total night owl," Hank told Nicole, "and I think she might have something to tell you about the night in question. But here's the thing. She's also a drunk. Don't call her before three-thirty in the afternoon. If you call before she's drunk, guaranteed she will not talk to you. Get her after that, just wind her up and let her go."

The following afternoon, after playing with her shoeless son, Nicole reached out to the ex-stuntman's ex-sister-in-law around four o'clock. The woman's speech was indeed slurred, but she was coherent. "I don't like talking about this," she said.

"I understand," said Nicole. "I really appreciate it."

"I'd come home from work after midnight as usual. Was sitting on the sofa watching some movie, just trying to unwind. Hank liked to keep the windows open on cool nights, which didn't sit well with me. I like having my house locked up tight. Out of nowhere, I heard a blood-curdling scream from outside. I muted the television and heard more screaming—it was a woman's voice, no question, high-pitched, loud and haunting. This was sometime between one and three A.M. I truly felt that she was being hurt. It was startling—startling and frightening." She had assumed it was spousal abuse. She went to the window but by then the screaming had stopped. "Next day, I told my sister about it. A day or two after that my sister told me there'd been TV cameras and police on the street." But by the time the bodies were found five weeks later, she had moved out. Nicole was the first person ever to interview her.

The account of the screaming spooked Nicole. She reported the interview in the group text, and the other women felt equally uneasy. They had always discussed the actual physical murders in the abstract. This woman's account, if accurate, indicated that the attack on Angela, and perhaps on Joel too, was very violent. So much for their theory that the couple had been painlessly drugged before being discarded over the side of the road. They had imagined a death in which the couple did not unnecessarily suffer, but now they knew that the reality was likely far more unsettling. The account forced them to imagine Angela's final moments—terrified in her own home, fighting for her life—and reminded them that the murderers were still out there.

Nicole followed up with Hank in hopes of corroborating his unstable sister-in-law's account, perhaps by speaking with his estranged ex-wife. He said he'd reach out. Over the next several days, Hank texted Nicole repeatedly, oversharing about his wife's clinical depression, claiming he'd also done bomb detection for Homeland Security, and advising her to be safe "with Antifa out there." Nicole realized she was dealing with a low-key lunatic—whom she had to keep texting and talking to because she so badly wanted his ex-wife's story. Nicole looped in the others on her unfolding drama.

> **Nicole:** Update. Hank's ex thought he was sleeping with her sister. Because I am obviously on the phone with Hank AGAIN. And he's calling me sweetie

Nicole: Hank just sent me his official headshot to "put a face to the voice"

Marissa: Clearly, Hank is your new quarantine boyfriend

Nicole: If Hank didn't live in New Mexico I would be concerned

Jeannie tried texting the ex-wife directly, hoping to aid Nicole's effort. A few days later, Nicole cold-called the woman, after Hank helpfully gave her some tips to get her talking. "She's ill," he said, "and nobody tells her what to do."

No luck. She wouldn't answer or respond to Jeannie's texts.

Nicole: I feel bad for you guys. Because I feel like everyone should experience Hank. And it's selfish that he's all mine

Jeannie: So selfish!!

Samira: I don't want to take away your special bond. You need something that is just yours

Nicole never received corroboration, and eventually Hank stopped texting and calling. It was a bonkers interlude, and a weird way to pass the time on a family vacation, but at the same time a reminder of the pain people like Hank's ex-wife have to deal with every day. The team put the scream into the timeline with an asterisk and tried to push the image of Angela's final moments out of their minds.

Out in Utah, Marissa kept abreast of these developments by text. Nicole's phone call inspired her to take another run at the couple who lived directly across the street, the wife whose husband told Jeannie she might have pivotal information. Marissa slipped away from the house to a nearby creek to make a few calls, and finally reached the wife. She was reticent at first, nervous about sharing what she knew even after fifteen years, but after some gentle prodding she started talking and didn't stop.

She said that Joel and Angela were early risers who were particular about their garden. The neighbors rarely spoke. They almost never had any visitors, and until the commotion across the street in the days following their disappearance, the woman had had no idea they had any children.

"We had a new puppy who required a lot of attention, including middle-of-the-night walks. I was outside around two A.M. one night that weekend, and I noticed lights on in the second floor of their house and strange behavior. They had thin curtains, not blinds or shades, and I saw a silhouette of a woman—I think it was a woman—moving around in what I assume was a bedroom, kind of back and forth. I heard a low mechanical humming noise, and I realized she was vacuuming. And I wondered why anyone would be up vacuuming at two in the morning."

She said she had not told the police these details when they came to the door a few days later.

"I don't know, it really didn't seem relevant at the time. It was someone vacuuming. Later, after their bodies were found, a reporter came to our door and we got to talking and I did share with him what I had seen. But I never saw it reported in the newspaper, and no one ever asked me about it since."

Marissa said, "You said there was a commotion and the children were outside the house. Did you speak to them?"

"After the police left, one of the men saw me and crossed the street to talk to us about what was going on. That's how we found out they were missing. I do remember him saying, in the course of conversation, something like, 'I think maybe they just went over a cliff somewhere.' Words to that effect, right? And he even said, 'Oh, you might suggest that to the police if they question you again.' Those words came back to me when the bodies were found off the cliff. It seemed like he had tried to plant the story with me. And this is why I didn't want to say anything to you. Because that was no accident."

Marissa said, "Was this guy handsome, tanned, an inch or two over six feet tall? Or was he shorter, with brown hair and narrow eyes, maybe five foot six?"

"The shorter one," she said.

Samira: That makes several times Greg said this

Marissa: He was planting this story everywhere

Nicole: Was it Marie vacuuming? The cleanup after the murder?

They debated adding this detail to their timeline. Because it was single-sourced—her husband didn't share the same memory—it also went in with an asterisk. They decided to pass their findings along to Detective Fonseca, so that he'd keep feeling their progress.

Detective Fonseca: No! That's outstanding! Could they identify who was vacuuming?

Marissa made it clear that they could not—but receiving exclamation points and general positivity from Detective Fonseca felt pretty good. He didn't comment on the allegation that Greg had tried to establish the car accident narrative in advance, which reaffirmed their hunch that Fonseca believed both Andrew and Greg were somehow culpable.

The week in Utah passed quickly, and the change in scenery did everyone good. They had few interactions on their trip, making stops only at a supermarket and hardware store. Brian drove straight home, and despite no one having any symptoms, out of an abundance of caution he insisted that the family all test for Covid. The girls hated the nasopharyngeal PCR test, the long swab probing deep past the nasal cavity to scrape the rear roof of the mouth, but their tests came back negative. So did Marissa's.

Brian was positive. False positives were rare, but he tested again. Positive.

Pre-vaccine Covid was scary, due to the unpredictability of the virus and its effects on the body, but it was kind of amusing that, of all of them, Brian had contracted it. He dutifully isolated himself in the converted carriage house in their backyard, Marissa delivering food to his door. A few days later Marissa got it. Brian was negative by then, so they swapped locations, Brian taking care of the girls inside the house while Marissa bunked in the carriage house in the backyard.

When the symptoms hit, she understood that this was not the colds or flu she was used to. She experienced some of the brain fog she'd heard people talk about, though she never lost her sense of smell or taste. She slept a lot but never deeply nor well. She felt sludgy, wrung out.

One night she awoke from this half-sleep to the sound of rattling. She pushed off her quilt and sat up, slow to realize that someone was trying to turn the doorknob a few feet away from her.

What is Brian doing up so late and why is he coming in here?

The rattling stopped. Marissa felt uneasy. She quietly reached for her phone and opened the app that linked to their home security cameras.

There was a man in her backyard. He was walking from the converted garage she was inside of back along the flagstone walkway, crossing the thirty-foot-square expanse to the kitchen door at the rear of the house.

The night vision image of the man was ghostly. In her Covid haze, Marissa thought to herself, *Why is Brian walking like that?*

The figure stopped, never reaching the main house, turning and starting back to the carriage house. Marissa looked up from her phone as the man's shadow fell over the shaded glass door before her.

The knob rattled again. She looked down at the foot or so of space between the bottom of the door shade and the floor. She saw a pair of tennis shoes. Not the sandals Brian would have slipped on to walk Cecil.

Fear broke through her Covid fog. *Who is this stranger?*

A single pane of door glass separated them. The interior shade swung a bit from the man's exertion as he stubbornly shook the doorknob—and it took the movement of the shade to convince Marissa that what she was experiencing was real. This was no Covid dream.

Marissa fumbled her phone touch screen, dialing 911. The rattling stopped, the shadow gone. She whispered to the operator: "A man is trying to get inside my house."

The operator told Marissa to stay on the line. Marissa didn't dare switch back to the camera view on her phone for fear of losing the telephone connection, so she had no idea where the intruder was. The operator pressed Marissa for information on exactly where she was in relation to her house, which Marissa relayed, speaking quietly but quickly, telling the operator that she had Covid and she was terrified. When she wasn't speaking, she heard nothing over the sound of her own frantic breathing.

Where had the man in the tennis shoes gone? Was he inside her house? She relayed her concern to the 911 operator. "Please—hurry."

Inside the second floor of the house, Marissa's oldest daughter awoke to the sound of sirens. Red-blue-and-white police lights flashed rapidly through her window up onto her bedroom ceiling at a dramatic angle. She rose blearily and walked down the hall to her parents' bedroom at the front of the house.

Brian stirred when he saw her. "I'm scared," she said—and that's when the siren registered for Brian, not a sound out of a dream but from a police car right outside the house.

He pulled on a mask and went into the hallway. His youngest stood there in her pajamas, scared stiff.

"*Occupants of the house,*" boomed a voice over a loud-speaker, "*make yourself known.*"

Holy shit. Brian grabbed the girls and moved them down the stairs in one huddled, petrified unit. Flashlight beams slashed inside through the first-floor windows. Cecil was howling and spinning in circles.

Inside the carriage house, Marissa could barely hear the 911 operator over the deafening siren symphony. Someone banged on the door the man had tried to open. She was afraid of being shot accidentally.

The operator told her they knew she was coming out. Marissa raised the wide shade, and police flashlights blinded her. She unlocked the door, which slid open, bringing her face-to-face with eight police officers and two barking police dogs. She was trembling so violently, she could barely move.

Brian and the girls got outside into the backyard, but they had to keep their distance because of Marissa's Covid. This meant there was no possibility of a reassuring hug. The sight of them sobbing made Marissa switch to crisis management mode. She called out across the yard to the sobbing girls, "I'm okay! Dad's got you. We're all right!"

The police dogs went through the neighborhood, officers checking the narrow alley adjacent to the house and all neighboring fence gates. The dogs never got a scent. The police stayed a while looking for signs of egress in the backyard, but it seemed the prowler had hopped the fence just out of camera range. He was gone and never found.

Marissa had to remain quarantined in the carriage house, so Brian gave her Cecil for the rest of the night. Marissa and Brian and the girls spoke via phone, sleep an impossibility at that point. She did her best to calm them down. "This is why we lock our doors. This is why we have an alarm. This is why we have cameras." Settling the girls' fears had the effect of settling Marissa's fears as well. Only after she got off the phone did her thoughts start to spin up again. No one in the house slept well for many nights after that.

The next morning, they reviewed the security camera footage. The night vision was murky and indistinct. Judging by the height of the carriage house doors, the would-be intruder—wearing a ball cap, face-shielding N95 mask, and a bulky, ill-fitting jacket—appeared to be a short, stocky man. She had no way to prove that this eerie trespasser was Greg Medina.

The fallout from the team's spouses was immediate. All of the strains the case had placed on their relationships burst into plain view. The team had been more mindful of the dangers of Covid than of the two potential killers they were pursuing.

Brian didn't need to say much, having gone through it himself. He knew Marissa had been chastened by the thought that she might have put her family in harm's way. "Don't we already have enough to worry about?" he asked her. It seemed to him that all the cleansing benefits of their one-week escape to Utah had vaporized overnight.

For her part, Samira wasn't totally convinced the break-in was related to the case. What it did do was awaken her to all the possibilities of what *could* happen, now that some of the ghastly particulars of the murders were coming into focus. She was most concerned about what Ward would say. He had never stopped worrying about both physical danger and legal action, but she noticed that during their rare outdoor gatherings with others, he would brag to friends about Samira's "murder case" and urge her to tell her story.

Nicole's Paul was similarly in awe of everything she had accomplished, despite his concern about her preoccupation with the case and his frustration with how time-consuming it was. She already had a full-time research job, on top of being a full-time Covid-era mother, and now this hobby had ballooned into a third full-time occupation.

Jeannie's wife, Tamara, was relieved they lived on the other side of the 405, putting some distance between them and the break-in. Jeannie agreed, although the distance, along with the curse of Covid, kept her from most in-person team get-togethers. Tamara's long work hours meant Jeannie was sometimes unavailable for evening Zooms, which really hurt. Jeannie would be occupied by something while her phone was blowing up over some new discovery or juicy new lead. She often felt like the "fifth Beatle," and found herself catching up on developments late at night, well after the fact. It sucked that she couldn't be more a part of the other three women's worlds, but she never felt excluded. Covid was already isolating enough, and she needed the connections this case was giving her. It was too important to her to consider letting go.

Walking away was not in any of their natures. The team pledged to be even more prudent going forward. Each family took extra precautions, from testing existing home security measures to restricting access to their personal information online.

Marissa texted Detective Fonseca about what had happened. She thought this provocation by the man she strongly suspected to be Greg Medina might spur him to share more of what he knew. He sympathized with what she'd been through and offered to look at the security camera footage, which Marissa forwarded to him. He had met with Greg Medina in person, but declared the footage inconclusive as to the identity of the prowler. Marissa was losing hope there was anything that would ever make him open the police file.

*G*oing *through Carrie Watkins's handwritten notes from the* days and weeks following her parents' disappearance, Marissa noticed entries such as "Questions for Cully" and "Save for Cully." This referred to Pasadena Police Department Detective Adam Cully, who had initially been assigned to the missing persons case. She hadn't realized how involved Detective Cully was in the initial phase of the investigation, before it became a homicide case and was handed over to the Crescenta Valley Sheriff's Station and Detective Fonseca. Because law enforcement agencies in different jurisdictions often didn't communicate with one another or coordinate information, maybe there was another opportunity here for the team to discover something that had slipped through the cracks.

Detective Cully had since retired, and a Google search returned someone with that same name working as a sales representative for a family-owned liquor distributor to bars, restaurants, and convenience stores whose office was not far from Pasadena. From the carriage house where she was finishing up her Covid quarantine, Marissa dialed the company phone number. A recording gave her Cully's private number, as, like almost everyone, he was working from home.

"Hi," said Marissa. "Is this former detective Adam Cully?"

"Yes. Who is this?"

Marissa gave him her spiel, which rolled off her tongue much more smoothly than it had when she began five months ago:

"I'm an investigative journalist and I'm working on a cold case from 2005 and was hoping to speak with you about it."

"Okay," he said, his voice thick with suspicion. "What case?"

"The disappearance and murder of Joel and Angela Watkins. Do you remember it?"

A sigh. "Oh, yes."

"I'm working with a team of investigators and we've interviewed more than fifty people in connection with the murders. We've also consulted with retired Sheriff's Department homicide detective Raymond Fonseca, do you remember him?"

"I sure do."

"Would you be open to answering a few questions?"

"Huh," he said. Marissa heard a noise on his end that sounded like a door closing, followed by the creak of a chair. "What are your credentials?"

"No credentials, I'm one of four independent journalists working on this unsolved case. We've done quite a bit of work already. I got your name from Carrie Watkins, the deceased couple's daughter?"

"Tell you what," he said. "You tell me what you think happened and that will determine whether I speak with you or not."

Marissa hadn't expected to audition for this. Her mind raced over their working theory, wondering what it was he needed to hear. He hadn't sounded happy to hear Fonseca's name. Perhaps Cully would be more amenable to sharing information than the detective who took over the case from him. This was a huge opportunity to gain police insight into the early days of the investigation.

"Sure thing," she said, reminding herself that she had faith in their investigation and everything they had learned, and launched into their version of the narrative up to that point:

By the summer of 2004, Joel Watkins's business had been in decline for a few years. He was struggling financially, both professionally and personally. In an attempt to close the gap on his cash flow issues, Joel entered into a factoring agreement with Pacific Heritage Bank & Trust. Essentially, for every invoice Wattkins LED initiated to a client, the bank would front the money, and the client would pay the bank directly. The limit of his line of financing was almost $1 million. However, the factoring deal could not make up for his declining sales, and Joel was overextended and becoming desperate. By the beginning of 2005, with knowledge and assistance from his son and son-in-law, Joel began generating fraudulent invoices. Unaware of the fraud, the bank continued to pay Wattkins LED for these invoices and awaited repayment. By May 2005, bank officials had become suspicious. There were several hundred thousand dollars outstanding, with each of the unpaid invoices totalling approximately $20,000. The vice president of the bank, with whom Joel had a long-standing professional relationship, met with Joel, who reassured him that the money was coming in and that he was holding meetings with investors and planned to sell the company within a matter of days. In reality, he had been unable to attract any buyers. In the meantime, Joel had come clean to his wife, Angela, about the financial trouble they were facing, and Angela became distraught. She reached out to her father to request a loan of $400,000, which her father declined, advising her to sell their house instead, unaware that the highly mortgaged property would not net enough to cover the debt. Family members who interacted with them at this time noticed tension between Joel and Angela.

As recently as two days before their disappearance, all seemed normal. On Thursday, May 26, Angela's Mercedes was taken in for regular service. Joel worked most of the day at the office on Friday, May 27. The only telephone conversations he had on his mobile phone were with his wife and his son-in-law. That same Friday, the son-in-law got into a dispute with an employee at his company who had not been paid for a few weeks. The son-in-law paid the employee with a check from Wattkins

LED—a separate business entity from the son-in-law's company—which bounced when the employee tried to cash it.

On Saturday, May 28, Joel went to his office as he usually did. He spoke to his father-in-law but avoided discussing their financial situation, saying only that he would "take care of it." He emailed the bank vice president a misleadingly upbeat message and set a meeting at the office for the following Monday afternoon. Angela, from their home, called her brother-in-law in a state of confusion about a phone number written down in her checkbook. Joel placed a call to his son-in-law, one of more than a dozen phone conversations they'd had over the past few days, and received a call from his wife at 10:59 A.M. He then powered off his work cellphone and left it in his office. Neither Joel nor Angela was seen alive or heard from again.

The son-in-law claimed that Joel was supposed to meet him at the son-in-law's office on Sunday afternoon but that Joel never arrived. The only potential concern the son-in-law showed was to leave a message on Joel's mobile phone voicemail at 1:30 the next morning.

Monday morning, Joel's administrative assistant arrived at work to find that Joel was not there. His son, who arrived for work around nine, said he didn't know where his father was.

Across town at this same time, the son-in-law's unpaid employee arrived at his place of business to find the son-in-law asleep, having apparently spent the night in his office.

At 2:30 P.M., the vice president of Pacific Heritage Bank & Trust arrived at Wattkins LED for a meeting to discuss the unpaid receivables. The administrative assistant said she thought that Joel was at a doctor's appointment. The son waited until the end of the day to call his grandfather, asking if he knew of his father's whereabouts. He then called his sister, Carrie, who had not spoken to her father in the prior two weeks. Carrie became alarmed and drove to her parents' house.

She arrived to find the side entrance door to the garage unlocked, the alarm not set, and the entrance to the home through the garage unlocked. Her father's 2000 Ford Explorer was gone, but her mother's 2002 Mercedes was there, unlocked, its undercarriage dirty, with soil and twigs near the driver's side as though someone had stamped their boots on the garage floor. This was uncharacteristic, as her mother was a neat freak. Later she would learn that the front right tire was flat—just two days after the vehicle had been washed and serviced at the dealership. Carrie searched the house, but her parents were not home. She noticed a vacuum cleaner lying on its side on the floor and a dining room chair pulled out of place. She left a note for them to call when they returned. She and her brother called area hospitals, and then Carrie contacted the police to file a missing persons report.

Five weeks later, Joel's Explorer was found at the bottom of a ravine off the Angeles Crest Highway. Joel and Angela Watkins's bodies were recovered approximately three hundred feet above the vehicle in advanced stages of decomposition. The airbags had not deployed, and the gear shift was set in Park.

"Is that enough?" Marissa asked, without a hint of attitude in her voice.

"Plenty," he said, followed by a pause. "What's this case to you?"

Marissa searched for words and landed on one. "Unsolved."

He grunted softly. "Fair enough."

He started talking. He'd been inside hundreds of houses in his career, so he didn't remember any particulars about the Watkinses' except that it wasn't treated like a crime scene. No yellow tape. Family members and sheriff's deputies came and went. He recalled that the family was cooperative until they weren't. He felt he'd built a rapport with the younger daughter but soon found himself edged out of the investigation.

"I'm the one who noticed the flat tire," he said. "Didn't know about the service appointment, though. About a week or so after the bodies were found, the homicide detective reached out to me, asking for my files. I sent over copies and never heard from him again. I was off the case."

Marissa sought to use the bitterness in his voice to her advantage.

"Detective Fonseca is retired now too," she said. "He eventually brought the case before a grand jury, but they declined to bring charges."

"And how's he feel about you doing this?"

"He's hopeful. But not very helpful. He won't share any of his files with us."

"Integrity of the case," said Cully.

"That's a phrase we've gotten used to."

Cully explained that he was four years retired but still worked as an investigator part-time as a "hire-back" for the District Attorney's Office. "Tell you what," he said. "Let me dig through my hard drive, see what I've got. So long as you agree to keep this confidential and me out of it, I'll share whatever I have with you."

The team held an early evening Zoom, and after Marissa recapped her conversation with Cully, it was as if a dam broke. Their enthusiasm was cleansing, helping to lift the cloud that had descended on them since the prowler incident. Finally, an offer of cooperation. Cully's file notes would be from the earliest days of the investigation, and they were optimistic they would find treasures in there, leads that could potentially provide them with weeks of work.

A few days later, the team got an update: Cully had scoured his hard drive and couldn't find any files from the Watkins case. "Give me a few more days," he said helpfully. "I have a friend who can pull them for me at Pasadena."

More waiting. By now they were used to it. In the meantime, summer was winding down. Marissa signed up for two online journalism courses that fall, and Samira was considering doing the same. Covid summer seemed endless.

> Nicole: I threw my back out doing nothing. It's like a big spasm

> Jeannie: Heat/Ice/Drugs

> Nicole: Booze?

> Jeannie: OF COURSE!

Marissa heard from Cully again. He was on vacation in Reno but promised to check in with his buddy at the Pasadena Police Department later in the day. He said he should hear soon.

> Marissa: Hi Raymond. I hope you are well! Just wanted to check in. We are still working hard on the Watkins case—exploring some new avenues.

> Detective Fonseca: I was wondering if you gals felt defeated and gave up or not. Glad to see you're undaunted.

Marissa sent a screenshot of this exchange to the team chat.

> Marissa: I despise being called a "gal." Especially in this context.

> Samira: Glad it wasn't just me

> Nicole: I think he actually thinks using "gals" is nicer than girls. Marissa, just write back and tell him we didn't quit like the "dudes" did

When Cully got back to Marissa, he explained that the Pasadena Police Department had begun tracking computer access and would not authorize releasing official files for a fifteen-year-old dead case to Adam Cully's friend. The women felt deflated, having foolishly put their entire investigation on hold waiting for these files. It was a momentum killer.

Other factors made them feel that they were in a holding pattern too. Covid fatigue, for sure. Fall was just around the corner, which meant Zoom school was soon to start up again—something each mom was dreading, as it was hard on their kids as well as a huge hassle for them. The prowler incident continued to cast a shadow on things; being super careful wasn't as fun as going all out. And the case was just plain difficult. Always two small steps forward, one giant step back. The top of the mountain looked no closer now than it had at the beginning of the summer. They were all fried. And Covid lockdown meant they were still on house arrest.

They had hit another crossroads. They decided to meet in person at summer's end. Jeannie drove out to the Westside and they walked along the beach, windy and warm, talking about anything other than the case. Eventually the sun dipped low, the light glowing orange. They went back to Marissa's house and sat around her backyard in beach chairs, enjoying some socially distanced tequila where the prowler had stood just weeks before.

Their anxiety about the case was such that they began tossing around some Hail Mary ideas. "We've talked about taking a field trip down to the crash site," said Marissa, recalling the time she'd started to hike down there solo. "Maybe there's some unrecovered evidence still lying around."

"What about contacting Marie Medina?" suggested Nicole. "She's a weak link for sure. We could press her. 'We have witnesses who saw you vacuuming your parents' bedroom the night of their disappearance.' Push it a little."

Jeannie said, "I'd like to see Marissa buttonhole Greg. 'What was so important that you and your father-in-law spoke by phone eleven times in the two days before he went missing?'"

"I wish," said Marissa. "'Why did you try to break into my house?'"

"Okay," said Samira. "Maybe we're getting carried away."

They laughed about their frustrations. These were desperation moves, too dangerous to attempt, emblematic of the serious doubts that had crept in. The tequila worked like truth serum, and their worries and insecurities came tumbling out.

"Maybe it's just too much for us to solve," said Jeannie. "We don't have all the tools we need."

"It was definitely easier in the early days," said Nicole. "Starting from zero. Every revelation was a win. We had no concerns about talking to the wrong person or drawing the wrong conclusions. This just gets harder and harder."

"And less rewarding," said Marissa. "I know. Reality's tough. We're wading through mud. In the early days of quarantine, working the case gave me structure and purpose, a direction. Even that's lacking now."

Samira sat forward. "I wasn't going to say anything, but maybe we need to address the one huge inconsistency we haven't confronted. If, as we assume, Andrew and/or Greg were behind Joel's and Angela's deaths, why did they make it look like suicide? Suicide as a cause of death would void the couple's life insurance policies and cost them the money they needed. Also, why would they ditch the car in a ravine where it might never be found? Declaring a missing person dead takes years. If they killed them for money, that makes no sense. Those two aren't master criminals, but they're certainly smart enough to realize that."

The others nodded. It was a high wall they couldn't get over.

"I've thought about this," said Jeannie. "Maybe money

wasn't the reason for the crime. What if they had a different motive? Don't ask me what, exactly—but maybe Joel's and Angela's deaths were intended to wipe away other crimes?"

"Now that's interesting," said Nicole. "As frustrated as I am with Detective Fonseca, I keep coming back to one thing he said that amazing day we met in the park. He said, 'You can't look logically at an illogical act.' Maybe that's our problem. Maybe we need to think more outside the box."

Jeannie said, "I just wish we knew for sure that there is a 'there' there."

"There has to be, right?" said Nicole. "Somebody killed them."

The conversation was intense and surprisingly emotional. They felt pressure from many angles—from their spouses and children, from the demands of the case, from their promises to Carrie Watkins and her aunt and uncle. As the night turned cool, Marissa looked for consensus. "What do we want to do?"

"I think we have to reassess," said Jeannie. "Is there something we're missing? Something we've overlooked? Or are we looking for something that doesn't even exist?"

Nicole said, "I agree that we can't go on this way. I don't mean quit."

"We've learned a lot," said Samira. "We've learned the hard way what not to do. Maybe now we need to look more closely at some things that make us uncomfortable."

"Such as?" said Nicole.

"Well," said Samira, "we've been so focused on Andrew and Greg as the bad guys, because they *are* bad guys. But are they *the* bad guys? Look at Joel. He was committing crimes too."

Jeannie quickly agreed. "They were all connected in this. We need to know how."

Samira said, "I can't believe I'm saying this, but—I actually think we need to go deeper."

Nicole said, "We have to consider everything and everyone."

Marissa let out a soft chuckle. "Honestly, this is not how I expected this conversation to turn out."

Nicole was adamant. "I don't want to let this go."

"Me neither," said Marissa. "I don't want to let Carrie down."

Their implicit commitment to Carrie Watkins sealed the deal. They resolved to regroup, lay out a clear plan of action, and plunge back in after Labor Day.

Mexico kept coming up.

The duck hunting trips Joel Watkins took multiple times each year. Joel was a consummate workaholic, yet he always made time for these three- and four-day excursions without his wife, and always with the same two friends, Amos and Hugh.

Their names and telephone numbers were printed on an emergency contact list Angela had compiled two months before the disappearance, the list Carrie had shared with the team. They also appeared numerous times in Joel's personal cellphone. Amos's ringtone was the whistling theme song from the movie *The Good, the Bad and the Ugly,* and Hugh's was the Los Lobos remake of Ritchie Valens's Mexican folk song "La Bamba." Other than perhaps his son-in-law, Greg, these men appeared to be the only two good friends Joel had had.

The three men regularly flew together to Mazatlán, a popular tourist destination on the Pacific coast of Mexico. The reason the team hadn't reached out to Amos or Hugh yet was because they were both retired firefighters. The team had committed too many unforced errors in the past, and there was no way to know what connections these two men might have had with law enforcement. But as the women recommitted themselves to the case, they realized that they needed to talk to Amos or Hugh, preferably both, if they wanted to find out more about Joel's trips to Mexico.

Marissa checked in with Detective Fonseca ahead of time, asking his opinion on Joel's friends. He told her they had potentially negative information that could be misleading and indicated that he believed they were not trustworthy.

Treading carefully, the team took to social media first. Both men's Facebook profiles were public. After much reverse chronological digging on Amos's page, Jeannie came upon a photograph of Joel with Amos and Hugh wearing lightweight camouflage and broad-brimmed hats, proudly dangling dead ducks with colorful plumage by their webbed feet. It had been posted in October 2016, eleven years after Joel's death, with the caption "Forever Friends."

It was a bit of a shock seeing a photograph of Joel other than the one from his missing persons poster. He wore round sunglasses and a wide smile. Jeannie alerted the others to the post and instructed them to read through the comments below.

A friend had left a note: "Two great guys, miss you both!"

Hugh had responded: "Thanks! Sadly, you never met our buddy Joel. He and his wife passed on several years ago. A true friend, much missed."

A woman named Matilde Prieto had commented below that: "*Muy amados, mis amigos perdidos hace mucho tiempo, siempre en mi corazón.*" Jeannie copied the words into Google Translate: *Dearly loved, my long lost friends, always in my heart.*

To which Hugh had replied directly: "always, *siempre.* Peace."

This exchange brought them to Matilde Prieto's Facebook page. Now in her midfifties, Matilde lived alone in Mazatlán. She had a grown son of whom she seemed very proud, posting often about his achievements. On her son's page, they learned that he lived in Mexico City and worked in banking. He posted few personal photos, but Marissa kept looking at a professional picture of the handsome young man posed in a suit and tie.

Marissa: Put me in my place if this is totally off the wall, but does Matilde's son resemble Joel??

They all scrutinized the photograph. Did this young man resemble Carrie? They agreed that it was possible. Samira reminded them that Joel's will specifically stated that no other heirs of his would be entitled to any of the estate. *Oh, boy.* Could Joel have been supporting single mother Matilde and her well-educated son financially? Could this support—perhaps extortion?—explain Joel's insatiable need for cash?

Marissa: I've got a funny feeling about this 😬

Jeannie: Trust your intuition. Let's dig.

Marissa didn't share this with the others at the time, but her hunch was informed by a peculiar and life-altering event in her own life.

In the spring of 2018, Marissa watched a segment on the *Today* show about detectives solving crimes using investigative genetic genealogy. Back when it was the thing to do, she had registered with 23andMe, the personal genomics testing company that had you spit into a test tube and drop it in the mail to learn your ancestry and genetic predispositions. She remembered receiving her results but apparently had never looked closely. After all, she thought she knew her family tree. Her father came from a large Ashkenazi Jewish family, and her mother was the only child of a Quaker couple who had died when she was young. The morning news show prompted her to dig out her results and take a second look at her report, especially the "DNA Relatives" page. She recognized an uncle to whom she knew she was related, and then three pairs of initials. She had no idea what they meant, but the sense of dread they triggered in her was all too familiar. Marissa checked with her sister, and both of them got on the phone with their mother to confront her. "Well," Marissa's mom said with a sigh, "I never told anyone this, but I was adopted."

To Marissa's mother, her adoption was a dark secret, a

source of shame, and something she chose never to divulge. This revelation rocked Marissa. She had known instinctively that something was off with her family, which had contributed to or at least partly explained her lack of a sense of belonging. She sat with the knowledge for a week, processing the deceit, trying to understand it from her mother's perspective, trying to make it make sense. She decided that the only way to do so was to set out to find answers.

With what little information she had, Marissa dug into researching her ancestral roots. She eventually tracked down a woman who lived in Washington State, and after Marissa reached her by phone and explained her reason for calling, the woman told her that her own mother, on her deathbed, had confided that another biological daughter—Marissa's mother—might come looking for them one day. The woman to whom Marissa was speaking was her mother's half sister. Marissa eventually met the woman, her aunt, at a restaurant, and sitting across from her she recognized the same unique jawline as she and her mother have, something countless people had commented on throughout the years.

Marissa wondered whether her mother's shame about having been adopted had manifested itself in her adult life in secretiveness and reckless financial decisions. One thing Marissa knew for certain was that seeking out and finding answers to this mystery had given her a profound sense of self-understanding as well as a new level of self-confidence. Research and investigation had proved immensely satisfying, and she felt she had a knack for it. This was the turning point that had inspired her to consider reinventing herself by taking journalism classes. Suddenly and happily, she had understood exactly what she wanted to do with her life.

Matilde's son was friends with Amos and Hugh on Facebook, which seemed interesting. The team went back through their interviews and voluminous notes to tally up all the times people had mentioned Joel's trips to Mazatlán. There were many holidays and long weekends. Could Joel have been visiting a second family down there? Marissa located an agency that tracked down birth certificates in Mexico, which were public records, and paid a small fee to perform a search. They were very interested to see who was listed as the son's father.

Samira dug further into Amos's and Hugh's Facebook accounts, looking for other friends from Mazatlán. She was puzzled by the fact that Matilde did not have any friends listed on her profile and shared this anomaly with the team. Something was brewing.

> Marissa: I have an hour to myself. Should I call Amos?

> Samira: Should I call Hugh? Hit them at the same time so they don't have time to call each other?

> Marissa: Yes!

Marissa dialed the number in Joel's cellphone log, seated before the team's prepared list of questions. Amos didn't pick up, and she left a message on his voicemail.

After three rings, Hugh picked up Samira's call. Since the team were already messaging back and forth, Samira started to live-text their conversation.

> Samira: talking to Hugh right now

> Samira: he's in the car at In and Out Burger

Samira had grown more confident in her cold-calling skills and felt she knew how to play this conversation. Hugh had already placed his order and was waiting in the typically long drive-through line. She identified herself in the usual manner. There was a beat of silence after the mention of Joel Watkins.

"I don't know if I should talk to you," he said. "Who are you again?"

A woman's voice asked Hugh, "Who's Joel Watkins?"

Samira: trying to decide if he wants to speak with me

Samira: passenger in his car (a woman) asked who Joel Watkins was

Nicole: I AM DYING

Samira: not sure if he realizes that I can still hear him talking

She listened to him explain to the woman in the car with him that Joel was an old hunting buddy. "Well," he said, resuming his conversation with Samira, "why don't we talk now, because I may not talk later." Samira suspected that the presence of this woman, who turned out to be Hugh's fiancée, might color his responses—but she also felt that this woman was the reason Hugh had decided to speak with Samira at all, rather than have to answer to his fiancée.

Hugh told Samira that he met Joel sometime in the early 1990s, and that they had been introduced by Amos. He called the Watkins family "a great family," yet seemed to know next to nothing about Angela or the kids. They went hunting maybe three times a year, usually an all-inclusive package in Mexico with lodging and gear provided. He related a long-winded story about Mexican *federales* stopping them one time, looking for a trio of "gringo fugitives," which felt like a stall, having nothing whatsoever to do with the reason Samira was calling.

"Maybe you can help me with this," said Samira, trying to get the conversation back on track. "Do you know anyone by the name of Matilde Prieto?"

"No," said Hugh. Then he added, "Maybe I might have heard the name."

His fiancée said, "Maybe you heard it from Amos."

Hugh said, "That's probably it."

Samira rolled her eyes. "Did Joel ever express any concerns to you about his personal or professional life?"

"No," said Hugh. He recalled that he had been scheduled to meet Joel for lunch on a Tuesday, and that was when Amos called asking if he had seen Joel, saying that Joel's son had called and said he might be missing. Joel never showed up for lunch that day.

"Do you have a theory about what might have happened to him?" Samira asked.

"I don't," he said. "You probably know more about it than I do." Then he said that he was at the window, and she heard him take possession of his Double-Double and Cherry Coke.

"Thanks so much for talking to me," said Samira.

Samira: ok off

Samira: you can bet he's going to call Amos

Marissa: TELL US EVERYTHING

Samira spoke to each woman individually, as none wanted to wait for a Zoom quorum. "I mean, he really gave me nothing," Samira told them, "but I find it very odd that a man who had such a long history with Joel never knew his kids." He had clearly lied about not knowing Matilde, whose "dearly loved" Facebook comment he had replied to. The team consensus was: These guys stink.

When Amos failed to call Marissa back, she asked Carrie to reach out to her father's old friend for them, hoping she'd have better luck. They knew they were on to something. Carrie said she would, and the team sent her a script of sorts to recite if asked about the women. *A team of investigative journalists approached me about looking into Joel's and Angela's deaths. It remains an unsolved case at the L.A. County Sheriff's Department, though the case is still open. Elements of the story that have surfaced recently are such that I was hoping you could help shed some light.*

Carrie connected with Amos and reported back that he was amenable to speaking but seemed very guarded. Marissa received a text message from Amos on her burner phone the next day: "Dear Marissa: Against my better judgement I am responding to you." He said that if he had any information he thought might help solve the mystery, he would not hesitate to share it. "Unfortunately, I do not. Nevertheless, I will converse with you."

They set a time for a call and Marissa reached him at home. After some initial conversation and a few kind words from him about Joel Watkins, Marissa focused on the disappearance. Amos recalled that Joel's business had been shut down, but he was not aware that it was shuttered just days after Joel had gone missing.

"Really?" he said, sounding genuinely surprised. "Wow, that stinks to high heaven."

Marissa paid out some rope, asking what he thought might have happened, "in your opinion."

"At the time, I assumed the business had gone under and Joel committed murder-suicide. When it came out later that he was the victim of a homicide—well, let's just say that never made any sense to me."

"Why not?"

"If Joel owed someone money, killing him off seems like the last thing that person would do." He went on to say that he suspected that the "chippies"—the California Highway Patrol—might have looked at the crash the wrong way.

"Maybe you can help me out with this," said Marissa, going in for the kill. "Do you know anyone in Mexico who Joel might have confided in? Anyone worth speaking to?"

"No. That was a long time ago."

"Were there any bars or clubs you frequented down in Mazatlán? I imagine the nightlife there is pretty fun."

"We always had a good time, but I don't see how that matters."

"Was it a 'What happens in Mazatlán' kind of thing?"

"I mean, look. We were all married at the time. There were some strip bars down there. I don't want to muddy a dead man's reputation."

"No, of course not," said Marissa. "Would there have been any reason at the time to think he had run off to Mexico?"

"Well, he loved it there."

"The reason I ask is because someone named Matilde Prieto keeps coming up in our research. Do you have any idea who that is?"

"Uh—vaguely. Like I said, it was a long time ago."

"Or her son?" Marissa cited him by name.

"Sorry. Nope."

He shut down after that, sensing that Marissa had the goods on the Mazatlán trips. As soon as she ended the conversation, she texted the team.

> Jeannie: I agree he's lying. But let's say Matilde and Joel were having an affair and her son is his. How protective will they be about this at this point?

> Marissa: These are old fashioned, private guys. I feel like they would take it to the grave . . .

Jeannie: So glad they have such honor . . .

Samira: Also it could be that all three guys messed around a bit and its more about keeping that a secret

Marissa: The more I think about it, the more I'm convinced that he is Joel's son.

Samira: I'm worried we tipped our hand and they already called Matilde.

They decided to craft a note to Matilde and send it via Facebook. "We are working with a team of reporters, experts, and interested parties to find out what happened in the 2005 tragic death of Joel Watkins. We understand that you knew Joel well and his death is a painful memory for you. We would love to speak to you about Joel and any details you might have that could help us find resolution and bring about justice."

A few days later, Hugh reached out to Marissa by text. He said he and Amos had spoken and they were impressed with the work the team had done. They had been operating under the assumption that Joel's death was an accident for all these years, but now they were convinced there were suspicious circumstances, and they wanted to help get to the bottom of it.

Samira: Interesting change of tone!

Jeannie: Hmmm. 🫤

Marissa: I'm calling him at 3:30 💁‍♀️

This second conversation with Hugh was enlightening on a few fronts. Right at the top, he told Marissa, "You guys have a lot of names and I'm wondering where you got them from." Later, awkwardly and without prompting, he brought up Matilde, saying the three men used to "hang out with these two waitresses and one of them had a son." It was obvious to Marissa that he was trying to get out in front of the revelation and normalize it—and potentially inoculate himself against any incriminating photographs that might exist. The others concurred.

> Samira: I think they're agreeing to speak with us so they can find out what we have

> Jeannie: I'm with you guys—this is suspicious. And since we're not men who need our egos stroked, the "we're impressed with you" just isn't going to snow us

A few days later, a digital copy of the son's birth certificate arrived in Marissa's inbox. There was no father listed on the form next to "El Padre," just a series of dashes.

Marissa shared their Mexico suspicions with Fonseca via text. The retired detective was completely unaware of Joel's potential secret family.

> Detective Fonseca: That's outstanding! Matilde is a potentially good source for motive. They may have spoken about the problems Joel was having.

But Matilde never replied to their Facebook message. Covid ruled out any travel to Mexico, though they considered it. The team couldn't let this go. Even if it ended up having little or no bearing on the case itself, it was such an important step toward understanding Joel Watkins. And Fonseca could be right—maybe Joel confessed to Matilde things he never confessed to anyone else. Maybe she would be more forthcoming with the team than Amos and Hugh had been.

A few days later, as the women were messaging about the case, Marissa admitted something.

Marissa: I did something impulsive today

Samira: What did you do oh hi baby

Samira: Oops. I was doing voice dictation and my dog jumped in my lap

Samira: What did you do?

Marissa: I wrote to him

Matilde's son. It was a softer version of the approach they had sent his mother. Marissa had dispatched it via Facebook, and over the next several days she had checked her page regularly. It was a desperation move. Marissa had no intention of sharing with this young man the team's theory about his parentage; she just wanted more information on Joel.

The other women applauded her chutzpah in reaching out. As Nicole said, this was badass Marissa at her finest.

But Marissa's message to the young man was never opened nor read.

"I've had a great life and a great family and I messed it all up."

At breakfast at a Denny's several days before his May 2005 disappearance, Joel Watkins bared his soul to a man to whom he had hoped to sell his company. Jeannie had tracked down this investor from the call log on Joel's work phone. Joel had evidently been counting on this transaction more than the investor thought, as Joel became, in this man's words, very disturbed and worried. "I'm in deep trouble. If I can't find someone to bail me out of this, I don't know what I am going to do." He admitted to submitting phony invoices in order to collect via his factoring scheme. He pleaded with this investor for a loan, but the friend did not have the money to do so. Joel said to him, "The people I borrowed money from are not good people."

Jeannie thought it extraordinary that Joel was so candid with this man. Every other interviewee described Joel as reserved, controlled, unflappable. This struck her as another example of Joel's growing desperation toward the end. He had reached a crisis point.

The team puzzled over the last remark about borrowed money, considering that Joel had $14,000 cash stuffed into a deposit bag in a table drawer at home. Had he been defrauding the bank in order to generate cash to pay back a large loan they had not yet uncovered?

Marissa and Samira had been trying for months to book a call with Joel's certified public accountant, the one Hal Durban said came into the office once a week and with whom Hal had a falling-out over accounting issues, which had led to Joel's letting Hal go. "*I had a disagreement with the CPA about how to book some things. It didn't seem right to me.*"

The CPA remembered Joel as a very generous, personable, and easygoing man who never raised his voice, even when the news was bad and times were difficult—and there had been difficult times. In 2000, Joel had been forced to sell his home, a great blow to him personally. The CPA said that Joel loved his wife dearly and wanted to please her, which was why he went against the CPA's advice and purchased the home on Shadow Peak Road three years later. It was well outside Joel's reach financially, but he wanted it for Angela.

The business had made a lot of money at one time and then it went away quickly. During the boom times, Wattkins LED would use contract labor for lighting installations, hiring workers for $30 an hour and billing the customer $120 an hour—making as much or more money from the labor upcharges and installation fees as they did from the sales of the lighting fixtures themselves. The boom lasted five or so years, and when that started to fall off, they began having cash flow issues. The CPA claimed to have no knowledge at all of the factoring scheme. He added that Joel tended to employ secretaries and assistants who did not have adequate accounting experience.

Did the CPA ever think it strange that Joel relied on him rather than on his son, who was employed by the company? "Only in retrospect," he said. "Maybe he didn't trust his son."

By the end, the business was operating on a skeleton staff. One week, on his scheduled day to visit the office and go through books and records, the CPA arrived to find the doors locked and no notice posted. He phoned several people, including Joel, who did not answer. One of the salespeople eventually got back to him and told him Joel and Angela had disappeared.

No one had ever contacted him about the shutting down of the business, which he'd found puzzling and suspicious. The accountant knew neither Andrew Watkins nor Greg Medina well. Of Andrew, he said he was eloquent and suave. When the business experienced its downturn, the CPA had advised Joel to let Andrew go. Andrew was drawing an annual salary of $75,000 and making additional monthly draws on his business account adding up to as much as $25,000 per year. But Joel refused, instead laying off other employees with smaller, commission-based salaries.

Andrew Watkins reached out to the CPA many months after his parents' deaths, requesting help with Joel's estate. The accountant referred Andrew to an attorney friend and that had been the end of it. As to the son-in-law, Greg Medina, the CPA recalled speaking with him only once. He said Greg talked about business in a way that indicated he knew little of what he was talking about.

The one-in-thirty call ratio paid off again when Jeannie took a flyer on contacting other tenants operating in the office building where Wattkins LED leased space. An accountant whose office was next to Wattkins LED at the time of Joel's disappearance reported that he knew Joel only by sight, from passing in the hallway or riding together in the elevator. But this man's office had a view of the door to the stairway, and he remembered noticing that during the last few weeks leading up to his disappearance, Joel spent much of his time out on the secluded fourth-floor landing talking on his cellphone. Sometimes this man could hear Joel's side of the conversation, and to the accountant's ears it sounded like Joel was "dealing with not nice people" trying to collect money. The accountant made it clear that he had zero evidence of this, but he specifically and colorfully recalled what he termed "fear-like emotion emanating" from Joel. The man stressed that he had never known Joel to take phone calls in the stairwell until the final few weeks of his life.

This was compelling hearsay from a third party with no skin in the game. To Jeannie's ears, this man did not sound like someone who wished to insert himself into an investigation. On the contrary, he seemed annoyed by the whole thing. Interestingly, Joel's work phone was missing two months of calls. There was nothing in his call log after March 11. This was the phone later discovered on his office desk. They checked with Joel's wireless carrier at that time, AT&T, and learned they no longer maintained data records from as far back as 2005. Either Joel's cellphone had been turned off for two months, or the call log had been deleted around the time of his disappearance.

This raised the question of whether Joel might have been using a third cellphone during this critical period of time. The "third phone" theory became a minor obsession of theirs, as it would explain much, and it was potentially still in existence somewhere. Might that phone have been in the car at the time of the crash?

This pushed Marissa to call Detective Fonseca and once again plead their case for getting phone records from the police file. "I truly don't want to step on any toes, but we desperately need the access to break this case."

"I understand that you think so," he said, "but I am in an impossible spot legally."

"How about a yes-or-no question?" she asked, and did not wait for his consent. "Did Joel have a third cellphone?"

"A third cellphone?"

"That's right."

"I can't answer that. Same as always. I just can't."

Marissa: So annoying but his confusion sounded like he had no idea about a third phone, had never considered it

Jeannie: I guess we'll just have to solve the damn thing to find out what's in that car.

With their frustration with Fonseca mounting, they considered consulting a forensic cellphone data retrieval company. Actual retrieval of information from a 2005 flip phone was an impossible task, they realized, but even discovering whether or not information had been deleted would tell them something. They decided to wait, as Joel's phones were some of the few pieces of evidence in their possession, and they were reluctant to let them out of their sight.

A few days later, Marissa received a text from Carrie requesting an update. This was a moment the women had been dreading. Carrie had asked for complete transparency when they first met, to which they had readily agreed—never imagining they might one day have to tell her that she may have a half sibling living in Mexico City.

Carrie's husband, Henry, joined her on the five-box Zoom call. The team took turns bringing the couple up to speed on everything they had learned since their in-person meeting: the neighbor interviews; the Mercedes car wash; the "third phone" theory; Pasadena detective Adam Cully raising and then dashing their hopes for a peek at the police files.

Then it was Carrie's turn. Amos had spoken with her after his conversation with Marissa. He admitted to Carrie that he had been reluctant to divulge much to the journalists, especially anything that might reflect poorly on her father. He confessed that "indiscretions" had taken place on their weekend hunting trips. Visits to pool halls and strip clubs where "Joel had favorites." They had become particularly friendly with two women down there, to the point of exchanging Christmas presents with them for a few years. While Amos did not go into any detail about the relationship, he insisted that it was nothing more than "a good time." The hunting trips ended after Joel's death and they had not maintained contact with the women since.

The team let Carrie know that that last part was a lie, laying out the two friends' Facebook interactions with a woman in Mazatlán—likely one of the women to whom Amos was referring. Both Amos and Hugh had unfollowed this woman's Facebook account after speaking with the team, which of course was no coincidence.

Before they could go any further, Carrie interrupted. "How old is this woman you're talking about?"

Marissa answered. "She's close to sixty now."

"Does she have any children? Between the ages of fifteen and twenty-two or twenty-three?"

All four women watched Carrie's and Henry's expectant faces in their box on the screen.

Marissa answered, "Yes."

"Half Caucasian?" Carrie asked.

Marissa nodded. "Seemingly, yes."

The stillness was broken by Henry reeling backward suddenly. "I told you," he said to Carrie. "I always said . . ."

"Ugh," said Carrie, nodding, shocked. "You did."

Henry continued, "I always said I expected someone to come knocking on the door someday."

The women were relieved that Carrie and Henry had arrived at the conclusion themselves. Carrie absorbed the blow well. She asked if the team had a photograph, and Marissa immediately texted her one. They watched Carrie and Henry study the image on her phone in real time.

"Okay," said Carrie, "well, he does look like . . . Okay." She remembered she was being watched and turned her phone over, setting it aside. "I'll study this later."

Marissa stressed that none of this was confirmed. Nor, at present, was there any apparent connection between Joel's Mexico dalliances and his and Angela's murders.

Carrie was graciously quick to absolve the team of any guilt. "Honestly," she said, "in terms of consequence, this means less to me than the two A.M. vacuuming and Greg force-feeding an alibi to the neighbors."

The team agreed. Drizzling a measure of truth over a batch of lies to obfuscate and confuse the listener was probably how Greg had survived being sued dozens of times. Jeannie said, "Why wasn't he more alarmed when your dad didn't show up at the meeting they had agreed to that Sunday?"

Carrie recalled how passive her brother Andrew had been in the days following their parents' disappearance. Normally a take-charge guy, he literally took charge of nothing—other than shutting down his father's business for good. "I remember asking him about his passivity," Carrie said, "which was so unlike him. And he kind of stopped and turned to me and said, 'You don't think I had anything to do with it, do you?'"

The team members audibly gasped.

"I know," said Carrie, shaking her head. "Looking back now, I'm like, how did I miss all this? Why did I not see it right away?"

Henry said, "Because you were so distraught."

"I was the only one, apparently," she said.

They touched on their frustration with Detective Fonseca, suggesting that it might help if Carrie could make her displeasure known to him. They wished they had more concrete answers and apologized for introducing this Mexico revelation to her memories of her parents.

Carrie said, "Even going down a wrong path is more than what was being done about my parents' murder a year ago."

Her saying *Thank you* and *Keep going*, after all the time, effort, and emotion they had devoted to the investigation of her parents' murders, was more satisfying than they'd expected. Parenting was by its very nature so thankless that being valued here was reward in itself.

The team stayed on after Carrie and Henry dropped from the Zoom call, decompressing. They had been spared dropping the bomb on the poor woman but had borne witness to the emotional moment.

"She wants this solved so badly!" said Samira. "Almost as bad as we want to solve it for her."

"We'll get there," said Nicole. "And now I'm closing my laptop before Paul divorces me."

They all clicked "End Meeting for All" and returned to their families.

As October rolled around, the Centers for Disease Control reported one million total Covid deaths worldwide in ten months, one-fifth of them—two hundred thousand—in the United States alone. Food insecurity reached an estimated 52 million people in the United States, 17 million more than before the pandemic. The president tested positive for the virus one month ahead of the 2020 election and was admitted to Walter Reed National Military Medical Center. After suspension and later resumption of the professional basketball season, the NBA finals were played inside a sterile "bio-secure bubble" before virtual crowds on the grounds of the closed Walt Disney World in Orlando, Florida. COVID-19 vaccines had reached Phase 3 clinical trials with hope that a rollout would begin by year's end. Everything was still generally shitty.

Going back and reviewing the raw B-roll news footage of the nighttime discovery of Joel and Angela's vehicle, Marissa noticed that at the end of the on-site remarks by the California Highway Patrol spokesman, the young officer spelled out his name for the stringer recording the incident: T-I-R-P-I-N-G. She reached him by telephone at CHP's Southern Division Headquarters in Glendale, where he had since been promoted to captain, and was pleased to learn that Captain Tirping remembered the night in question well. He had returned to the site the following day when Joel's and Angela's remains were brought up, telling Marissa that that was the first time he'd ever seen anything like that. Marissa gave him the short version of the circumstances surrounding the case and the current state of their investigation. He seemed curious and wanted to be helpful: "Wow, I had no idea they never solved this. You've really piqued my interest." He promised to "poke around" and see if there were any unofficial files tucked away. "I'm not sure what I can talk to you about, but call me back here at this time in three days."

Three days later, Marissa called him. "I have the full MAIT report right in front of me," Captain Tirping said.

"Full what?"

"Multidisciplinary Accident Investigation Team report. The main pieces are the Evidence Report, which lists everything inventoried from the incident site, and the Mechanical Inspection Report, a comprehensive analysis of the condition of the vehicle. It's very interesting."

"Interesting how?"

"Unfortunately, I ran this by my superiors and they won't allow me to share the contents of the files with you. I wish I could help."

Marissa was ready for this. "We've heard that a lot," she said, telling him she completely understood that police agencies were unable to make investigatory materials available to the public, something she and her colleagues had come up against time and time again. "Could you give me the report number so I can make a targeted public records request?"

He did so. Marissa sensed that he genuinely wanted to share information with her, so she kept him talking.

"Is there a full accounting of the vehicle's condition?" she asked.

"Oh, yes. Very comprehensive."

She let him know what they already knew, trying to sound casual. "No airbag deployment. Gearshift set in Park." Then she added something they thought they knew but hadn't confirmed. "Seatbelts not worn."

"Correct."

Bingo. "And were the vehicle's keys recovered?"

"I really can't tell you that."

"But if the keys were not recovered, that would definitely point to this being murder and not a road accident, wouldn't you say?"

A pause. "Safe to assume, yes."

She pushed. "You're so helpful, I really do appreciate it. Was there anything found in the car that jumps out at you? Or found near the bodies? Or outside the car—anything at all?"

She heard pages being flipped, then a sniff or a snort— a sound of discovery, something along the lines of an *aha* or a *hmm*.

Then he spoke. "Is there a Mexico angle to your investigation?"

Marissa: There is something related to Mexico in there

Nicole: STOP

Marissa: That's all he would say. He SO wanted to tell me info, but couldn't.

Jeannie: Omg!! Well done!!! What could it be?

In the moment, it felt like a hit, although ultimately these chips of information chiseled out of the law enforcement bureaucracy only revealed how little they actually knew. Another tantalizing fact glimpsed, but the evidence remained out of reach. They all felt that they were at the limit of what they could do with the tools they had. The information was out there. They were working harder than ever to uncover things that were known yet hidden away from them. It seemed that no amount of dedication on their part would earn them the access they needed.

Early on, Marissa had assumed that any progress made would be duly rewarded. She believed that everyone thought as the team did, simply wanting this mystery to be solved. Now it felt like they were actively being thwarted. She vented to Nicole on the phone that night. "We aren't being unreasonable."

"Hell, no," said Nicole.

"How are we doing anything that gets in their way? This is a fifteen-year-old cold case! No one else was doing anything to investigate it until we came along. And they act like we're trying to make trouble."

Nicole said, "Take the handcuffs off us so we can help you put them on the killers!"

Nicole had reached an associate of Joel's who was living and working in Mexico. This south-of-the-border connection got her attention, and the businessman was happy to talk. He said that he knew Joel was into some shady business practices and this man was a pack rat who saved everything. "I've got records on an old hard drive. Let me dig it up and get back to you." This tantalizing offer kept the team on the edge of their seats for days—but the businessman ghosted Nicole. The number she had reached him at was no longer in service. They never knew whether he was for real, or whether something had happened to him. Another promising lead that fizzled.

Ben Dealer, Joel's archrival with an office in the same building, was another time-sucking red herring. The team had heard lots of stories about him and his CIA fictions in interviews, and they went about tracking down various aliases he had used through the years. Dealer was apparently a dangerous, unstable individual, someone they wisely never attempted to contact personally, but he ultimately proved to be nothing more than a fraud with mental health issues. Another distraction that probably could have been avoided with a little guidance from Detective Fonseca.

Six weeks after their end-of-summer low point, they found themselves again fighting off malaise. Fatigue and disappointment returned, though the team never once turned their exasperation on one another. Detective Fonseca became the focus of their frustration. Of all the women, Jeannie felt she understood his position best. He simply did not have the authority to open his books for them. At the same time, they, as amateurs, could not competently move forward without some access to the police files. The two sides, which should have been the same side, had reached an impasse.

Nicole suggested they try applying political pressure by going around the L.A. County Sheriff's Department to the L.A. County District Supervisor's Office. Perhaps with Carrie Watkins's help, they could lobby to persuade the LASD to release the police files to the family. This would be a power move, but requesting Carrie's assistance in taking the investigation public was a huge ask. There was no guarantee she would say yes. In fact, Samira and Marissa felt certain she would decline.

Left with no other choice, the team decided to take one more run at Fonseca. They weren't asking for or expecting full cooperation. Only guidance. They felt they had earned it.

Marissa reached out to set a meeting. Fonseca responded that he would be happy to meet to "hear what they had." The one-way street again. Marissa texted back that they hoped he might share something with them in return.

> Detective Fonseca: I still can't turn over the files to you. I don't have the authority and it would be unprecedented for them to be released at all.

They knew from watching *I'll Be Gone in the Dark* that that wasn't true. After consulting with the team and shaping a response, Marissa texted him back.

Marissa: We are at a crossroads here. We have opportunities to move ahead and have conversations with relevant
people in this case. There are well-meaning people who
want to offer us assistance but can't. But without corroborating information, we are putting ourselves in harm's way. We
need to be able to proceed with the satisfaction that we
understand all the facts and dangers. If you can't share the
actual files, would you at least be able to discuss some
pertinent facts with us?

Detective Fonseca: My hands are tied. I have tried to give
you some direction. If that is not helpful, then I understand
and wish you the best.

Their reactions among themselves were salty. They cleaned it
up considerably in Marissa's response:

Marissa: We appreciate your honesty. And we recognize
your position. We want your feedback. All we are asking for
is some actual guidance in the form of facts.

He suggested a Zoom call, but the women wanted to meet
in person. They gathered midmorning on a mid-October day
in the same public park where they had met before. Not much
about the surroundings had changed, but the women had. The
first time they'd met, the women had made their pitch. They
had been rank amateurs looking for validation. Their air of
eager supplication from the first meeting was now long gone.
They were through being patient and accommodating. Kind
understanding had taken them only so far. They were invested
in this case now. They felt they had sweat equity. Surely Fonseca
could bend the rules for them if he wanted to. Why didn't he
want to?

With masked children cavorting in the enclosed playground thirty yards deeper into the park, they stood around the same bench as before, Fonseca with his hands tucked into the pockets of his barn coat, his posture indicating a willingness to listen but also a readiness to shrug. The conversation was not recorded, but the women remembered it all too well. They were surprised at how contentious it became, and so quickly.

"We've come to a bit of a wall," Marissa told him. "Despite the dozens of interviews and reviewing all of the publicly available documents in this case, there is still key evidence that we need and that evidence is only available in the police files. Phone records, suspect interviews, police reports—all of this information will get us further along."

Nicole said, "You can redact whatever you want."

"We understand your side of things," said Jeannie. "We respect that—we do. But we can be of help. We want to be of help. I think we want the same thing."

"We are aware of other cases where files have been released and it's made all the difference," said Samira. "This wouldn't be an unprecedented move for you to release the files to us."

Fonseca's eyebrows lifted in surprise. He was not prepared for a full court press. "That's just not the way that I work. I have to protect the integrity of the case."

"But with you retired, and no movement from the department on reopening the case," said Samira, "we are the only hope in getting this solved."

"That may be true," Fonseca replied, "but I'm not willing to risk losing the chance to bring this to trial over something as simple as a chain of custody issue."

They tried a different tack, asking specific questions, trying to get him to open up while reminding him of what they'd found out on their own.

"If you weren't able to bring murder charges against Andrew

and Greg," said Nicole, "I don't understand why you didn't at least arrest them for participating in the factoring fraud."

"The bank did not want to pursue that course of action. They did not want those charges pressed because it would bring their negligence about the factoring scheme into public light. They screwed up big-time handling Joel Watkins, and they knew that. They got back a percentage of their loss and walked away. For my part, I didn't want those two for white-collar crime. I wanted them for murder."

"What convinced you that Joel and Angela were murdered?" said Samira. "Was it that the car keys were not found with the wrecked Explorer down in the canyon?"

He saw the trap being set before him and sidestepped it deftly. "I never confirmed to you whether or not any keys were found."

"We confirmed it independently," said Samira.

He said nothing.

"You're not going to ask us how, because that would tip your hand," continued Samira. "And why would we tell you how when you're not giving us anything?"

"What was the Mexico connection in the wrecked vehicle?" asked Marissa.

He couldn't hide his surprise at the question. He shook his head. "I can't tell you that."

Marissa sighed in exasperation. "This is incredibly frustrating. You acknowledge that we are the only ones working on this case, but you'd rather it stay unsolved than cut through some red tape?"

A barn coat shrug. "My position won't change."

"We are out of options," said Marissa. "One thing we are considering is going to the county supervisor. Using political pressure. Carrie Watkins said she'd consider it," she fibbed.

"Go for it," said Fonseca, incredulous. "You're welcome to

call the District Attorney's Office. Walt Kramer's the ADA in Major Crimes. See if he'll take your call."

Fonseca smiled knowingly, nodded to the team, and started back to the street. The women watched him go, letting him get out of earshot before turning to one another, startled that the meeting had ended so abruptly.

"Wow," said Jeannie. "Okay then."

Marissa said, "I don't know if we just shot ourselves in the foot or what."

"He thinks we're Karens," said Nicole. "Wanting to speak to his manager."

Jeannie chuckled. "He knows better than that. He's just had it."

"He's bullshit," said Samira.

"He definitely did not expect to get attitude," said Jeannie.

"Look," said Nicole, "we said our piece. It needed to be said."

"He doesn't think we'll do it," said Marissa.

"Do what?" said Jeannie.

"Call this assistant district attorney."

Jeannie looked from Marissa to Samira and Nicole. "*Are* we going to do it?"

"Wow," said Nicole.

"What do you guys think?" Samira asked.

They discussed it. Nicole's attitude was, *What's one more phone call? What's one more door slammed in our faces?*

They agreed to think about it further. No taco lunch this time. They all had kids to get home to. Samira called Marissa on the drive back.

"That got heated!" Samira said.

"Did you think he was taunting us at the end?"

"No. Do you?"

"Like challenging us. Not in a good way."

"I think it is a risk," said Samira. "We could get a hard no this time, but permanently. Like, cease and desist."

"I'm so pissed," said Marissa.

She had already decided what she was going to do, but waited until she was home before texting the others.

Marissa: I'm calling him now before I lose my nerve.

Marissa sometimes acted impulsively, and on those occasions Samira and Jeannie were usually able to rein her in. But in this instance, no one said *Don't*.

Marissa checked on the girls, then went up to her phone-call closet. She looked up the District Attorney's Office and called the main number. She asked for Walt Kramer and was transferred, expecting to get a voicemail or his assistant.

A man answered with a brusque "Hello?"

Marissa gave her name.

"And?" the voice said. "Who are you?"

Wait. Was this him?

Marissa started talking. Intimidated at first, she found herself rambling. She said something about the team.

"What 'team'?" he said. "What is this you're talking about? Who are you?"

She couldn't get her footing. She said something else—God knows what—then referenced Joel and Angela Watkins by name and spoke about the car wreck.

Incredibly, ADA Kramer remembered the case immediately.

"That's my case," he said. "I keep all my cases. Bottom of a canyon, deceased male into some shady financials. Inconsistent statements from the son and son-in-law who had information they did not want to share."

"Yes!" said Marissa.

"Look," he said, "I don't know why you're calling about

this, and I don't know what you expect to get, but you aren't getting it from me."

The only way to settle herself down was to settle into the case they'd been investigating for six months. In that time Marissa had learned that building a case is telling a story. Once again, the team had to prove themselves. It fell to Marissa to sell it here, now or perhaps never.

She took a breath and started slowly. She laid out their discoveries methodically. She detailed a bit of their process. He asked a few questions here and there, and she kept going. By the time she finished, thirty minutes had somehow flown by.

"Okay," he said. His manner was blunt and also weirdly energetic. As with Detective Fonseca, he spoke and operated like no one inside Marissa's world. "My specialty here in Major Crimes is circumstantial murder cases, cold cases, okay? So the fact that you don't have any hard evidence whatsoever doesn't scare me. I need to speak with Raymond Fonseca to get his read on this and on you. Now, I am going to call you back. I'm not a bullshitter. When I say I'll call you back, I will call you back."

That was it. He ended the call. Marissa pulled her phone away from her ear and looked at the screen. *What the fuck just happened?*

However many dozens of phone calls Marissa had made since she started looking into the Watkins case, this was the first one she had done without at least googling the person ahead of time. She looked up Walt Kramer now and learned that the Major Crimes Unit he worked in handled the most prestigious assignments in the Los Angeles County District Attorney's Office—headline-grabbing cases, such as the Michael Jackson investigation, the Nipsey Hussle murder, the Robert Durst case. He was the real deal.

She sent these articles to the other women, excited to share news of their progress.

Marissa: I just had a long and very intense conversation with the ADA. He remembered the details of the case clearly and the suspects.

Marissa: He said basically, "If your motivation is to help, let's sit down. You have to be willing to turn over everything that you have."

Marissa: He's so intense, guys. We need to discuss what to do.

Nicole: We are either about to hit a brick wall or maybe get inside

Jeannie: Wow.

Samira: Fingers crossed 🤞

The next morning, Marissa shared with the team a screen-shot of a text she received overnight from Detective Fonseca.

Detective Fonseca: Kramer called me last night. I have to talk to the Unsolved Lieutenant from Homicide to work out logistics. When I speak to him, I will let you know and we can go from there.

Samira: Bet this is happening faster than he thought

Nicole: 💯 💯 💯

Nicole: I read the article. This guy is no joke. It's really exciting.

Nicole: Also it is IMPOSSIBLE to get work done while trying to home school an uninterested kindergartner.

Marissa didn't have to wait long for a reply. ADA Kramer called her later that same morning. "Why are you giving this retired detective such a hard time?" he said. "It was a big investigation, confusing financials, and he was working a full caseload."

"We never meant to do that," explained Marissa. "We just desperately wanted to move this case forward."

"Well," said ADA Kramer, "in that, you've succeeded."

Marissa: Just talked to him. We gotta talk ASAP. Shit is getting real.

Marissa: He's reopening the case and assigning a new detective

NEW LIFE

The next day everything changed.

The ADA called Marissa twice more. He was bombastic, fired up, but also warned her and her colleagues to be extremely careful not to say anything that would jeopardize the case. He implored them to proceed with caution at all times. "Remember, you're dealing with murderers. Be wary."

He was most interested in the financial aspect of their investigation and the behavior of the son and son-in-law leading up to the disappearance. What could have motivated them to kill? He said he was working on getting a homicide investigator who would want to see everything they had.

A congratulatory text from retired Pasadena detective Adam Cully put all this in perspective for them. "You guys should be incredibly proud. This is huge."

They were proud. It *was* huge.

They set about organizing and repackaging their voluminous research for fresh eyes, focusing on their timeline and key witnesses. Their great worry now was about what kind of cop they were going to get. Based on everything they'd experienced, a lot was riding on this assignment.

A call to Marissa from Sheriff's Department Homicide Investigator Lee O'Farrell alleviated their concerns.

Marissa: Just had a GREAT conversation with Detective O'Farrell. He is very eager to chat with us. Also, he's much more open

Marissa: Said brake lights were not activated and evidence
points to it being very likely that the bodies were in the
back of the car

Samira: I knew it! Angela was in fetal position!!!

Nicole: You've said this the whole time!!!

The team made plans to meet in person, outdoors, at the LASD Homicide Bureau in Monterey Park in the coming weeks. In the meantime, while working on their presentation to Detective O'Farrell, Samira had discovered something in the Wattkins LED financials. In reviewing images of several Wattkins LED company checks drawn on the Pacific Heritage Bank & Trust account, she noticed that one of the signatures looked completely different from all other Joel Watkins signatures—the letters stilted and slanting in the opposite direction. She compared the handwriting to Andrew's signature from the family estate probate documents, and both form and angle were identical.

Marissa: You just tied him to the fraud, Sam!!!

Jeannie: They are going to be throwing darts at photos of
us in their jail cells.

Samira: Don't mess with citizen detectives!

Nicole: GO SAMIRA!!!!

Andrew Watkins might not have had the authority to sign any financial documents, but that hadn't stopped him from forging his father's signature.

As October turned into November, a post-Halloween surge in Covid infections led to another modified lockdown. Their options were to wait until this new wave passed before meeting with Detective O'Farrell or do it over the dreaded Zoom. The meeting became virtual. The team did a review and rehearsal ahead of time. Their master presentation was divided into sections titled "High-Level Characters and Motive," "General Narrative," and "Overarching Assumptions." It was satisfying to utilize their professional skills on a pitch that was literally about life and death.

Detective Lee O'Farrell did not disappoint. He was in his midfifties, baggy-eyed, completely bald, with a graying brush mustache trimmed tight and rimless eyeglasses hooked over long ears. He was engaging from the start, speaking to them from a seat at his dining room table amid dishes and silverware already set out for Thanksgiving dinner.

The team had shared documents with him ahead of time to make the financials easier to follow. As to motive, they explained that Greg's debt exposure was overwhelming. He and his wife, Marie, had tax lien judgments against them totaling close to $400,000. In addition to unresolved lawsuits, Greg's total debt topped $600,000 at the time of his in-laws' disappearance. He had submitted over $80,000 in fraudulent invoices through four separate companies to Wattkins LED, with Andrew Watkins involved in three of the companies. Greg also solicited another business partner of his into acting as a dummy out-of-state company to process another fraudulent invoice. Then there was Greg's $100,000 repayment request to grandfather-in-law Terry, followed by a call to Terry from Andrew saying that Greg would go to jail if he didn't get the money—which Terry never gave him.

They also learned some things. O'Farrell casually tossed out bits of information over the course of the conversation that they grabbed at like diamonds. It was amazing. He mentioned that, while the pathologist had not been able to conclusively determine cause of death, it did *not* appear that Joel's and Angela's necks had been broken. He spent time taking them through the condition of the Watkinses' Explorer. Running the engine, putting the car in Drive, and pushing it over the edge would have resulted in a crash that looked most like an accident. Shifting the vehicle into Neutral and rolling it off the road would have looked most like murder. But leaving the gearshift selector in Park with the engine turned off? That was a neither/nor. The transfer case, however, was in Neutral. He explained that this was an intermediate gear box that transfers power from the transmission to the axles of all-wheel-drive and four-wheel-drive vehicles, one reason such vehicles are ideal for towing. In fact, the California Highway Patrol accident reconstruction theorized that the Watkinses' Explorer could have been towed to the Angeles Crest Highway. The question was—why? Why not simply drive it there? And what of Angela's Mercedes with its flat tire just two days after getting serviced?

At one point during a discussion about Joel Watkins's actions leading up to the disappearance, O'Farrell slid a thick binder into camera view, flipping to a page for reference. The team realized they were looking at the murder book—the case file of the Watkins investigation—right there on this man's dining room table. All the information, all the secrets! Jeannie wanted to reach in through her screen somehow. Marissa actually caught herself leaning over her laptop, as though she might be able to see more of the thick book by looking down.

O'Farrell read them a passage from an interview with the bartender at the Keg and Cask near Joel's office in Pasadena. The bartender recounted that Joel would regularly come in three to four times a week, order two double shots—four ounces—of tequila around noon, then return in the early evening for two more double shots. Never food. This matched the credit card charges on the bills Carrie had shared with the team. The bartender also reported that on the Wednesday before his disappearance, Joel drank more than two doubles, becoming so intoxicated that the bartender took his car keys and had an employee drive Joel home. The following night, Joel returned to collect his keys, drank his two double shots of tequila as usual, then settled up and left at seven-thirty. That was the last time the bartender ever saw Joel Watkins.

Marissa related the story from the neighbor across the street who was walking her puppy when she saw someone vacuuming at two A.M. the weekend of the disappearance/murder. She inquired about the vacuum cleaner Carrie had found lying on its side on the floor in the dining room. Had the vacuum cleaner been kept as evidence? Had the contents of its bag been examined or preserved?

The team watched wide-eyed as he flipped through the magic book of answers, running his finger down what must have been an inventory of items booked into evidence.

"No," he said. "No vacuum cleaner, no vacuum cleaner bag."

A gut punch. The contents could have yielded trace evidence or even hair for DNA testing. Another devastating law enforcement oversight.

Tantalizingly, O'Farrell referenced video evidence. He had a forty-five-minute recording of Fonseca's interview with the family at the sheriff's station during which Andrew had refused to take a lie detector test. Also recordings of the interrogations of Andrew Watkins, Greg Medina, and Bonnie Salazar, among others. Security camera footage from multiple locations within Joel's office building. Videotaped search warrant executions of Andrew's house and Greg's office.

Could they see this evidence? O'Farrell didn't say no. "Let's do this one step at a time."

They could tell he remained skeptical about solving the case after so many years, but that was okay. After everything they had gone through to get to this point, they were under no illusion that every piece of material they sought would be immediately provided. Talking and sharing, comparing notes—this was a win.

It had been stunning to get actual answers to their questions about the case—even surreal. They became obsessed with getting their hands on that murder book. They soaked up every bit of oral intel O'Farrell had shared, but craved documentation. They converted their notes and updated existing timelines and narratives. Furthermore, he referred to them as "ladies," not "gals." An upgrade right there.

"This is happening," said Nicole on their follow-up Zoom.

They felt cheered. This arrangement was good for both sides. They were getting access, and O'Farrell was getting four dogged sleuths determined to solve his case for him.

Several shorter Zoom sessions with O'Farrell followed over the next few days. They felt his comfort level with them growing. If anything, they offered him too much detailed information when asked. They continued to pick up previously unknown facts in the process—some helpful, some disappointing.

Incredibly, despite the expense of airlifting the Watkinses' wrecked Ford Explorer out of the Angeles National Forest, the vehicle had since been destroyed. This seemed inconceivable to the team, but O'Farrell explained, "Saving every vehicle from every criminal case would mean maintaining parking garages the size of those at LAX. We did retain evidence samples taken from the vehicle, such as hair and blood from the edge of the shattered sunroof."

"Were those samples tested for DNA and such?" asked Nicole.

The answer was no. Again, this floored the team. "Never submitted or processed," O'Farrell said, leafing through the pages.

Something else to add to their to-do list.

"Joel's wallet and Angela's purse were never recovered," he told them.

"Wow," said Jeannie. "Nowhere at the crash site or at the house?"

"Missing in action," O'Farrell confirmed. "Though a few items recovered from the wreck site—a Blockbuster Video rental store membership card, for example—could have come from a wallet, or just as easily from the glove box."

Samira wanted to be clear. "No identification was ever recovered from either spouse?"

"Correct."

This detail seemed critical. Animals wouldn't have run off with Joel's wallet or Angela's purse. The killer or killers must have disposed of them.

O'Farrell also confirmed that Joel Watkins had left his place of business alone on the Saturday of his disappearance. "He was not abducted or forcibly taken from his office," he said. "The clothes he wore to work that day were recovered from the washing machine in the home, unwashed, with dirt on the jeans."

"From gardening," deduced Marissa. "So he had come home and worked in the yard."

"And Angela was a neat freak," said Nicole. "Where was the washer and dryer?"

O'Farrell checked a diagram of the home's interior. "Mudroom entranceway from the garage."

"She had him put his dirty yard clothes directly into the washer rather than let him track dirt into the house," said Nicole with certainty. She added, "Maybe I should do that with my kids."

This revelation tightened up their timeline considerably. No neighbors recalled seeing Joel or Angela working in their yard the next day, which confirmed what the team thought they knew—that the disappearance/murder occurred sometime between Saturday afternoon and early Sunday morning. The scream was heard by the neighbor around two A.M. This narrowed the window of time down to roughly twelve hours.

After the November Covid surge receded following the Thanksgiving school break, O'Farrell proposed an in-person meeting at a public park not far from his home, offering to share with them more insights into the case. He arrived that morning looking slimmer than his Zoom box had indicated. He walked with a slight limp, telling them that since Covid had struck, he'd committed to walking three miles every day. "I've dropped seventeen pounds," he said proudly.

He led them back to his car, an unmarked black Chevrolet Caprice parked near the entrance. "I want to show you something," he said, popping open the trunk with his key fob.

Inside sat seven banker's boxes with LASD markings and chain-of-custody stickers on the lids and sides. The boxes were labeled WATKINS #1, WATKINS #2, and on up through WATKINS #7.

"Oh my God," said Jeannie.

It was all right there. They were completely unprepared for this emotionally. What they had hoped might happen at their first meeting with Fonseca was happening at their first meeting with O'Farrell.

"I've got about an hour, maybe a little more," said O'Farrell, enjoying their shocked reactions. "Why don't you give me a hand with these?"

The cartons were heavy, but the women's adrenaline allowed them to rush them to the nearest picnic tables. O'Farrell hovered nearby as the women paired off at opposite ends, removing the lids, revealing a trove of file folders and sheaves of paper bound by black binder clips.

This wasn't the murder book. This was better. This was all the raw case data that had been distilled into the murder book.

Witness statements. Search warrant applications. The CHP MAIT vehicle reports. Detective Cully's original missing persons report. Raymond Fonseca's own handwritten notes in small wire-bound notebooks. Telephone records for Joel, Angela, Andrew, Greg, others.

After months of subsistence eating—a Thanksgiving feast. There was no time to waste, no time to get organized and methodical. They brought out their cellphones and began laying out documents on the picnic table, snapping picture after picture.

Joel's and Angela's unredacted autopsy reports were in there, photographs included. Jeannie refused to look at them, but the others forced themselves to. The images were, of course, hideous, and Angela's corpse curled up in the fetal position was something that could never be unseen. Adding to the strangeness of the moment was the presence of children racing around nearby, laughing and calling out to one another through their masks.

As O'Farrell watched, the women pored through documents, often calling out a particularly exciting find.

"I have Dennis Ladd's interview with Fonseca!" said Jeannie, holding up one of the spiral notebooks.

Samira waved a stapled sheaf of pages. "Andrew's phone records!"

Marissa called back, "I have Greg's!"

The California Highway Patrol MAIT report that Captain Tirping had spoken of listed an inventory of everything found in and around the Watkinses' Explorer. Nicole found much of it routine as she ran her finger down the items: Pep Boys store receipts, Joel's Costco membership card, reference cards for the cellphones.

Then she stopped.

"Guys!" said Nicole. "The Mexican connection in the car?" She read it out loud. "*One guidebook 'MAZATLÁN BY NIGHT: Adult Action Guide.'*"

"Oh, Joel," sighed Samira. "Thirty-eight years of marriage. And Amos and Hugh—we knew they were liars, but wow."

"He kept that in his car?" said Jeannie. "Isn't that insanely brazen? Clearly, Angela never drove or rode in it."

Nicole read aloud another entry. "*One black/dark gray polyester and suede-leather glove, right-hand, size Men's Large.*"

Jeannie said, "Add O. J. Simpson to the suspect list."

"Wait—what the hell? *One Blockbuster Video laminated membership card located at incident scene near victim vehicle. Front side of card contains red residue resembling blood.*"

"Blood?" said Marissa. "Are you kidding me?"

Jeannie added, "I've got the evidence list here. I do not see any glove on it."

Samira was flipping through the phone records. "Okay, so, that first Monday back when Joel didn't show up for work? Andrew called Joel's cellphone several times, called Carrie in the afternoon, called his grandfather Terry—but not Angela at home to see if she's okay?"

"Super sketch," said Nicole.

Jeannie said, "Not calling his mother is so fishy!"

"Even murderers should call their mothers!" agreed Nicole.

"How about this," said Marissa. "From Dennis Ladd's police interview, a direct quote from Joel via phone that last Saturday morning, 'Angela and I are probably going to jail.'"

"Wow!" exclaimed Jeannie. "Check this out. Detective Cully's missing persons report. *On 6-2-05, I received an anonymous call from a person who worked at Union Bank of California. The caller told me that on May 27th, at approximately 1520 hours, Joel and Angela Watkins came into the bank and cashed two checks that totaled $27,557.57. Caller related that the checks were out of a mutual fund in Angela Watkins's name, payable to Angela Watkins. Caller stated the Watkinses both acted natural and did not seem under any sort of duress.* Friday afternoon before the disappearance—cashing out mutual funds?"

Samira said, "She was trying to pull money together. To stay afloat or pay somebody back."

Jeannie echoed, "'Both acted natural'? Of course they did. Always keeping up appearances."

"If I remember correctly," said Marissa, "they had like sixteen grand in their bank account. And another fourteen in the hallway drawer. So much cash flying around."

"Ha," continued Jeannie. "Someone who called in a tip. A woman was one hundred percent certain she saw Joel and Angela at the Pasadena Taco Bell on the Wednesday after they went missing, ordering breakfast."

Marissa said, "If they hadn't already been dead, that Taco Bell breakfast would have killed them."

"No!" cried Jeannie. "Ben Dealer again! He called Pasadena PD ten days after the disappearance."

"What?" asked Samira. "Read it."

"Cully interviewed him at his office. *Dealer stated that they had a tolerable relationship, but Watkins had cost him a lot of money when they were partners due to Watkins's drinking and poor business choices. Dealer related that on one occasion a female showed up at the office and claimed Joel Watkins had hired her from the bar where she worked. The female had a napkin with Watkins having written on it that she would have a starting salary of $50,000 a year, signed by Joel Watkins.* Oh my God. *Dealer related that they ended up having to pay the female one year's salary to terminate the agreement.* A cocktail napkin contract."

"Oh, Joel," sighed Samira yet again.

"Jesus," said Jeannie, continuing. "*On another occasion, Dealer walked in Watkins's office to find Joel Watkins having sexual intercourse with a female on Watkins's desk.*"

"Could be an HR issue there," Samira added dryly.

"Remember, though," Nicole cautioned, "Ben Dealer is a lying lunatic."

"Yes, but this: *Dealer said that on 5-18-05, Joel Watkins came in his office*—nine days before the disappearance, sworn enemies—*and told him he needed to ask a favor. Dealer stated*

Joel Watkins seemed as if he had very low energy and had lost weight. Here it is. *Watkins told Dealer he was having trouble with his 'factoring company'*—that would be the bank?—*and making collections on his invoices. Watkins asked Dealer if he could invoice to Dealer, Dealer pay Watkins the sum of the invoice, and Dealer collect from the bank. Dealer was not sure if what Watkins was asking him to do was above board and Watkins assured him it was.* Right, sure. *Dealer says he contacted Dennis Ladd about this, but never agreed to do it. Dealer provided me with copies of invoices he has received from the bank where Joel Watkins had alleged that Wattkins LED had provided services in the amount of $19,890.00.*"

"Always twenty grand," said Marissa, "every single time."

Samira added, "If Joel went to Dealer asking for help, he was truly desperate."

"Good old Herschel Wensinck," said Marissa. "This is the day after the bodies were found. *Wensinck told me he had heard the report on the news about the Watkinses being found at the bottom of Angeles Crest Highway. He stated the news surprised him because at the beginning of the missing persons investigation Wensinck was talking with his employer Greg Medina, at which time Medina told Wensinck, 'maybe his in-laws drove off a cliff.'*"

After their time was up, the team returned the cartons to O'Farrell's car, thanking him profusely. They celebrated with tacos afterward, reconvening on the sidewalk outside the Mexican restaurant, processing everything they had seen. The speed at which they had devoured the evidence was dizzying. Nicole reported that her phone said she had taken a total of 293 photographs.

They thumbed through their findings, AirDropping images to share. One item that chilled them was Joel's final email, sent from his office at 10:20 A.M. on Saturday, May 28. The subject line read "RE: Monday Meeting," following an exchange with his bank representative that had originated early the day before.

FROM: joel
SENT: Friday, May 27, 2005 7:08 A.M.

I have a meeting with a company this morning and another one this afternoon. I expect to finalize deal today with one of them that wants to buy into the company, which would provide Wattkins LED with strong financial assistance moving forward. If I get back in time today I'll give you a call otherwise I'll call you on Monday to discuss all. I will have Bonnie go over all the items in question regarding clients not receiving our invoices.

Thanks and have a good day.

SENT: Friday, May 27, 2005 10:48 A.M.
TO: joel
SUBJECT: RE: Monday Meeting

I'd like to meet with you on Monday at your office to discuss this, go over the aging report and the banking relationship. What time is good for you?

SENT: Saturday, May 28, 2005 10:20 A.M.
FROM: joel
SUBJECT: RE: Monday Meeting

Had a very productive day yesterday and it looks like we're going to be wrapping something up by mid-week. Monday is good, anytime after 1:00p. See you then.

This final email was not at all truthful—but was it a lie or a wish? Ten minutes later, after speaking by cellphone with Greg, Joel had called Dennis Ladd and told him, "I'm in trouble. Angela and I are probably going to jail." Dennis reassured him that they would figure something out and they set plans to meet for lunch on Monday, ahead of the bank meeting. So perhaps Joel still had hope that things would work out.

But had Joel also said something like *Angela and I are probably going to jail* to Greg on their call? Did Greg realize that he and Andrew would be implicated too? Was that what pushed them over the edge—figuratively over the edge for Greg and Andrew, literally over the edge for Joel and Angela?

Something else from the phone records jumped out at Samira. Andrew made zero cellphone calls in the two weeks leading up to and including his parents' disappearance. None. After placing a call at 6:53 P.M. on May 16, his cellphone was turned off and unable to receive any calls. He did not use it again until May 30, the Monday following his parents' disappearance. That timing was extraordinarily suspect, but what did it indicate?

Additionally, before powering down his phone for two weeks, Andrew had received numerous phone calls from a number beginning with 999. The team learned that this was an exchange associated with telemarketers, but also with international calling cards. One of these calls lasted more than six minutes, a long time to be telling a telemarketer "No, thanks." The phone report listed only numbers, however, no names. Upon further examination, Samira realized that these were not in fact telephone company records but merely telephone company bills. They needed to know who Andrew had been talking to. This was something to follow up on with O'Farrell.

One question that had lingered since the very beginning of their investigation—*How was the Sheriff's Department so*

certain this was a double homicide and not a traffic accident?—
had now been answered. The Explorer's transmission was set in
Park. The ignition switch was in the Off position. There were no
keys in the ignition or recovered nearby. The emergency brake
was engaged. The airbags did not deploy. The transfer case was
in Neutral. All damage noted, including the braking system
components, was, according to the CHP MAIT report, the apparent result of collisions as the vehicle made its descent in free-
fall. The front seats had been electronically moved all the way
forward prior to impact, indicated by the floor rails being intact
and undamaged. At that positioning, it would have been impossible for a man of Joel's size or even a woman of Angela's size to
sit up front. The lack of stretching of the webbing material of
the seatbelts indicated that neither the driver's nor the passenger's restraints had been in use at the time of the crash. The
front and rear seats had been bent forward as though struck by a
heavy, unrestrained object. "Based upon the facts surrounding
this collision, it is believed that one occupant of the vehicle was
unrestrained in the rear seat and the other occupant was unrestrained in the rear cargo area."

During the vehicle's descent, one corpse had been ejected
through the sunroof and the other through the right rear cargo
window. Hair and blood had been recovered from both surfaces.

Angela's Mercedes was a notable omission in the reports.
The team had hoped for some insight into what might have
caused the flat tire. Now it appeared that they would never know.

Apparently, one police theory was that Greg had lured Joel
and Angela to his place of business that Saturday or Sunday.
Once inside, his warehouse's cement walls and lack of windows
offered ideal concealment and opportunity as a murder site.
Could an impromptu meeting at their son-in-law's office explain
the casual attire Angela and Joel had been found wearing? In any
case, a search of Greg's business premises had not turned up

anything of value. A few drop cloths had been seized as evidence after cadaver dogs picked up a scent—but these were tested at the crime lab, and nothing incriminating was found.

It was a lot. It was all so much. They had gotten what they had been craving for months, but for the moment they were more confused than ever. It was like discovering a hidden treasure and then realizing they lacked the means to carry it all away with them.

For months, the team had gone back and forth over whether Andrew or Greg was the lead perpetrator. Both had been, as the official report stated, "deceptive and uncooperative during the course of this investigation." They understood now why a grand jury had been unable to recommend pressing charges. There was no physical evidence linking Andrew or Greg to Joel's and Angela's murders.

O'Farrell followed up with them on their phone records request, and it was another disaster. Yes, all cell records, call detail, and cellular tower location records had been received and examined by an LASD Homicide crime analyst in 2005 and 2006 for any pertinent tower location data—specifically for any evidentiary information regarding Andrew Watkins and Greg Medina. No incriminating evidence had been found. Additionally, Joel's cellphones—the ones the team now had in their possession—had also been analyzed, and nothing was found that impacted the case. Accordingly, no reports had been generated.

The data had been stored in a digital ShareFile in 2006. In 2011, when the case was "booked up" and all material placed into banker's boxes for storage, the digital files were burned onto five DVDs labeled "Digital CD Evidence." Those disks were included in the case material the women had reviewed. Disk #5, the one that should have contained the raw cellphone data, was blank. The disk burn had failed for some reason, and the copy process was never double-checked. That raw information—names of callers, geographic phone locations—was lost forever.

A few days later, after a bit of haggling over logistics and chain-of-custody issues, Detective O'Farrell swung by Marissa's house with a hard drive containing most of the video files in evidence. These huge digital files included the family meeting with Detective Fonseca at the sheriff's station and a three-hour interview with Greg Medina. O'Farrell insisted that the files remain on the device and would not allow them to be uploaded onto the team's Google drive. The team could only view these files in the detective's presence.

O'Farrell had something else for her. It was a low-capacity USB-A memory stick with a wire evidence tag affixed to the end loop, labeled with the case number and the words "Joel Watkins" and "Optimus recorder." She remembered something from the crash site inventory list: *One Radio Shack Optimus digital recorder; plastic case, gray and black in color, worn-weathered, functionality not determined, contents not checked; battery compartment opened and two AA batteries removed to prevent damage from alkaline battery corrosion; located at incident scene near victim remains on "fall line" approx. 30–40 ft above victims.*

The handheld digital recorder's memory contained a WAV audio file thirty-six minutes and forty seconds in length. This O'Farrell allowed her to copy, but first he insisted that she put on headphones and listen to it right then.

The recording began with a quick succession of short clips of what sounded like a car radio, interspersed with a series of beeps. She realized that the device was being started and stopped, as though by someone testing its controls and capability. Suddenly, at thirty-three seconds in, amid background noise that could have been highway traffic or distant ocean waves, a woman's breathy voice was clearly heard.

"Joel Watkins, um, recording here at the hotel . . . Um, you're registering, I'm sitting in the car . . . I thought I almost lost my ring . . . Sick to my stomach . . . Found it under the car, hallelujah . . . I'm sitting out here looking at my beautiful stone while you're in registering . . . Adios amigo . . ."

Jaw-dropper. The unknown woman narrating pleasantly, flirtatiously, with a very slight Mexican accent, sounded young, though that may just have been her playful tone. Marissa went back and listened again. She deduced that the woman had become bored waiting for Joel to check in to their hotel, and while playing with a ring Joel had evidently given her—a ring with a stone—she had dropped it, then found it. The young woman then discovered the voice recorder in his glove compartment and decided to leave him a little message.

That short snippet proved to be the clearest audio segment on the entire recording. After another minute or so of beeps and distortion and car radio noise, there was a brief, muffled exchange between Joel Watkins and *"Dennis"*—who must have been Joel's friend Dennis Ladd—which seemed to involve some sort of private joke between them. They sounded as if they had been drinking, mentioning something to do with a *"key word for 1998,"* indicating that the early part of the recording went back to the boom times for Joel.

There followed a stretch of many minutes when the recorder was in a crowded location, perhaps a bar, before exiting—then footsteps, someone entering a car, the engine starting, and driving away. Marissa reasoned this part of the recording had been made by accident.

At about the nine-minute mark, she made out a car radio playing with a commercial mentioning *"2004 family films."*

Then came a series of heavily distorted, one-sided conversations of Joel driving and apparently talking on a cellphone that was not hands-free. It was clear the conversations were about money. *"Hey, it's me. Yeah, um, I just left the office. Yeah, can you hear me? Okay, I left the office to pick up the check. Yeah, we have to meet up tomorrow. Yes, given him twelve thousand, roughly."*

At the fourteen-minute, forty-two-second mark, a long conversation began, much of it inaudible until about two minutes in. *"Okay, but, but, Greg, Greg, I need your help as quick as possible. I really, I really do. I'm just desperate."* Greg's voice responded inaudibly. Joel's car windows must have been open. Marissa strained to listen. *"Okay, please do. Right, right. He probably has* [inaudible] . . . *I'm at a point where they're just really putting the squeeze on me at the bank. I'm doing something criminal. That's the problem."*

Marissa's mind raced. It was incredible hearing Joel Watkins's voice. In her imagination, Joel was a figure of great mystery, so hearing him speak humanized him. That said, here was Joel not only discussing his financial trouble with his son-in-law on a recording, but also apparently referring to, and confessing to, the fraud.

"Yeah, no one's giving me [inaudible]. *But you know, we don't have enough* [inaudible] *over ninety days. And they want to know the exposure. Yeah. This bank, you know. Anyway, so I, like, really need your help, Greg. I really do."* Greg responded inaudibly. *"Okay, talk tomorrow. Thanks, bye."*

She could not believe this recording existed, never mind had survived a car wreck, followed by fifteen years of cold storage. Why had Joel recorded these conversations? For his own security? He was asking Greg for help. He said he was desperate. He sounded scared.

There was one more one-sided conversation with Greg at the twenty-two-minute mark. The recording started in midcall. *"All* right, Greg, I've already left the office. You want to meet in L.A. somewhere or do it here?" Greg responded inaudibly. "Well, I'll be in tomorrow, but what do you mean [inaudible]." The conversation continued for another ninety seconds, comprising one- and two-word answers from Joel. "Right." "Okay." "All right." "Well, obviously." "That will be fine." It ended with Joel saying, "Oh, shoot," as though the call had been disconnected.

Then another unproductive conversation and more radio noise. The team knew Joel to have been a gadget guy and an early adopter of electronics back in his solvent days, so his owning and playing with a voice recorder made sense. The time jump from 1998 to 2004 indicated that he had merely been experimenting with the device. At the nine-minute mark was when he started recording his conversations.

She uploaded the audio file for the others. When they caught up later, none of them could believe it. They had to know what Greg was saying on the other end. It could sort out the entire case. This being Los Angeles, each of the women knew someone related to the music business, and they reached out to their contacts for help enhancing the audio. This eventually produced four different versions, each with improved quality and reduced background noise—but Greg's side of the conversation remained inaudible and unrecoverable.

Joel did not sound threatened on the recording. Perhaps Greg was withholding help? Help in the form of money? Notably, as far as any of them could tell, there were no recorded conversations between Joel and Andrew.

The young woman's recording at the beginning was by turns haunting and distasteful. The fact that Joel had apparently kept this device in his glove compartment with the guidebook of "adult action" was difficult to understand. This wasn't something he'd toss into his car at the airport upon returning from Mexico—or was it? Had he no concern that Angela might stumble upon these irrefutable documentations of his infidelity? Samira had been right all along. There were two sides to Joel: the loving, doting husband and generous, well-regarded employer, and the persistent philanderer and embezzler–slash–money launderer.

Each of the women reviewed the confidential police video recordings in O'Farrell's presence over the next several days. Nicole came over and watched them on a monitor in Marissa's converted garage, where she had taped to the wall a long piece of Kraft paper containing their evolving timeline.

For the family meeting at the sheriff's station, the camera view was high in a wall at the deep end of a conference room looking down and out over a long table to the far wall and a door. Andrew Watkins sat closest to the camera; other than when he entered the room to take his seat, only the back of his head and shoulders were visible. Carrie and Henry sat farther away in profile on the left side, Greg and Marie even farther away on the right, near the far wall. Raymond Fonseca held court from the head of the table at the center of the fixed image.

This scene had already been described to them by Carrie, but watching it unfold was gripping. Greg appeared oddly relaxed and made a few strange statements. At one point, he suggested that Angela had complained of being stalked in the weeks before the disappearance. At another, he asked, "Don't you think it's weird that all of Angela's lingerie was missing?"

Fonseca seemed surprised. "I didn't know that," he answered flatly.

"There was some in her bathroom sink, but the rest was gone."

A bizarre thing for any son-in-law to say.

Andrew sought to control the conversation, asking question after question, at times challenging Fonseca's assertions. The team felt renewed respect for Fonseca in the way he handled Andrew. They were under the impression that Fonseca had summoned the Watkins siblings to the sheriff's station, but in fact it was Andrew who had requested the meeting. Perhaps Andrew, and maybe Greg, wanted to glean some information about how the Sheriff's Department's investigation was going. The search warrants for Andrew's and Greg's homes, computers, telephones, and places of business would not go out until the coming weeks.

Andrew Watkins's refusal to take a lie detector test was jarring. He didn't want his siblings to take a polygraph either. During Greg's marathon three-hour interrogation, he vacillated between weeping, pleading, acting defensive, and professing his love for his in-laws. At one critical juncture, Fonseca confronted Greg regarding his 1:30 A.M. Monday phone call to Joel. Fonseca told him that that call never took place, according to the phone records, and furthermore that Greg surely knew Joel was in bed every night no later than ten. He bluntly accused Greg of trying to establish a timeline for an alibi, but Greg stuck to his guns, insisting he had tried Joel's personal cellphone at that improbable hour.

What did appear true, however, was that Joel had been closer to his son-in-law, Greg, than to his own son. Greg played off his eleven conversations in one day with his father-in-law like it was no big deal, while claiming he could not recall what they had discussed.

Likewise, Marie, Joel and Angela's daughter, had been Angela's closest contact, but she said little at the family meeting and showed almost no emotion. The polygraph tests she failed had not been videotaped, nor were any transcripts of her questioning, if they existed, among the case evidence. Fonseca had once referred to Marie as a "nervous squirrel" in conversation with Marissa, so perhaps that explained it. Nicole was certain that she herself would fail a lie detector test even if she was one hundred percent innocent. Or perhaps Marie had good reason to be nervous.

Coincidentally, around this time in early December, Marie reached out to her sister Carrie regarding an impending scheduled cash distribution from their grandfather Terry's trust. Marie had hired a financial consultant since her split with Greg, and the consultant had a few questions she was unable to answer. Carrie shared a screenshot of her sister's text with the team, who all agreed this represented a prime opportunity for Carrie to try to squeeze some information out of her older sister, if she was willing—and Carrie was. The women wondered whether, now free from Greg's grasp, Marie might be more willing to talk about what she knew. Maybe they could even get her to flip on her soon-to-be-ex-husband.

Carrie replied to Marie, setting a time and place to meet for coffee. Recording someone without their knowledge is illegal in the state of California—not that the team didn't consider it. Carrie promised to give them a complete download afterward. The women waited anxiously.

Marissa: No word from Carrie yet

Samira: Pins and needles

Jeannie: Let's hope Marie doesn't try to poison her with an arsenic-laced 🧁

Carrie reported back that her sister remained convinced that their parents died by suicide. When Carrie pointed to evidence that the car had been in Park and the airbags did not deploy, Marie said, "Well, maybe they jumped off the edge after it." Carrie felt almost as if Marie were trying to convince her. When asked if she knew that Greg and Andrew had been implicated in their father's financial fraud, Marie answered that she couldn't see either one of them murdering their parents. As a non sequitur, the reply was startling, but what had shocked Carrie—and shocked her anew as she retold it—was that Marie did not ask any follow-up questions about their participation in the fraud, nor did she deny it.

Marie claimed not to remember where she had been on the weekend their parents disappeared, which the women found completely unbelievable. They knew where Marie had been that weekend, or at least where Greg had claimed she had been: after a two o'clock movie matinee, they had returned home and remained there all night. However, Greg's cellphone record showed a call placed to Marie's cellphone at 8:30 P.M. Was he claiming to have called his wife from inside his own house? It made absolutely no sense.

Marie said she was still angry with the Sheriff's Department for "treating their family so cruelly." About her failed polygraph tests, Marie said the police were "harsh" with her afterward despite her having been "totally honest." She suspected the Sheriff's Department lied about her failing the lie detector test in an attempt to trick her into confessing something that wasn't true.

She did speak about a message she had received from the grave. Marie planted orange blossoms in her backyard because they were her mother's favorite flower, and one day Marie consulted a medium who told her that "someone was holding orange blossoms and saying, 'I'm sorry.' "

But it was the women who were sorry—sorry for putting Carrie up to this task. Marie sounded like a true flake.

> Marissa: The fact that she is attached to these fantasies while dismissive of hard facts is WEIRD.

> Samira: Still doesn't explain why your best friend who is also your mother would disappear with no note, no cryptic "goodbye" call, no nothing?

Jeannie: She really couldn't be any more different than Carrie.

Samira: She's starting to be a suspect to me again

Carrie gave her sister Detective O'Farrell's contact information. Marie said she would contact him but never did, and when O'Farrell reached out to her, Marie did not return his call. A few days later, Carrie forwarded the team a text from Marie: "Carrie, I would love nothing more than to help this get resolved and help you heal your pain. I have dealt with the same pain, being so deeply wounded, and it had consumed my life for so many years. I am very sorry that you are still there. But I have closed the door to that part of my life, moved on, found closure and some peace. I do not wish to further engage in this investigation and open back up such a horrendously painful part of my life. I wish for you the same. Please respect my wishes. I sincerely hope we can continue a cordial relationship."

A lot of woo-woo words from her older sister saying no.

Marie had also promised to pass along Detective O'Farrell's number to Greg—and, surprisingly, she did so. Even more surprisingly, Greg reached out to O'Farrell. "He said he wants to help," O'Farrell reported. "He's okay with talking to me but claims to know nothing about any of the fraud or Joel's business dealings at the time. He seemed very curious when I said I want to go over some additional clarification and transcripts from a voice recorder Joel had been found with."

The women were stunned that Greg agreed to cooperate. Was he hoping to learn something about the renewed interest in the case? They wished they knew the location of the meeting so that they could stake it out. Marissa especially wanted to eyeball Greg to see if his manner matched that of the prowler captured on her home surveillance cameras. Once again, the women waited anxiously for a postmortem report on an interview with a major suspect. They thought for certain that Greg would back out.

O'Farrell called later and the team conferenced in everyone. "We sat and talked for twenty, thirty minutes," he said. "He downplayed his role in the factoring fraud, though he did acknowledge it was occurring. He said Joel took advantage of him."

"Of course," said Jeannie. "Greg is the true victim here."

"He said he leans toward suicide as the cause of death, due to Joel's and Angela's depression and Joel's desperation for money at the end. I reminded him of the condition the vehicle was found in, the undeployed airbags, and he admitted that didn't add up. The only alternate theory he offered was that someone at the bank might have been complicit in the fraud."

"He's trying to shift the blame to the bank manager?" said Samira. "I think that reflects more of how Greg thinks than any sort of reality."

"He didn't give me much," said O'Farrell. "I showed him the transcript of the voice recording of Joel talking to him, but he claimed to have no recollection of his side of the conversation. Bottom line? The man wasn't nervous at all. I detected no potential guilt giveaways, verbal or nonverbal. He did not bite at shifting blame and demonstrated a desire to cooperate."

Another letdown. The team were reluctant to accept O'Farrell's verdict on Greg, the man they had been chasing for so long.

Jeannie: I think Greg's secret weapon is that he's a sociopath who shows no fear and can lie without feeling a damn thing. But he is such a lazy, incompetent, inconsistent fuck that he leaves breadcrumbs right to his door.

Marissa: I want to sit down and talk to Greg. With a camera crew. Am I crazy?

Jeannie: Wonderfully crazy

Marissa: I actually know the answer to that question

With Covid still raging, it remained as easy as ever to reach people by email and telephone, so it was notable when a person was unavailable.

One man, Wayne Abrams, was a true anomaly. His name appeared in Fonseca's police file notes as a past business associate of Joel's. Abrams was connected to multiple businesses, some of them overseas, one of which was involved in the factoring fraud. Wayne Abrams was also in Joel's phone records, having spoken with him twenty-seven times between January and March 2005 before ceasing communication two months before the disappearance. Additionally, Samira was fairly certain that in one of the one-sided conversations on Joel's voice recorder, he addressed his caller as "Wayne"—though, owing to the poor quality of the audio recording, this could not be confirmed.

They called Abrams several times without receiving a call back. Eventually Marissa did get a call, not from Wayne Abrams, but from someone who claimed to be Abrams's business partner. Abrams was unwilling to speak with Marissa, he said, but wished to convey through the caller that "his only relationship with Joel Watkins was that he had tried to broker a deal for Wattkins LED to go public." The caller said that this would be Abrams's only comment on the matter before hanging up.

The problem was that this didn't make sense. There had been a time back in 2000 when Joel explored the idea of taking his company public, but it had never come to fruition. So why had Wayne Abrams been talking to Joel in early 2005, the year of Joel's death? And why didn't he want to explain why?

It was one loose thread among many and came at a time when the team were overloaded with input from the police files. Otherwise they might have pursued Wayne Abrams more persistently. Later they would count themselves fortunate that they hadn't.

Never satisfied, the women wanted to look at the inventoried security videos from Wattkins LED's office building, currently missing from the evidence cartons and feared lost like the phone records. They weren't anticipating a "smoking gun" revelation but hoped the CCTV footage would resolve several minor inconsistencies in their Saturday timeline. Additionally, they wished to sync up Joel's stairwell cellphone calls with their newly acquired phone records, still speculating about a third cellphone.

O'Farrell proved to be a true mensch. He was liaising between the District Attorney's Office and the Los Angeles County Sheriff's Department as a hire-back, a retiree recalled to the force on special assignment on a year-to-year basis, working full time on several cases at once, and yet he was always responsive to their requests, even if it took him a few days.

He learned that the original VHS videotapes had been turned over to LASD in 2005 and booked into the evidence system. They had since been stored inside the huge Central Property storage warehouse in Whittier. He likened the situation to the end of the movie *Raiders of the Lost Ark,* when the ark in question was crated up and tucked away deep inside a government storage facility of identical crates, lost forever.

Incredibly, he located them. In O'Farrell's presence, Brian transferred the eight-hour VHS cassettes to digital media files for Marissa. This took some time, as the files were huge and the recordings had to be chopped into pieces before uploading them to the team's central drive. The women divided up the files among them, each studying a selection in detail, taking notes on important times, and then later pooling everyone's findings.

The process was incredibly time-consuming. The surveillance tapes had run constantly, each cassette tape having been recorded over many times, so that the resulting images were ghostly and faded. Fortunately, the time stamps in the upper right corner were clear enough. They had color footage from early Friday morning, May 27, through Monday evening, May 30. There were six different camera locations around the office building: the stairwell, the lobby doors, the exterior front entrance, the first-floor elevator, the parking lot, and a rear entrance. Each woman went frame by frame through the videos in QuickTime, stopping whenever there was movement.

Nicole: My eyes hurt. Also I have yet to see one person

Marissa: SO tedious

Jeannie: This is more annoying than the phone records

Nicole: Phone records were a dream

They worked on and off as their patience and families allowed. Marissa got her first hit on day three and sent around a screenshot.

Marissa: I think this is Joel talking to Angela on Friday

She sent a screenshot of a somewhat ghostly Joel Watkins in a blue or black shirt and blue jeans standing atop a half-flight of stairs, one hand on the red or orange handrail, the other holding a flip phone to his ear. The two-lined time stamp read 05-27-05 FRI / 11:42:32.

Jeannie: Wow!!

Nicole: WOAH!!!

Samira: Okay, this just might work

They kept going. Jeannie confirmed images of Bonnie Sala-zar, a corpulent woman who wore socks with sandals. They got to know a cast of characters by sight, including Hawaiian Shirt Smoker, Coffee-Drinking Stair Climber, and Creepy White-Haired Lingering Guy in Yellow Jacket. Samira's tally grew to fifty-two pages of logged notes.

Jeannie: I have a Hawaiian Shirt Smoker that is out every 45 minutes. I'd so fire this guy if I was his boss!

Nicole: I have yet to see one person. I'm staring at a pair of doors. I keep pausing on a planting in the lower left corner thinking it is a human. My eyes are burning

Jeannie: If the plant starts talking use the safe word and we'll get you out

They discovered that Bonnie had returned to the office on Sunday, despite what she told the police in her original inter-view and later on the phone with Marissa and Samira. In his police interview, Andrew mentioned that Bonnie had come in over the weekend but was never asked why he thought that or how he knew. She remained inside the office, out of sight of any surveillance cameras, for close to an hour before leaving, but it did not appear that she brought anything in or took any-thing out.

The most important find was Joel speaking on his phone in the stairwell at 11:09:20 A.M. Saturday morning. He wore a loose gray T-shirt and blue jeans—clothes fitting the description of those found in his home washing machine, dirty from gardening, after his disappearance. But according to Joel's cellphone bill, his final call—the one when he told Dennis Ladd that he was in trouble and would probably be going to jail—occurred at 11:02 A.M. Joel was not visible on any surveillance cameras at that time, so presumably he had made that call from inside the office.

There was no record of a cellphone call at 11:09 A.M., and yet there he was on videotape, talking on a cellphone.

Marissa: I think he definitely had a third phone.

Samira: I wonder if Joel ever had a "Mexico" phone

Jeannie: Whoa. That's a thought!

The "third phone" theory looked less like theory and more like probability. Did Joel have this third phone with him when he disappeared? Could it have been in his Explorer's glove compartment along with the voice recorder and the pervy *Mazatlán by Night* adult guide? If so—where had it gone?

The third phone theory consumed them. The team had physical evidence establishing that Joel and Angela were victims of homicide. They had financial evidence establishing that Andrew Watkins and Greg Medina were culpable in the financial fraud scheme. What they did not have, and desperately needed, was physical evidence connecting Andrew or Greg to Joel's and Angela's murders.

The team already knew that many things had never been recovered. Joel's wallet. Angela's purse. The Explorer's key. Maybe also the mate of the mystery glove retrieved at the crash site. And now a potential third phone. It seemed to them that there was only one location where one or more of these critical pieces of evidence might still be.

They had previously talked about embarking upon a fact-finding mission to the crash site. It would mean hiking a hundred feet below Angeles Crest Highway to search the Explorer's final resting place, the fall line, and three hundred feet above it where Joel's and Angela's corpses had lain. Now it seemed like something they had to attempt.

"I've thought about this a little too much," said Marissa, reminded of her earlier insane impulse to hike down solo. "There's no chance of walking straight down. The only way to do it would be to climb down an access point a mile or more south of the turnout where the SUV went off the road. There will be a long trek along a stream winding north, followed by the climb up the canyonside to the site. Then, of course, back to the starting point again."

"I don't know," said Jeannie. "It's been fifteen years since the crash. At least one brush fire has burned through the site—probably more."

Nicole reminded them about the fifteen-year-old flip phones and voice recorder coming back to life. "It's a long shot, but this whole investigation is a long shot. Think about Joel's wallet lying there on the ground waiting for us to pick it up."

"We might find something we don't even know we're looking for," said Samira. "Police never fully searched the area." At the time the corpses were recovered, the ravine was considered a motor vehicle accident site, not a crime scene.

Aside from the hike being illegal, as they would be trespassing in a national forest, there was difficulty in pinpointing the exact site. The road would not be visible from the bottom of the canyon, and there were no landmarks to guide them. Paper maps and even Google Earth wouldn't be enough.

Jeannie cold-called a Southern California mapping specialist who had developed proprietary cartography software normally available only to surveyors and photogrammetrists. He sourced military-grade satellite imagery to generate photo-accurate topographical geomaps. After a long conversation in which Jeannie explained what they were attempting to do and why, the man generously agreed to do something he'd never done before in his professional career: He allowed the team unrestricted access to his software.

While mapping out their route into the ravine, Jeannie made an intriguing discovery. The high-resolution images showed, within just a few hundred meters of where the Explorer had come to rest, other abandoned cars at the bottom of the ravine.

They thought they'd geared up appropriately. Samira ordered a metal detector and bear repellent from Amazon. They packed protein bars and plenty of water. Sunscreen and bug spray. Samira's GoGirl. Phone chargers, flashlights. They dressed in layers of REI gear, wearing sunglasses, ball caps, hiking boots. On a clear, cool December day they gathered at the start point at noon, took a selfie, and at a break in the traffic, started past the No Trespassing and Closed to the Public signs down the slope of the ravine.

The hike was emblematic of their entire investigation. It started out in high spirits and with high hopes. The terrain was steep and rough, but they were game. After pushing through heavy vegetation, they would stop for a tick check, but not too long, because there were snakes about and a mountain lion had recently been spotted in the area.

Marissa and Jeannie were in the front, picking their way through dense brush, when a profound rustling startled them— loud enough to make them think it was not just an animal but a person. For the first time, Marissa wondered if transients camped in that area.

"Hello?" she called out.

No response, thankfully, though the silence was scary too. They were in an area of Los Angeles that no one ever saw, and it was vast. As they continued ahead, the sudden sound of smaller, unseen critters darting away from them through the underbrush elicited shrieks that echoed off the canyon hills above them.

They bottomed out, crossing a dry riverbed before the land started rising again. Jeannie consulted the path she'd marked on her maps, but the actual terrain was deceiving. They had a lot of wild land to cover and were already at the two-hour mark.

Marissa, back near the area she'd once explored as a young camper—one of the reasons the original news footage of the wrecked SUV had resonated so strongly with her—was confident they would find the crash site. They discovered there was no cell service in the depths of the ravine, the women's minds returning to lions and transient hill dwellers. Once again, they had gone into this thinking they had thought everything through, only to find that they hadn't.

They had made many mistakes over the course of their investigation, but this trek, as they now realized with a laugh, was perhaps the dumbest. *What have we done?* They scaled a rocky ledge, helping each other clamber over the top, trying not to get hurt. One turned ankle and they were completely screwed.

Out of the great silence, a rushing noise. They reached a stream at least fifteen yards wide, probably no more than three feet deep at the middle, but rushing past with an absurdly swift current, flowing fast around large, craggy stones and fallen trees.

"Nope," said Nicole, taking a seat on a large rock. "No way."

Jeannie agreed. "Now what?"

Marissa and Samira had come too far to let this dissuade them. They explored to the left and to the right, hoping the waterway might narrow for an easier crossing—but no luck.

Samira tested a raised stone at the water's edge, stepping to another, then a third. She reached out for the trunk of a half-fallen tree leaning across the fast-moving stream, moving from rock to rock, and suddenly she was halfway across.

"Samira, what are you doing!" yelled Nicole. As often happened when their investigation hit an obstacle, one of them did something a bit reckless that moved them ahead. Usually that person was Marissa, but not this time. Marissa followed Samira, and Nicole's and Jeannie's concern turned to laughter and cheering. "Go, Samira!"

Nicole and Jeannie let the other two go on without them. Jeannie walked to the water's edge just to watch, and her boot tread slipped off a wet rock, her knee giving way, plunging her left leg into the icy water up to the shin. "Oh, hell!" she yelled, Nicole laughing at her, Jeannie laughing at herself, unlacing her waterproof boot and pouring out frigid water.

Samira and Marissa made it to the other side, turning back with their thumbs up and smiles of accomplishment, taking bows to Nicole's and Jeannie's applause.

"Great job!" yelled Jeannie. "But now what?"

Marissa and Samira scrambled ahead together, climbing a rise through dense brush, picking through some prickly thorns, and topping out at a beautiful, wide-open meadow. A vast expanse, wildflowers everywhere. This bucolic scene called Marissa forward, whereas Samira saw only how far they had yet to go. Splitting up and leaving Jeannie and Nicole behind was a nonstarter. There was light left in the sky, but they were way behind schedule, and besides, all four women had kids to get back to.

They returned to the rapid stream, crossing back without incident. The women retraced their steps, the sun dipping behind the hill crests high above, the temperature dropping several degrees. They made it back to their cars just before dark, feeling a mix of emotions. Disappointment and exhaustion, to be sure, but also amazement at the rash but fun expedition they'd attempted.

But they didn't give up. Even before all their scratches and bugbites had healed, they resolved to try again. Jeannie remained skeptical about their chances but agreed to chart a new path in hopes of avoiding the watercourse barrier. Nicole happened to listen to a podcast interview with Ashley Flowers, the creator and host of her own megapopular podcast *Crime Junkie,* in which she spoke of bringing along a burly bodyguard for protection whenever she went knocking on doors.

Unfortunately, none of their spouses were the burly bodyguard type, but maybe they had something even better. They reached out to Detective O'Farrell, inveigling him—and his department-issued handgun—to accompany them on their second attempt to reach the crash site. He didn't seem all that eager to join them until he heard about the other car wrecks in the same vicinity where the Watkinses' Explorer had come to rest. That intrigued him.

He met the team at the same start point on State Route 2, this time at ten in the morning. They felt a lot better about descending into the ravine with an armed escort. They left the metal detector behind this time rather than taking turns lugging it. In his LASD windbreaker and bleach-stained cargo pants, O'Farrell stopped to lean against a rock or tree every twenty minutes or so, relating cop stories from his career while pretending he wasn't winded. The women found him charming in his own way, and the hike was a bonding experience. It was nice to have someone outside their own foursome with whom they could discuss the particulars of the case. The women were worried about his getting across the water with his limp, but for some reason—perhaps a dwindling of runoff from the hills—the water obstacles they encountered this time were easily stepped over.

Despite doubling back after a few wrong turns, they found the terrain easier, and they made better time than before. About thirty minutes away from the crash site, they came upon a rusted, dented oil drum with several bullet holes in its sides. The barrel was empty, but the location was no place for idle target practice.

"What do you think was in there?" asked Nicole. "Or who?"

O'Farrell looked up the slope in the direction of the unseen road high above, from where the barrel had surely been tossed. "I think we'll never know."

Several hundred yards farther on, they came upon a wrecked car, its cracked windows and busted seams threaded with years of overgrowth. O'Farrell used a Leatherman tool to cut through the weeds and snapped a picture of the vehicle's VIN from the doorframe to check later. Again they looked up the steep, tree-covered slope, the road so high above them they couldn't even hear traffic. They could only imagine what it would be like inside a car crashing and tumbling down the incline at breakneck speed.

Not far ahead was another four-door sedan, this one lying on its flattened roof, too crushed to crawl inside.

The barrel and the other vehicles gave them the sense of trespassing in a graveyard. When they finally reached the area they believed Joel and Angela were recovered from, no one felt like celebrating.

They scoured the area, using dead branches to move aside brush. Samira and Jeannie tried to climb farther up the fall line but the angle was too steep and unforgiving. They examined the ground as respectfully as they could, hoping to find the third phone, the second glove, the keys to the Explorer, anything.

They found nothing. It had been fifteen years, after all—but they had gotten lucky before, and had hoped there was a chance they might again.

The team were disheartened at having come all that way for nothing and now having to hike back empty-handed, but

O'Farrell had a different take. He told them that wasn't exactly accurate. "You did find something," he said. "You learned that their car wasn't pushed off the road at a random location. This place is a dumping ground. Whoever got rid of the Watkinses' car here had done the same thing before."

Nicole's family put up a Christmas tree during the holiday break, despite being Jewish. Any activity was a welcome activity. School vacation during lockdown provided little change of pace from everyday lockdown, except that the kids had more free time to be filled. Accordingly, work on the case stalled out into January.

There were few upsides to 2020 other than having survived it. The families knew how fortunate they were to be safe and together. Life had slowed, but the kids were growing up as fast as ever—faster, it seemed—so this enforced time-out presented opportunities for small moments of connection that might have been lost under normal circumstances. There were benefits as well as challenges to being in quarantine, but you had to look for them.

New Year's Eve arrived and they were more than ready to turn the page. Confetti fell on empty streets in New York's Times Square. The Rose Parade was canceled. Jeannie's family spent the night with friends, making a point to dress up, dancing in the living room. It didn't feel normal, but it did feel good. Marissa's girls also insisted on dressing formally, all of the families Zooming with friends and relatives and playing Among Us and offering toasts to a better year.

Nicole's family got a loaner puppy—at least that was what she told Paul. The kids had seen other friends adopt Covid pets, and Nicole thought a new addition might liven things up around the house. Paul was resistant, but having contracted Covid, he wasn't in any shape to protest. Nicole assured him that the breeder had said they could give the dog, whom they named Matzo Ball, back if it didn't work out, which wasn't true. By the time the dog began stealing Paul's spot in bed, the die had been cast. But Nicole's instincts proved correct, as not only did Matzo Ball bring more love into their lives, but he was also a tremendous study buddy for their youngest, who, having been officially diagnosed with ADHD, was now resisting taking his medication and struggling with homeschool remote learning.

At the end of a long January week of back-to-remote-school headaches, wrangling a rambunctious, not-quite-house-trained puppy, and late-night deadline work on her paying job, Nicole had dragged Paul to a Covid-responsible outdoor neighborhood gathering. Tired as she was, Nicole relished interacting with friends in person over good tequila. She noticed Paul was sticking with water, content to sit in his camp chair rather than mix, complaining that he didn't feel right. He had just recovered from Covid, so it wasn't that. Paul was a seven-mornings-a-week boot camp guy in great health. Their hosts were one of those always-prepared-for-anything kind of families. As soon as they heard Paul wasn't feeling well, they insisted he use their blood pressure monitor. Nicole and Paul laughed as he hooked himself up—his reading was perfectly normal.

That night he woke up with stinging pain in his jaw and knew something wasn't right. Google informed him that jaw pain was a potential symptom of a heart attack. Paul's father had a history of heart issues, so he decided to act. He shook a sleeping Nicole, who mumbled and rolled over. Rather than wake her, he dressed, summoned an UberX, and rode to Cedars-Sinai Medical Center alone.

He waited in the emergency room, observing stringent hospital protocols, feeling like Covid was all around him. The elastic mask bands around his ears made his jaw ache. Eventually they called him in and hooked him up to a machine. To his surprise, everything looked normal.

Paul was unconvinced. "I am having a heart attack," he told them.

Reluctantly, they ran an enzyme test. Twenty minutes later, he was being wheeled into surgery.

Nicole awoke that morning a tiny bit hungover. Matzo Ball had taken Paul's place in bed, as presumably Paul had gone to outdoor boot camp. She reached for her phone, as usual, and read her husband's texts with rising horror.

Paul: Good news, it's not an active heart attack.

Paul: Going into surgery now, in case I don't respond to your texts.

Nicole lost her mind. She jumped out of bed to rush to the hospital, but of course the Covid protocols made seeing Paul impossible. All she could do was pace frantically with her phone in her hand, waiting for a call or text, some word.

In the end, Paul was extremely lucky. There was no muscle damage to the heart itself. He had three stents implanted, spent the night in Cedars-Sinai, and was home by Sunday and back at his office desk Monday morning. Among its many potential harmful effects, Covid is now known to exacerbate cardiac issues in people with underlying conditions. But it was one of the worst weekends of Nicole's life. Had Paul not gone to the hospital and not insisted on the enzyme test, Nicole could have lost him. Her life would have been destroyed. Not that she needed reminding, but it underscored for her how precarious life can be, how it can all change in an instant.

Later that month Samira's brother passed away in a tragic accident back in Indiana—the second family member she had lost during the pandemic. It was an especially heartbreaking time, made even more difficult by the realities of the ongoing health crisis. Travel remained limited, and many remained cautious about flying, particularly those who were high-risk or un-vaccinated. Samira's parents were elderly, considered high-risk, and had not yet received their second vaccination. Protecting them was always top of mind, and the thought of exposing them—even unintentionally—was a risk Samira wasn't willing to take. Because of these concerns, and the fact that many family members lived in different states, the family made the painful but thoughtful decision to postpone any memorial service. They agreed it would be best to wait until it was safer to travel and warm enough to gather outdoors. This made sense—but it didn't make it easier. This was a deeply emotional time for Samira, and the inability to properly mourn her brother alongside loved ones added to the weight of her grief.

Marissa: Oh god, Samira. I'm so, so sorry!

Jeannie: That is so unfair on so many fronts

Nicole: Covid is so hard

These family matters and health concerns further impeded their floundering inquiry. At the same time that their productivity slowed to a crawl, they sensed that O'Farrell was losing faith in the investigation. His North Star at every twist and turn in the investigation was the eventual criminal court case. Circumstantial murder cases were the most difficult to prove before a jury of twelve people, and O'Farrell's role often involved playing devil's advocate, examining the team's theories and deductions from a defense attorney's perspective. He knew from experience that ADA Kramer would not bring charges in a case he could not win, and remained focused on what could potentially persuade or dissuade prospective jurors.

Annoyingly, this meant O'Farrell would postulate wildly improbable scenarios to counter their assumptions. The women didn't mind having their work challenged until, after one particularly far-fetched demonstration, they realized he was giving up on them. He had gone so far as to locate a 2000 Ford Explorer, the same model as Joel's vehicle, and set a meeting with the team in a parking lot behind a Vons supermarket. Samira, unable to attend in person, participated via video call. They watched as he showed how the gearshift selector could be set in Park with the engine off while the transfer case was set in Neutral, which released the wheel axles for towing. But even with the vehicle instruction manual in hand, he had a difficult time pulling this off himself, needing to start over twice.

"The key could have popped out of the ignition due to the centrifugal force of the roll down the ravine," he told them. "Don't forget Joel Watkins was facing arrest and prison time, leaving his wife destitute. All those desperate phone calls to associates in the days leading up to the crash? And he was drinking heavily. Put all that together with Angela Watkins's confused state of mind, and a suicide pact is not beyond the realm of possibility."

The women knew his alternate theory was ludicrous. By phone, Samira said, "A sixty-year-old man who was desperate and depressed decided to expend all this physical energy fooling with his vehicle's transmission settings while his wife is waiting patiently in the car, then somehow rolled the SUV over a cliff and jumped inside at the same time? Who have you seen in your career who chooses to kill themselves in the most difficult and labor-intensive way?"

O'Farrell remained stubborn. "You'd be amazed at what I've seen."

They were not buying it. His theory was beyond implausible—but that wasn't the point. O'Farrell's focus was on the criminal case; their focus was on the truth. As they had with Raymond Fonseca, the team and the detective had reached an ideological divide.

"I think you guys have to think about letting this go," he told them.

Marissa's heart sank. She disagreed completely, knowing that without O'Farrell and ADA Kramer behind them, they had no chance whatsoever of solving this case.

"I understand what this is," she told him. "You're trying to knock down the one irrefutable piece of physical evidence we have in this case—the condition of the vehicle. But you yourself said the other cars in the ravine had been stolen, two of them used in other crimes. Joel Watkins didn't coincidentally push his car off the road at the same exact spot other criminals disposed of their evidence."

"It doesn't matter what I think," said O'Farrell, climbing out of the driver's seat of the Explorer. "It matters what a jury thinks."

Samira went on to list all the items that had been recovered from the crash site—Joel's Blockbuster Video store card with what looked like blood on it, the hair and blood from the sun roof and window, the mysterious glove—which had never been tested. "I feel like you're ignoring the physical evidence we do have rather than helping to develop the physical evidence we don't."

O'Farrell sighed before coming back at them with a surprising offer. "The lab criminalist who worked on the Watkins case is still with the department. What if I can get you into the crime lab, maybe let you go over the evidence file for yourselves. Would that satisfy you?"

Though it was clear he was only doing this to ease them off the case, there was no way they could pass up this opportunity.

"Don't get your hopes too high," he said. "Only sworn law officers are allowed inside. Maybe Kramer can pull some strings. I'll let you know."

A few days later, word came through: Only one of them would be allowed in. The team decided Marissa should be the one to go.

She met O'Farrell outside a modern building near Cal State, east of downtown Los Angeles. The LASD Crime Laboratory was one of many offices inside.

"The plan is to review tests done fifteen years ago," he told her, "and to see what evidence they still have. If you want anything tested now, you better be ready to make a compelling case as to why."

He badged her inside. For the purposes of this meeting, she was an outside investigator.

The criminalist received them inside her office. She was pleasant and professional, having since risen to head of her department, and answered questions without a hint of defensiveness. O'Farrell had clearly briefed her on Marissa's concerns.

"The reason why the hair and blood samples from the vehicle were never DNA tested," the criminalist explained, "is that there was no reason to believe anyone other than Joel and Angela Watkins had been injured in the car crash." She said that the presence of a single glove might appear enigmatic when included on a list of evidence, but people kept all manner of things in their personal vehicles. "Had it been a latex glove, for example, rather than a man's leather Isotoner, that certainly would have warranted further examination." The substance on the Blockbuster Video store membership card? "It was listed as 'red residue resembling blood' on the CHP report, but that was a misidentification by an untrained patrol officer. It was clear to my eye that it was not blood, which would have turned quite brown over the five weeks between the automobile wreck and the recovery of the belongings."

Marissa nodded and smiled while seeing the team's hopes being dashed left and right.

The criminalist showed her a rendering of the interior of the house on Shadow Peak Road. "This location was never considered a crime scene and therefore never processed as such. The only items the forensics team collected, such as Angela Watkins's hairbrush and Joel Watkins's toothbrush, were selected as sources of DNA for possible future identification—which, as it turned out, was not needed." She showed Marissa another map, this one of a location that *was* treated as a crime scene, though not until many months after the fact: Greg Medina's office and warehouse. The map highlighted every location that had been tested for blood. Marissa thought something about the rendering was off, but she didn't say anything, instead trying to take a mental snapshot.

The meeting was brief, shorter than Marissa had anticipated. Disappointingly, she was never invited into the actual working laboratory. She thanked the criminalist for her time and exited the building with O'Farrell, who asked if the meeting had answered her questions. "Some," admitted Marissa. O'Farrell didn't press the point and said goodbye.

"We've lost him," Marissa told the team via conference call on her way home.

The criminalist's rendering of Greg's offices bothered her, and once Marissa was able to access their drive, she saw why. Their own hand-drawn map of Greg's office, courtesy of Herschel Wensinck, Greg's disgruntled employee who had kept meticulous notes, was different in one glaring respect. She called the nervous little man and asked him about an alcove he had left unlabeled on his map.

"That was storage," he said, without having to think about it. "A windowless space—too big to call a closet, too small to call a room."

"What did Greg keep in there?"

"Depended. Junk, sometimes. Sometimes nothing."

"There was a door? Did it lock?"

"Probably," he guessed.

"I just came from the L.A. County Sheriff's Department Crime Laboratory, and they'd made a rendering of Greg's office, but in their map there was no alcove."

"It was definitely there," said Herschel, "just like I drew it. In fact, when Joel would come visit Greg, sometimes they stepped into that room and closed the door to speak privately."

Samira had reminded Marissa of something when Marissa told the team she was reaching out to Herschel. "A while back, one of my associates spoke to an associate of Greg's who had phoned in a telephone tip to police in 2010," she told Herschel. "Like you, this man was owed quite a bit of money by Greg. He'd never collected, so his tip was considered the product of this grudge, and as far as we can tell, nothing was done about it. But this man said something interesting. He said that Greg had a friend who was staying inside Greg's shop—sleeping there nights—at the time of Joel Watkins's disappearance. Do you have any memory of that person?"

"I do, yeah," he said slowly, remembering. "I don't know if we were ever introduced. But I do remember him being around, and Greg did have a bed in his office."

"The tip caller claimed that Greg's friend was a homeless drug addict."

"I mean, I wouldn't be surprised. He was shady-looking. He did have a car, because I would see it parked in one of the reserved spots. A Chevy pickup."

Marissa thanked him, eager to end the conversation and loop in the others.

"Wait," said Herschel. "Was I working with a couple of murderers back then?"

"Maybe," said Marissa.

The team developed another loose theory on the fly. Greg's druggie friend owed him. Joel had called Greg that final Saturday and said words to the effect that he was going to declare bankruptcy or even go to the police. Greg invited Joel to visit him at his office. Maybe he even suggested bringing Angela too.

Greg wasn't a killer. But perhaps his friend was. As Marissa said, "People do crazy shit on drugs." He could have killed them both in the storage alcove. Then he and Greg could have driven the Explorer and Greg's friend's Chevy to the crash site, using the Chevy to push the Explorer over the edge.

Like most of their scenarios, this theory matched some elements of their timetable while contradicting others—including Angela's late-night screams and the Mercedes's flat tire. But it was something to go on.

They ran this development past O'Farrell, who said all the right things, but they could tell he agreed to accompany them to the former site of Greg Medina's offices under the assumption that it would be another dead end—this one fatal. Had Joel and Angela been, say, strangled in that storage room fifteen years before, it was doubtful that any forensic evidence would remain. But if blood had been shed? That might still be visible. The team could not let it go. They needed to make sure the forensics team hadn't missed something in that hidden room.

Greg's former Pasadena office was now owned by a printing company. As with most businesses during Covid, they were running with a skeleton in-person staff. O'Farrell wore a police windbreaker with the word "Homicide" on it, which got the employees' immediate attention. He explained that they were working on a murder case from fifteen years ago and one of the suspects used to lease this space.

Their eyes lit up.

"Oh my God, was somebody murdered here?"

"Would you mind if we take a look around?" he said.

The other two employees joined them in the rear warehouse, aghast. Marissa recognized the door to the storage room ahead on her left. It was unlocked. The women peered inside. It was windowless, just as Herschel remembered. The room was being used to store a variety of printed signs, but there was plenty of open floor space. The walls and floor were unpainted. The space could very well have been unchanged in the ensuing fifteen years. Was this the very room in which Joel and Angela were murdered?

The team brought out blacklight wands they had purchased and turned them on. They searched the entire room for blood, which would not reflect or glow under ultraviolet light but instead look black. With O'Farrell at their backs, they hoped they might solve the murders right there. It felt as if everything had been building to this moment.

Please, Marissa remembers thinking. *Please let this be it.*

They found nothing.

All along this journey, the women had believed that if they worked hard enough, they would eventually find a smoking gun. Instead, it seemed all they had found was failure. Every promising lead proved to be a dud, and now even their leads were drying up. It felt as if they had exhausted every avenue, and they had to admit that they did not know where to go next.

Carrie reached out, asking for an update. This was a true break point. Samira, a project manager in her career days, dreaded the thought of failing to deliver results to a client. All they had really done for Carrie was to reveal her late father's secret life and maybe the existence of a half brother in Mexico— leaving Carrie in a worse place than she was before they got involved. For the first time, the team discussed making a graceful exit and how to go about doing so. They would never give up wanting to know what happened, but despite their best efforts, it looked as if the case was going cold again. They decided to present the facts as they currently understood them and leave the decision up to Carrie.

They returned to her backyard to sit again with Carrie and Henry. Carrie's aunt and uncle, Gwen and Bill, were present via Zoom on her laptop. The women took turns running through their findings, and they were honest about having lost traction. They felt confident in their theory but lacked the evidence to support it. "None of us feel good about this," said Samira, "but we've exhausted pretty much every lead we've had."

"There is one thing we've thought of," said Marissa, "and it's something we're quite reluctant to do, so we're just going to put it in front of you to see what you think." She told her about a 2019 podcast titled *Your Own Backyard* by Chris Lambert, which detailed the unsolved 1996 disappearance and murder of a nineteen-year-old college student named Kristin Smart. "Because of that podcast, some listeners came forward with new information, and, long story short, it resulted in two arrests."

"Not that we know anything about producing or hosting a podcast," Nicole interjected.

Jeannie said, "This is not anything we want to do."

"This is more an indication of how desperate we are at this point in time," agreed Marissa. "This is kind of a Hail Mary."

"And this wouldn't be a for-profit thing," said Samira. "Our intention is only to crowdsource information regarding your parents' murders in hopes that someone, somewhere, will hear it and come forward with previously withheld information."

"And obviously," said Marissa, "we wouldn't do anything like this without your and your family's approval."

The women felt a little gross pitching her this. It was an awkward exchange. Carrie looked pained.

"My family's privacy is really important," she told them. "Even if this might help, I'm not sure I could handle the fallout from my brother and sister by making everything public."

The women understood completely. In fact, they were relieved.

Gwen and Bill chimed in from their kitchen, offering to fund the team out of their own pockets in order to keep the investigation going. It was a true show of faith as well as a terrifically sweet gesture, but the team refused outright. "We've simply hit a wall we can't get over," Marissa explained. "The last thing we wanted to do was let you all down."

The women felt the weight of having labored so hard on this for so long.

"You've done amazing work," said Carrie. "We're so appreciative that you picked up this torch that had been unlit for so long. No matter what happens, you've given me hope again. I'm thinking of that scene in the original *Star Wars* when R2-D2 projects the holographic image of Princess Leia and she says, 'This is our most desperate hour. Help me, Obi-Wan Kenobi. You're my only hope.' That's how I feel about your team."

It was an extraordinary thing to hear, coming at a time when they felt as if the Death Star had just blown up their home planet. They didn't know what they were going to do, or how they were going to do it, but in that moment, they all understood they weren't going to stop investigating. They just had to find some new way forward.

A NEW HOPE

In her former career, when Nicole trained researchers, she always pointed out to them that you can read the same story ten times and pull out something different each time depending on what you are looking for. Alternatively, if you don't know what you're looking for, you probably won't find it.

With Nicole's maxims in mind, the team slowly began going back through their work from the beginning in order to see if anything was worthy of reappraisal in light of all they had gleaned from the raw police files.

Marissa took a fresh look at the financials, which was her bailiwick. Carrie's faith in the team, her trust, which once lifted her up, now weighed her down. *You're my only hope.*

That was why, several weeks after that emotional meeting, instead of watching her masked daughter rotate through non-contact soccer drills, Marissa was sitting in her car reviewing case files on her laptop. One business that had been implicated in Joel's factoring scheme was a small local insurance company. Marissa could find no connection, business or personal, between Joel and this company, unlike other participants in the scheme. The president of the company at the time of the fraud had a distinctive name, Vincent Grassilli, that was very Google-friendly.

The first several matches for her search were versions of the same Pasadena police blotter entry from May 18, 2006. *Vincent E. Grassilli, 56, was found dead May 17, his body buried in a shallow desert grave. He was reported missing by his family May 7, having been kidnapped from his place of business.*

Marissa sat up as though she'd been shocked. Grassilli was murdered one year after Joel and Angela went missing. Later news stories named two men who had been arrested in connection with the abduction and killing.

A third murder! Marissa's first instinct was to tamp down the excitement welling up inside her. Many months of setbacks had conditioned her to lower her expectations rather than raise them. But this felt like a true breakthrough. This felt potentially huge.

Marissa checked the Watkins files when she got back home. Grassilli had been interviewed by police in 2005 concerning his part in the fraud scheme, about which he claimed to have no knowledge—but there was no notation about his subsequent murder.

Marissa: Is this something? Tell me this is something.

Nicole: Jaw on the ground

Jeannie: OMG

Nicole: Great find Marissa!!!!!

Samira: Text O'Farrell

O'Farrell's attitude did a one-eighty at the news of a third murder. Both of Grassilli's killers had been found guilty and sentenced to fifteen years to life. They were still incarcerated. They had claimed it was a robbery gone wrong, but Grassilli was not known to carry or have access to large amounts of money. Neither man had any personal connection to the victim. One of the assailants had been in significant debt at the time as a result of prior loan defaults.

Like Joel Watkins, Vincent Grassilli had no criminal record when he was kidnapped and murdered. "It could have been a paid execution," speculated Marissa. "A murder for hire."

"I can't believe you found this," said O'Farrell with genuine excitement. "Keep going."

O'Farrell was back. Marissa shared this find with ADA Kramer. "It is incredibly suspect to have two people associated in a criminal scheme kidnapped and murdered within one year," he told her. "This is significant. Those dots need connecting."

The women were cheered by this discovery, but also puzzled, since it tested their long-held theory of the Watkins murders. Neither Andrew Watkins nor Greg Medina had anything to do with the Grassilli murder. After focusing their investigation primarily on family members for the past year, they realized they once again needed to reassess everything they had learned and broaden their inquiry into Joel's business itself.

Nicole discovered a link between the insurance company and Wattkins LED. Wayne Abrams, the past associate of Joel's who spoke by telephone with him twenty-seven times between January and March 2005—the man who had refused to speak directly with Marissa and had his "business partner" contact her instead—had been in business with a senior officer in Grassilli's insurance company.

Samira: Damn super sleuthing, Nicole!

Jeannie: Excellent work!

Wayne Abrams's intermediary had claimed to Marissa that his only relationship with Joel was that he had tried to broker a deal to take Wattkins LED public. This led Jeannie back to Joel's notebooks from 2000 at the time he was weighing the IPO that had never come about. Amid Joel's hasty scribbling, illegible words, and marginal notes was an email address. That address was dead, but Jeannie connected it to a physical address in Carpinteria in 2000. She looked up the occupant at that time and found it was a man named Dominic D'Alessandro.

Jeannie: Guys, hang on to your hats.

Dominic had been indicted by the Securities and Exchange Commission (SEC) in 2007 for securities fraud, conspiracy to commit securities fraud, money laundering, conspiracy to commit money laundering, and wire fraud.

Nicole: Oh God

Jeannie: It gets better. Meaning worse.

As Jeannie started to read, she felt her body tighten. Dominic D'Alessandro's father had been implicated in a notorious and massive scheme in the 1990s that became one of the largest investment and accounting frauds in history. The complicated scam involved the use of a shell company to take an overvalued business public for the purposes of a "pump-and-dump" scheme—that is, artificially inflating the price of a stock through misleading financial information (the pump) in order to sell the owned stock at an inflated value (the dump). Once the stock is sold, the share price collapses, and investors bear the loss.

This particular scheme fell apart when the owner of the original business was forced to file for bankruptcy, which accidentally revealed everything. That owner went to prison for a long time, while the people behind the investment part of the scheme—the architects and the muscle—did not. One of them was a man named Abrams—Bernard Abrams.

Bernard Abrams was Wayne Abrams's father. Jeannie went deep on researching Abrams père, who apparently was notorious for concocting financial schemes that allowed mobsters to gain footholds in legitimate businesses. Her research turned up court testimony from the 1970s that linked Bernard Abrams to several crime families on the East Coast and elsewhere. Her heartbeat quickening, Jeannie looked again at Dominic D'Alessandro and discovered that he too had a connection to the mafia.

Jeannie felt the ground opening up at her feet.

Marissa: Oh my dear lord

Jeannie: I fear we have stumbled into the mafia, for real.
There's more.

It was too much to deal with on her own. As soon as she could get free, Jeannie drove to Marissa's. Nicole couldn't get away, but Samira came over, and the three women sat at the backyard table on their laptops. As they dug further, they discovered that Wattkins LED *did* go public in 2000—sort of.

Apparently, both Wayne Abrams and Dominic D'Alessandro had followed in their mobster fathers' footsteps. They helped Joel and Wattkins LED complete a reverse merger—by which a private company becomes a public entity by purchasing control of a public company—with a shell company that had been implicated in the 1990s case. Now, it seemed to have come to life again with Wayne Abrams and Dominic D'Alessandro at the helm. This was a way to take Wattkins LED public without the expense or regulatory reviews associated with putting it on the New York Stock Exchange or the NASDAQ. This new entity was registered with the name Wattkins LED LLC.

In a reverse merger of this type, private company shareholders normally receive a majority of the shares of the public company. That should have been Joel Watkins. However, the Form

8-K filed at the time of the 2000 transaction, required by the SEC to notify shareholders of material changes within a company's structure, listed two other men as the owners of Wattkins LED LLC. One of those men was Wayne Abrams.

Assuming this reverse-merger scheme operated in the same manner as the earlier schemes, Jeannie theorized what had occurred. Joel had been induced to invest in a product or service represented by Wayne Abrams and Dominic D'Alessandro to have tremendous upside financially. Perhaps at son Andrew's urging, Joel threw good money after bad, going deeper into debt on this speculative venture until he had no way out. The notes and diagrams in Joel's notebooks outlined not what could have happened, but what *had* happened. One year later, Wattkins LED LLC itself was reverse-mergered into another company and continued operating as a shell company under a new name.

The women puzzled through it. This was a lot of financial maneuvering to take in.

"He was just so desperate for cash," reasoned Jeannie, "he became involved in a game far more complicated than he could have imagined."

Marissa said, "This is unbelievable, Jeannie! I am shocked by this turn."

"One little goddamn email address in a twenty-year-old notebook," said Jeannie.

"I'm still wrapping my head around it all," said Samira. "So stupid, Joel!"

Marissa and Samira were awed by Jeannie's discovery. Jeannie wished she could enjoy the moment more, but all she saw was danger. She had feared all along that something like this might happen.

They kept Nicole apprised via text.

Nicole: You guys are KILLING it!!! But this is some scary shit.
Joel's "bad people" statement is getting real

Joel's company was one of many rolled up into this massive pump-and-dump scheme, which was confusing and purposefully complicated in order to shield the fraud from the SEC. In layman's terms, it functioned something like a pyramid scheme. But instead of individual investors paying up the pyramid, one owner or group of owners sits atop a pyramid structure of businesses. The small businesses near the bottom, such as Wattkins LED, are rolled up inside shell companies. Money moves through these companies, giving the appearance of sales and profits, which allows the companies to attract financing. The money keeps accruing and flowing to the top, but the foundation is built upon little or nothing. In the 1990s case, drug money was laundered through the entity. They could not be certain, but it seemed very likely that the same thing had happened here. The scheme was not built to last and would eventually collapse of its own weight, but not before those at the top had siphoned out as much money as possible, leaving the zombie companies at the bottom dead and drained.

In 2011, the SEC caught on to this ploy and issued an investor bulletin cautioning investors about reverse mergers. Marissa reached out to the SEC prosecuting attorney on the original 1990s fraud case, but even two-plus decades later, the woman refused to discuss it.

"I'd love to know how much money they raised in penny stocks," Jeannie said. "And who they defrauded with this scheme."

Marissa said, "All we know for sure is that Joel was messing with the wrong people."

"He was a real dumbass," said Samira. "Remember Gwen and Bill said he wasn't smart enough to engineer the factoring fraud?"

Jeannie said, "I bet it was Andrew who got him involved in the whole stupid scheme."

"Oh, I am sure," said Samira. "Andrew was one hundred

percent balls deep in it. Explains his intense fear after the disappearance. Maybe Greg as well."

"But, Jesus," said Jeannie, "I did not think this is where the case was going to go."

Their suspicions were further supported when Jeannie, over the next few days, took a deep dive into investor message boards dating back two decades. She believed she had found Andrew Watkins there, posting under the screen name Player8. Among other topics, Player8 posted news releases on Wattkins LED LLC and the companies it was later merged into with favorable comments. Player8 posted in these forums obsessively, many times daily from 2000 until May 19, 2005—nine days before Joel's death, and right around the time Andrew Watkins mysteriously stopped using his cellphone for two weeks—and then posted only twice more that year, and a couple more times in 2012.

Marissa: This makes so much sense. People said he spent most of his day "day trading."

Jeannie: Right! He so got Joel into this.

Marissa: This is amazing work, Jeannie. Feeling really confident that Joel was ready to break and/or file for bankruptcy and the mob had to shut him up

Jeannie: My concern is that the ADA will want to pass this on to the FBI. And while I would love to nail these guys, I'm rather uninterested in being subpoenaed and showing up as an informant against the mob.

Nicole: Jeannie you could tease your hair. And put on really intense makeup

Nicole: I'm on the Forever 21 site now finding you a leopard
print fur

The jokes belied their fear. This was serious stuff—far deeper
than the intrafamilial murder they thought they were investigating. They had uncovered a criminal conspiracy involving organized crime.

Later, they would learn that another man associated with
Wayne Abrams, a Russian national, had been convicted in a
separate pump-and-dump scheme in 2008. That case had been
brought in 2006, the same year the insurance company owner
was kidnapped, shot, and buried—leading the women to specu-
late that either Grassilli had started cooperating with the feds,
or the people who had him killed feared that he would.

Part of the discovery for that court case revealed conversations between the Russian gangster and another suspect as they
discussed paying members of a biker gang to "take care of someone" who had shorted them on a deal. On another occasion, the
man was said to have put a hit out on someone for $50,000.

The women were freaking out. And trying to think of the
best way to explain this to their spouses.

They didn't have all the answers.

But they had enough.

THE NIGHT IN QUESTION

The bartender smiled and brought Joel his double tequila with a wedge of lime, along with his car keys.

He kept it light, asking how Joel was doing, saying he'd never seen him like he'd been the night before.

Joel explained he'd had a long day Wednesday. He was better today. He thanked the bartender for making sure he'd gotten home, and the bartender moved on to another customer.

Joel looked at his keys on the bar. He threw back the double tequila and sucked the juice out of the lime, leaving the rind in the empty glass. The liquor landed and Joel sighed quietly and pretended to look at the television screen—his mind on the day before.

The woman from the bank had stopped by the office unannounced on Wednesday with a list of unpaid invoices. Joel showed her correspondence he had falsified between him and the late-paying clients and promised to follow up with them again.

Andrew saw the banker walking out but he didn't say anything. Bonnie was out that day and Oliver was easy to avoid. The office was so quiet now, just four people, but some afternoons as few as two. A shadow of what it used to be. Work used to be fun.

Joel couldn't remember much from the night before. Now it was Thursday and there had been no subsequent contact from the bank. Andrew asked no questions because he already knew or didn't want to know. Joel tried not to think about what the rest of his life would look like. He could only think day to day. It had been that way for a while.

He wanted to go home, but he didn't want to face Angela. He hadn't told her all of it, but he'd told her some. He'd had to. They were going to lose their home again. She believed they could dig out. She'd called her father for money. Joel hadn't stopped her but he knew this time it wouldn't be enough to save them.

The second mortgage hadn't been enough. The bank factoring agreement that had been his lifeline hadn't been enough. He'd maxed out nine credit card accounts and it hadn't been enough. Looking back now, it was clear that when he started submitting phony invoices to generate cash from the bank, when he'd crossed that line, that was the point of no return. Like starting a morphine drip for a dying man. There was no coming back from that.

His second double arrived and he again sucked the lime dry and swiped at his stinging lips with the cocktail napkin. He closed out using the company card at seven-thirty and thanked the bartender again, telling him he'd see him next time.

He found his Ford Explorer where he'd left it the night before. He got inside and started it up. He opened the glove compartment. His third phone was there. He opened it to reveal the screen. No messages.

Angela was reading when she heard the garage door open. She recalled her anger the night before. First, fear—the strange car in the driveway, the knock at the front door. Then Joel and the shape he was in. She never said anything about his nightly drinks on the way home, but this was way beyond. This was not him. This was the old him. He tried to tell her a funny story about something that happened on the ride home but he couldn't talk straight, and her anger made him scowl and go quiet—quiet except for his bumping and stumbling around the house.

She had faith that he could see them out of this but his condition last night shook her. He was a hard worker and devoted. Now that she had processed it and accepted it—the debt he had allowed them to take on again—she had begun to hope. He had done it before. When they lost the last house, somehow he paid her father back all the money he'd borrowed, and within two years they were living in a bigger house—this house—in Paradise Canyon. He had done it once and he would do it again.

But that didn't mean she had to be pleasant to him. He entered from the garage and she was relieved to see he wasn't drunk. The checks from her mutual funds were on the counter with the mail, as were the passbooks of the closed accounts. He saw them and said nothing. He switched on the kitchen television and ate the food she'd left for him. He wouldn't apologize for the night before. After thirty years of marriage, she knew what to expect. He would show her he was all right tonight, and he would put what had happened behind him and keep moving ahead.

Joel arrived at the office Friday morning at 5:45 and, after a workout, was at his desk just after seven. He sent an email to his point man at Pacific Heritage, saying that he had a morning and an afternoon meeting with investors interested in buying into the company and might not be back in time to call the banker later. This was all a stall to get Joel to Monday.

Andrew came in at nine. The office was so quiet, any coming or going was heard. Oliver had the day off. Bonnie came in around midday but there wasn't much to do and Joel suggested she take the rest of the day off.

His banker replied via email at 10:48 A.M. asking to meet Monday. Joel did not reply.

Because the office was so quiet, Joel took calls out in the stairwell. He had borrowed money from Greg in the past but at the moment Greg was tapped out, he said, and Joel believed him. Greg had already submitted three phony invoices to Pacific Heritage for $60,000 that he'd turned back around to Joel. Greg was having trouble making payroll himself and asked to pay someone with a Wattkins LED check. Joel knew the bank would cover the check.

He made one stairwell call with his third phone, the prepaid one Wayne Abrams had told him to purchase back in March. He left a message asking Abrams to please call him back this time.

He timed his calls so that he would be out of the office when Andrew left at one. Joel left after two P.M., unusually early, but he was worried the bank auditor might come back. And he needed to pick up Angela and cash the mutual fund checks. Later that evening, after the bank was closed, Joel deposited half of the proceeds from Angela's mutual funds into the business account at Pacific Heritage Bank via night drop. He put the other $14,000 in a drawer.

Saturday morning, alone in the office. Joel answered Terry's call at nine, offering to take Joel and Angela in with him for a time if need be. Joel assured him that he was going to take care of everything and hung up. When Wattkins LED was rolling, it had looked like Joel was on his way to being wealthier than Angela's father. Back then it was like sticking your hat out the window and catching rain. Before the climate changed.

At 10:20 A.M. he replied to the bank's Friday email: "Very productive day yesterday . . . wrapping something up by mid-week." He was lying about selling a company he didn't even own. The bank was on to him. It was only a matter of time. The receivables financing agreement was expiring in a week.

Greg called. Joel told him he was worried. Greg was taking Marie to a matinee and couldn't meet. He invited him to stop by his shop on Sunday afternoon to talk.

Joel went out to the stairwell and called Dennis Ladd. He told Dennis more than he'd planned to. That he was in trouble. That he and Angela might be going to jail. Dennis, who knew a lot but didn't know everything, reassured Joel that he'd find a way. He said to meet him for lunch on Monday before the bank meeting and they would figure something out.

Joel had long considered taking the soldier's way out, but that would leave Angela at these men's mercy, and he couldn't bear the thought of it.

He placed another call on his third phone, leaving another message for Wayne Abrams. Something about the bank, or something about not being able to pay him on the first of the month. Something that set off alarm bells. Joel went back inside, powered down his work phone, and plugged it into the charger. He looked around his silent office, dreading Monday. With the third phone in his pocket, he left for home.

Mail came early on Saturday and Angela did something she never did. She opened the credit card bill. When she saw the amount owed, she was shocked but not surprised. She only wondered where the money was going.

Joel handled the finances. All Angela had was her checkbook. In her distress, she flipped through it and noticed a telephone number in her handwriting that she didn't remember jotting down. She picked up the phone and called. It was her sister's number. After a confusing conversation with her brother-in-law, she rushed off the phone, her heart racing.

Angela was out front gardening in her wide-brimmed hat and cotton gloves when Joel went in for lunch and saw the open credit card bill. This was how they communicated. He put it in a drawer. Angela would not mention it.

He ate very little and headed out to do yard work. It was good physical activity but it did not take his mind off his troubles. Everything he did at the house now felt final, something that would soon be only a memory. Just like the other house they'd lost. Just like the house they'd raised the kids in. Just like the kids when they were young.

Their address was painted on the curb. In his distraction, he didn't notice the vehicle drive past twice.

He came inside and shrugged off his sweat-stained shirt and pulled down his dirty jeans and dropped them into the open washing machine as always. He carried a glass of water upstairs and heard the vacuum below, Angela cleaning up the bits of soil he had tracked in. She turned off the vacuum when she heard the doorbell. She hated people coming to the door. She heard the shower running upstairs and couldn't call for Joel. It was a man with a package. She realized she'd have to sign for it in her housecoat.

Joel toweled off and walked out of the bathroom. Two men stood in his bedroom and his breath left him.

Where's the phone?

Joel didn't understand their words in that moment. There was a roaring sound in his head. He was terrified and he needed to know where Angela was. He tried to call out and that's when the men took a step toward him. Joel was built solidly from daily workouts but here he was outnumbered and undressed.

Where's the phone?

The phone, he realized. He told them he would get it.

Get dressed first, he wants to see you.

Joel pulled on clothes quickly and without thought. He needed to see Angela. They followed him down the stairs, Joel gripping the handrail.

A third man stood against a wall in the living room, out of sight of the front windows, his hand over Angela's mouth. Her eyes were wide. She wasn't moving. The man's grip was the only thing holding her up.

Get her dressed, one man said. The third man pulled Angela to the stairs.

Joel led the two men into the garage and pulled the phone from his glove compartment. One man checked the call log. Joel was telling them he would get the money when the two men took him down to the cement floor. Joel was strong for his age and it took some time, ten or even fifteen minutes of exertion, before the blood stopped moving through his heart and his brain.

If the neighbors' accounts were accurate, Angela remained alive until late into the night when her scream erupted—either from the bedroom, where she was killed and which the assailants later vacuumed and cleaned, or perhaps from the garage, where Joel's body in the back of the Explorer would be the last thing she'd ever see.

Both the Explorer and the Mercedes were driven to the turnout on Angeles Crest Highway where the assailants had dumped vehicles in the past. They had all the time they needed. The Explorer was pulled up to the berm at the very edge of the sheer cliff. The vehicle was put in Park and the emergency brake applied to hold it at the precipice. The front seats were moved forward. The ignition was turned off so that no headlights would give away the crash site and no fuel leak would cause a fire. The emergency brake was released. The men pushed from behind and the tow-ready tires crunched over the berm, inching forward until gravity took control. The rear of the vehicle bumped off the edge, the SUV starting to flip end over end, and it was gone. The grinding, the thudding, the shattering glass sounded like a case of beer bottles crashing down a long flight of stairs. Then silence.

THE FINAL TWIST

The four women set a time to meet with Assistant District Attorney Kramer and Detective O'Farrell, inviting them to Marissa's converted garage. They invited Raymond Fonseca as well, and he brought along his former partner, also retired, a woman who had worked the Watkins case alongside him. They carefully prepped for their presentation, as always, though this one required extra effort. They had connected all the dots; now they had to explain how. They had updated their timeline on the long sheet of Kraft paper taped to the wall, illustrated with names and evidence highlighted throughout. A flowchart of merged companies was drawn on construction paper.

Marissa had ordered fancy doughnuts without thinking, which got a laugh from the retired cops, who were not offended by the "cops and doughnuts" stereotype. Kramer drank Diet Coke at ten in the morning. The team led off with the densest, most confusing part, the financial details of two Wattkins LED companies and the pump-and-dump scheme. With that established as background, they detailed the original fraud case from the 1990s, underlining the similarities and connecting the dots with the father-son Abrams and D'Alessandro lineages. They closed by bringing everything around to Joel and Angela Watkins.

After several years of financial success, the family business had begun to suffer losses and Joel became dangerously overextended. Desperate for cash, he'd had no luck searching for an investor to help turn things around. Eager to protect his generous salary, son and employee Andrew likely facilitated a meeting with investor Wayne Abrams. After Joel lost more money than he could afford to investing in the failed or phony product or service, Abrams proposed a complicated reverse-merger scheme that could provide Joel with cash, keep his business afloat, and even offer him and his son the opportunity to make money on a pump-and-dump scheme from the sidelines. It felt like a win-win-win, though in reality Joel had little choice. He had already lost his house and borrowed $200,000 from his father-in-law. Either he took this deal or he would lose everything.

Joel sold the use of his company while continuing to head the legitimate business. Meanwhile, the now publicly traded shell company, Wattkins LED LLC, was used as a vehicle to launder money and pump up its penny stock price.

More underworld figures bought into the scheme, and after two more reverse mergers, the company name disappeared from the stock listing. Joel entered into a factoring agreement with Pacific Heritage Bank & Trust in June 2004 in order to keep cash flowing as the lighting industry consolidated and sales dropped off. Joel approached friends and associates for loans to bridge the shortfall, but it was never enough. He fell into personal debt trying to make up the losses. The factoring fraud began in February 2005, and from that point forward the company was in a death spiral.

Bank auditors became suspicious when the phony invoices went unpaid. Joel knew an audit was imminent and that his company's finances would not stand up to Internal Revenue Service scrutiny. He had kept all this from Angela, but with things coming to a head, he disclosed most of the details and their dire financial situation to her on May 19, 2005. Though deeply upset, she tried to help, asking her father for more money, which he refused to lend her. She closed out some long-held mutual fund accounts, but it was nowhere near enough. Even the sale of their twice-mortgaged home would not come close to covering the nearly $1 million shortfall.

Joel and Angela—Angela by virtue of having been the original 51 percent majority owner of the company—were now liabilities the mob investors could not afford. A declaration of personal bankruptcy would expose the company's finances and the entire multicompany fraud and penny stock scheme, as it had in the earlier and much larger 1990s case.

Two days before a meeting with the bank, Joel and Angela were attacked in their home and murdered. Their bodies were driven to a remote ravine under cover of darkness and their vehicle was pushed over the edge, eventually coming to rest out of sight from the road seven hundred feet below.

Andrew Watkins's actions in the week that followed, culminating in the abrupt closing of the family business, aroused suspicion. Though he was not involved in the planning or execution of his parents' disappearance, he had likely been responsible for exposing his father to this ruthless organization. He knew essentially what had happened to his parents and why. Whether Andrew was warned to stay quiet, or simply feared becoming the next victim, he never divulged what he knew, ceasing cooperation with the police, refusing to take a lie detector test, and eventually relocating across the country to start a new life. Greg Medina knew of his father-in-law's financial concerns but presumably was not aware of the whole story, which was why he successfully passed his lie detector test.

In order to prevent the embarrassment of public disclosure of their mishandling of the factoring agreement, Pacific Heritage declined to pursue the matter beyond receiving a partial settlement from the Watkins Family Trust after the life insurance payouts. Joel and Angela were gone, all debts were settled, and the mafia's involvement was never exposed.

The ADA and the three retired detectives had all dropped their game faces halfway through the women's recitation. They were beyond impressed. After the team finished, following a brief, astonished silence, ADA Kramer started laughing.

"I can't believe it," Kramer said, going around fist-bumping each of the women. "You did more than just connect all the dots. You didn't just solve two murders, you exposed an entire criminal conspiracy."

O'Farrell had come into the meeting knowing most of the details, but even he was amazed at hearing it all laid out in narrative form. "I didn't think you could do it," he admitted. "I don't even think most top detectives I know could have cracked this case."

Fonseca shook his head and smiled. "Great work, ladies," he said, clearly at a loss for words. His partner looked stunned.

For months, the team had been told that something was missing in their investigation. The mob connection was that missing link. Now it was as though they had opened a door these four professionals never knew existed.

"If you had told me," said ADA Kramer, "that four moms would solve this convoluted fifteen-year-old case, I never would have believed it. Amazing work. Seriously amazing. Congratulations."

They were elated. It was everything they had dreamed of. "Okay," said Marissa. "What now?"

"You figured it all out," he said, "but now what do we do about it? We still don't have a murder weapon. We don't know the identity of the actual killers. And we are talking about members of various factions of the mafia—very dangerous, very connected people accused of capital crimes." He was pacing now, his hands on his hips beneath the flaps of his suit jacket. "They've already killed three people we know of. The murders are under my office's jurisdiction, but the conspiracy they are linked to is not. This is a federal case now."

The women looked at one another. Samira said, "Okay, then, can't you take what we've given you and give it to the FBI?"

"Well, you guys need to consider the possible outcomes," Kramer said. "I can't fully predict it. But I can tell you that if you brought this to the FBI, there is a good possibility that you would be compelled to testify and, with that possibility, that you and your families could wind up in the Federal Witness Protection Program."

They were stunned.

Witness Protection? Uprooting their families, relocating to a new state? Changing their names, their spouses' careers, their kids' identities? Blowing up their lives? This could simply never happen.

They pictured themselves living in a one-horse town in North Dakota, in a dusty pueblo in New Mexico, in minus-twenty-degrees Fairbanks, Alaska. It was absurd. How was it possible, after all the highs and lows of this case, all the hurdles they had overcome, the battles they had lost and won, that they had achieved their dream of solving a fifteen-year-old double homicide cold case only to have it immediately turn into a nightmare?

Kramer recognized the concern in their faces. "This is your choice. You don't have to bring this to the FBI. Even with your information, this will be a very tricky case to prosecute—especially with no murder weapon. The SEC has already prosecuted some involved, so it is very likely that the FBI have their eyes on these people too. That said, whether or not this case is prosecuted, you have achieved something incredible. Think of what you have done! And if you're at all undecided, maybe float this to Carrie and see how she feels?"

The women looked at each other knowingly. Becoming witnesses in an organized crime case was frankly terrifying. At the same time, the idea that this case would not go to trial felt heartbreaking.

There was only one thing left to do. It was something they had fantasized about for more than a year: presenting their findings to Carrie Watkins. Answering the question that had plagued her all of her adult life. But what should have been their victory lap now felt more like a death march.

Once again, they sat with Carrie and Henry on their backyard patio. The moment was heavier than the team could ever have imagined. This woman had been through such pain—losing her parents so mysteriously, losing her relationships with her older siblings, losing faith in law enforcement and the justice system—and now here they were to deliver another body blow. As proud as they were to be able to provide her with answers she had sought for fifteen long years, they knew that nothing they could say or do would ever make Carrie whole again.

Carrie held a notebook and pen, preparing to take notes. The team watched her face intently as Marissa cleared her throat softly and began laying out their theory.

"In June 2000, when your dad was experiencing cash flow issues, your brother, Andrew, introduced him to an investor. That investor secretly purchased your dad's company. That investor was also a member of the mafia."

Carrie's head dropped. Her pen fell onto her notebook and she cupped her free hand over her mouth. "Go on," she said after a few moments, but the women could tell that it had all clicked for her already. She never took down a single note.

Jeannie said, "Andrew appeared guilty because he was guilty—just not of murder. We think it's likely that neither your brother, nor certainly your father, knew exactly who they were dealing with until it was much too late. Unfortunately, as the walls closed in, your father sought assistance and guidance from probably the worst adviser he could have turned to—your brother-in-law, Greg."

Samira continued, "The week after your parents went missing was a tense one for your brother. We think the realization set in sometime on that first day, and that's when he became afraid. You said he was uncharacteristically 'passive' about wanting to look for your parents. With the bank closing in and the missing persons alert hitting the press that Thursday, Andrew was panicked about who might show up at the office or at his home. You said yourself that only after the business was closed forever on Friday and everything placed in storage was he able to relax."

"Once the immediate danger had passed," added Nicole, "Andrew and Greg almost immediately resumed their scamming ways, trying to recoup fictitious loans to your father from your grandfather."

They went on to relate their theory about the hired killers, based upon the mob's tactics in the past. It was awful watching Carrie visualize her parents' final moments in a way she had never visualized them before. Marissa hoped to soften the blow. "Maybe you can take solace in the fact that, despite appearances to the contrary, at least your brother and brother-in-law weren't the actual murderers."

"But they knew," she said, her face grim. "They knew."

The team then came to what was for them the most difficult part. Jeannie explained that with the investigation now a conspiracy case involving organized crime, the only way to continue was to go to the federal government with what they'd uncovered. "The main mafia figure is still alive and active. The ADA told us this would be a very difficult case to prosecute and that you and your family would have to endure years of legal proceedings. Additionally, it might mean that the four of us would have to testify against the mafia—"

Carrie stopped them there. She understood.

"There's no need to go further," she said. "No need to put

yourselves in danger. I have no desire to relive this in court. You've given me everything I need. You have no idea what this means to me. Now I have a story I can tell my son about his grandparents someday." She forced a smile to show them how grateful she truly was, despite the pain. "As far as I'm concerned, you did exactly what you set out to do. You solved it. I can't thank you enough."

This was the most profound moment for all of them: not presenting their findings to Carrie or bringing her closure, but realizing that she had come to care about them as much as they cared about her. They had handled this incredibly delicate situation with grace and consideration, which she recognized and reciprocated. It was over. All that was left was for Joel and Angela's daughter to grieve.

ADA Kramer told them they had made the right choice. Their ability as women to get people to trust and confide in them things that they would not share with law enforcement figures was their superpower in investigating and breaking this case.

"Seriously amazing work. You are four extremely bright, energetic, hardworking women, and I mean it, the door is open if you want to come work for me."

Investigators in the District Attorney's Office? It was intensely flattering and exciting to consider, at first. It would mean going back to work. Being back in an office setting. Professional investigators, doing work that mattered.

But it was little more than a passing fancy. They all agreed that while they wanted to do more of this, they didn't want to make it a job. Their actual superpower above all others was that they cared. That was why they had never given up. That was why they had succeeded. This had worked only because they were able to investigate a case that truly mattered to them.

The foursome gathered for lunch at Lulu, the reopened restaurant in the courtyard inside the Hammer Museum—back where it had all started, where Marissa and Jeannie had met for the first time just weeks before Covid shut everything down. Social distancing and mask mandates had been lifted for the fully vaccinated, and travel restrictions were being relaxed. Later that fall and winter, the Delta and Omicron variants would spark new waves of infection, but at that moment it felt as if they had turned a corner and the world was slowly reopening.

Their drinks arrived, and the women toasted Angela. Beautiful Angela. Porcelain Angela. The forgotten victim, collateral damage from her husband's crimes and indiscretions, financial and otherwise.

"That was one fucked-up family," said Samira. "The scariest part is, their kids were our kids' ages once. Angela and Joel were where we are now in life."

"May all our kids be Carries and not Andrews," said Nicole, raising her glass.

Providing catharsis and closure for Carrie Watkins had also provided catharsis and closure for them. They had given her the peace of mind that her father was not a crook defrauding his bank to enrich himself but instead a tragic victim of his own aspirations—a desperate man trying to dig himself out of trouble in order to stay alive.

They recalled with horror their own desperate near-misstep: their Hail Mary idea of doing a podcast to churn up leads. "We literally dodged a bullet there," said Marissa. "We would have put the mob right on to us."

"We would have become true crime story victims ourselves," said Jeannie. "Very meta."

But mostly they rode the high of having broken the case, of

having never given up. It had ended in a way no one saw coming, including them. Their Covid jigsaw puzzle was finally completed.

"Guys," said Nicole, "I can't believe it's over."

The thought of everything going back to "normal"—carpools, activities, dinner, repeat—was heartbreaking. But over the course of the last few months, when it seemed that the Watkins case might not pan out, O'Farrell had begun talking to them about other Sheriff's Department cold cases that might benefit from their involvement. He'd shared details from seven different unsolved crimes, each with a nickname like Russian Bride Case and Widow Drug Killing. All were interesting, but one case stood out. One case spoke to them the way the Watkins mystery had.

A serial killer case from the 1980s sought to link the previously unconnected murders of as many as twenty women in Southern California dating back forty years. Modern advances in DNA and genealogy databases would give the team an edge over previous investigations. Maybe this time the four of them would even get inside the actual crime lab. The case would involve a lot of legwork, as almost none of the victims or the circumstances were internet searchable.

This case appealed to them for two reasons. First, there was no mob angle, no chance of running afoul of hired killers again, no concern about being forced into witness protection. Second, many of the victims were still, to this day, Jane Does. Not only had their murders gone unsolved, but their identities were not known. This was an opportunity to give these women names, and in doing so, to tell their stories.

It had been joyful and fun. Dreamlike at times. The many frustrations of the case faded when compared to the development of the women's friendship and their strength and dedication as a team. They trusted one another, challenged one another, supported one another, and in doing so had achieved things they never thought they could achieve, at a time in their lives when they really needed it.

At the start of it all, they had felt adrift. They hadn't been their best selves because they had lost themselves. Each woman, separately, could not see what the next stage of her life looked like. Then Covid struck and everything stopped. Lockdown forced them to look at themselves and everything around them. Lesser concerns didn't matter anymore. They took stock and set about building confidence—and then they found one another, and lightning struck. If not for the case and the great "pause" of Covid, they would have chugged along, finding their way, but without an opportunity for such a profound transformation. They considered themselves no more special nor smarter than anyone else. The secret to their success was simple: They had worked like hell. They had discovered something they were really good at and made it something that was truly and solely theirs. The bond they'd formed, their connection coming at a time of such isolation and uncertainty, was a great gift.

Like a powerful current, this family story had taken hold of them, propelling them toward a new sense of identity. In the most unlikely of circumstances—the cold case of a brutal double homicide—they reconnected with the women they were before motherhood and found a richer sense of self along the way. Motherhood no longer defined them—it was now one of many hats they wore.

Another unforeseen outcome of this great adventure was the profound impact it had on what they treasured most: their children. Between time spent away from the kids, physically and mentally, and exposing them to "murder talk," they feared they might have been inflicting lasting trauma on them. It turned out to be quite the opposite. The kids gained independence and resilience during the women's all-consuming journey. They began to see their mothers as multidimensional people capable of seemingly impossible achievement. They learned from their mothers' examples that life is a series of opportunities to keep learning and reinventing oneself.

Most importantly, the women followed through on the promise they had made to themselves way back on that summer day in 2020 when they met Carrie. They had solved this for her, and they hoped that in doing so they had contributed to redefining her sense of self as well. Helping to heal her old wound brought them an indescribable sense of solace.

They closed the file on this life-altering case and wasted no time moving on to the next.

Jeannie: OK, guys, let's talk serial killers.

Samira: I'm ready!

Marissa: I already started the spreadsheet 🤪

Nicole: Let's fucking go!

Author's Note

When I first met Samira, Nicole, Jeannie, and Marissa in the converted garage behind Marissa's house in Los Angeles's Westside in September 2023, they presented me with a two-inch-thick three-ring binder titled "Key Documents" divided into fourteen labeled sections, containing legal documents, newspaper articles, notes, autopsy records, photographs, and much, much more.

Over the next eighteen months, I came to learn that this level of organization and professional presentation was their hallmark. Entrusting their incredible true story to a stranger, as well as sharing elements of their personal lives, represented a great leap of faith. This book was written with their cooperation but also, and more importantly, with their support.

This account is based upon that binder, along with comprehensive interviews with them, crime scene visits, the review of dozens of hours of recorded telephone interviews, more than one thousand pages of contemporaneous text messages (roughly ten thousand texts in total), and some other items we can't talk about. I also interviewed the L.A. County assistant district attorney with whom they worked, who appears in these pages, as does everyone other than the four women and their spouses, under a pseudonym. Identifying features, including but not limited to locations, dates, and physical appearances, have been recast where necessary.

Unrecorded conversations have been reconstructed from the women's memories and their corroborating notes. Transcripts of telephone interviews have been condensed and edited for clarity and to preserve confidentiality. Reproduced documents, such as the bank lawsuit affidavit, have been amended (for example, the name of the bank has been changed, as have specific dollar amounts) without materially altering their context. Creative license was taken in the section titled "The Night in Question" in order to illustrate the team's ultimate vision of the circumstances of the crime.

The women's step-by-step investigation occurred as presented here. Distinguishing elements of the crime and the people associated with it have been comprehensively revised for two reasons: as a courtesy to preserve the privacy of "Carrie Watkins" and her family, and to protect the personal safety of the Carpool Detectives.

About the Author

CHUCK HOGAN is the author of several acclaimed *New York Times* bestsellers, including *Prince of Thieves,* which was awarded the Hammett Prize and adapted into the hit feature film *The Town,* starring Ben Affleck. His most recent novel, *Gangland,* was selected as one of the *New York Times*'s Ten Best Crime Novels of the year and nominated for an Edgar Award. *The Carpool Detectives* is his first work of nonfiction.

Bluesky: @chuckhogan.bsky.social

About the Type

This book was set in Sabon, a typeface designed by the well-known German typographer Jan Tschichold (1902–74). Sabon's design is based upon the original letter forms of sixteenth-century French type designer Claude Garamond and was created specifically to be used for three sources: foundry type for hand composition, Linotype, and Monotype. Tschichold named his typeface for the famous Frankfurt typefounder Jacques Sabon (c. 1520–80).